LITERATURE AND
ETHNIC DISCRIMINATION

Rodopi Perspectives on Modern Literature

18

Edited by
David Bevan

LITERATURE
AND
ETHNIC DISCRIMINATION

Edited by
Michael J. Meyer

Amsterdam - Atlanta, GA 1997

90127

♾ The paper on which this book is printed meets the requirements of "ISO 9706:1994, Information and documentation - Paper for documents - Requirements for permanence".

ISBN: 90-420-0222-0 (bound)
ISBN: 90-420-0221-2 (paper)
©Editions Rodopi B.V., Amsterdam - Atlanta, GA 1997
Printed in The Netherlands

Table of Contents

There is a power above that can "bring down high looks; at the breath of whose mouth, our wealth may take wings, and before whom every knee shall bow." I would warn that ... the time may come when those who are despised and hated may be needed, when those whom they compel by oppression to be enemies, may be wanted as friends. What has been, may be again. There is a point beyond which human endurance cannot turn; the worm may yet turn under the heel of the oppressor.

Frederick Douglas, "A Lecture on Slavery"
Rochester, N.Y. December 8, 1850

"It takes two of us to discover truth; one to utter it and one to understand it."

Kahlil Gibran
Sand and Foam

Introduction

How are ideas for book generated? I am sure there are a variety of answers to that question, each depending on the writer's or editor's experience. For myself, however, I can safely say that the motive for this collection grew out of a National Endowment for the Humanities Seminar on Harriet Beecher Stowe and her famous novel, *Uncle Tom's Cabin*, which was held at the Newberry Library in 1992. Led by early-Americanist scholar, Mason Lowance of The University of Massachusetts, a group of 12 scholars gathered in Chicago for eight weeks to discuss a very controversial book about race and slavery written by a white woman and a Northern white woman at that.

As we got deeper and deeper into our discussions, it became evident that at least one of the participants, a woman of color, felt that Stowe had no business whatever writing a novel which purported to portray African American characters and their lifestyles accurately. In this scholar's opinion, a novel about race and ethnic discrimination was invalidated if the author was a member of the victimizing race rather than that of the victim. She contended that as a white person, Stowe used language to privilege her white characters and that her bias (albeit latent) against a racial other was revealed through the dialogue and speeches she placed in the mouths of her African American characters. She went on to argue that the power and dominance exerted by the ruling culture's mastery of language prohibited an accurate portrayal of the Southern Negro of the 1850's and 60's, creating instead a white (wo)man's stereotype, a Romanticized and domesticized picture of an ethnic minority which elicited pity rather than admiration, and whose words and speeches indicated white condescension and mockery rather than an attempt to record "real" and accurate speech patterns practiced by the racial other.

A large part of her argument rested on her belief that no white could accurately portray black culture for they were forever separate and isolated from them because of cultural differences. In her opinion, ethnic discrimination was all that *Uncle Tom's Cabin* could portray; it could not effectively argue the slave cause or proselytize for reform and change. Her reading of Stowe's work fascinated me, and I was determined to explore her contentions further. Therefore when the opportunity for this volume presented itself, I initially thought of a concentration on racial prejudice and a discussion of whether "white on black" or "black on white" could ever produce an accurate portrait of an "opposite" or "opposing" ethnic group.

Eventually, I decided that a wider focus was necessary, and I began to envision a study in which contributors would help readers see the variety of ways in which writers use language to portray the biases or prejudices faced by ethnic minorities of all types. Although my goal was for a balanced volume, I felt it was more likely that I would be barraged with a large number of essays discussing the black white dichotomy and bewailing the inequalities and misunderstandings between Americans of color and their Caucasian counterparts. Fortunately, contributors provided a wide range of essays rather than a limited scope. Karen Surman Paley's essay was one of the first to arrive, bringing with it the intriguing concept that college courses which emphasize the use of multi-cultural texts in an attempt to promote ethnic understanding and acceptance of those who possess a different background, may, in fact, create an opposite effect, reinforcing misconceptions and stereotypes rather than promoting a positive shift in opinion.

When considered alongside the original comments from the NEH seminar, Paley's analysis of how literature depicts and may even foster ethnic discrimination made it clear to me that even though universities are sincere in their attempts to foster unity and worldwide acceptance through offer a "politically correct" curriculum (minus ethnic and racial slurs), the attempt to protect students from such exposure is just as futile as our attempts to make up for years of discrimination in the workplace by demanding affirmative action programs for minorities, and those which will settle gender and sexual preference disputes as well.

Texts do and will continue to contain biases and prejudices based on racial and ethnic otherness. That does not mean we should shun them and condemn their authors for a limited perspective or for their shallow perceptions of so-called "differences." Instead our reaction to "otherness" must foster a heightened sensitivity of the tendency of all humans to judge individuals on the basis of their heritage; be it racial, genetic or ethnic, we tend to label that which is different as "strange" and perhaps even as "wrong" or "bad." Seldom do we look beyond outward appearance and see the full picture.

Ethnic discrimination as portrayed in literature provides readers with an accurate view of a world where dissension and conflict far outnumber acceptance and peaceful co-existence. To present books that suggest otherwise would be to distort reality and depict an ideal world. The discussion that follows presents quality works of literature that concentrate on ethnic discrimination while working not to promote its beliefs but rather to expose its flaws. In fact this volume even demonstrates how authors who are actual members of ethnic minorities may practice self-criticism as they depict their own ethnic enclave through satire.

As editor, I ask you to peruse each of these studies with an open mind. The range and variety is appealing. You will meet writers from the traditional American canon while also being exposed to third world writers whose work is as yet unfamiliar to a wide reading public. You will sample memoirs of Holocaust survivors and experience the silencing of Italian American women. You will see South African apartheid and tribal conflict in Nigeria as well as transplanted Asian culture in Canada and the idolization of the black body in Japan. Each essay demonstrates how language and books, empowered by the inspiration of their authors, effectively and powerfully communicate a wide variety of discrimination based on ethnicity. As you sample, may you come to know the ethnic "other" not merely in a politically correct way - in which you sample the difference and nod your head approvingly, validating all cultures as equal. Rather, may you experience a contemplative assessment of each critic's attempt to analyze the authorial motives and goals inherent in each work. By confronting the ethnic "other" in this way, I hope you will question as well as accept, thus engendering a wealth of understanding based on active engagement rather than on passive acceptance.

Dr. Michael Meyer
February. 1997

Dedication and Acknowledgments

The editor wishes to acknowledge and thank Justin Hardman of Hong Kong International School for his assistance with formatting this document and for correcting typographical mistakes. The project would have taken much longer without his meticulous help. Series General Editor David Bevan and Fred van der Zee of Rodopi were also been supportive and encouraging as this volume progressed, and all the authors were particularly tolerant and cooperative when revisions were suggested by the editor. I should like to dedicate this book my mother, Irene Stoit Meyer, whose love for books and learning was lovingly instilled in me during my youth. For countless stories read aloud, for weekly trips to the library and encouragement to write, I owe her endless thanks. This acknowledgment can't begin to repay my debt of love for the gifts she gave me, but it is a start.

1.

RELIGIOUS SKIRMISHES:
WHEN THE ETHNIC OUTSIDER
CANNOT HEAR "THE LOUDEST VOICE"

Teachers of freshman composition are being inundated with multicultural composition readers. They have names like *Crossing Cultures, Making Cultural Connections, Cultural Tapestry, and Multitude.*[1] According to Nancy Shapiro, "[T]he multicultural reader has become the hottest idea to hit textbook companies since the revolution in rhetoric from modes to process."[2] Their publishers believe that "culturally mainstream students ... need to have their horizons expanded."[3] The assumption here is that there is a cause and effect relationship between exposure and expansion. While Shapiro faults these texts for a lack of rhetorical diversity, favoring the personal narrative over more academic discourse, my concern is more basic. Does the ethnic narrative in these texts actually break down cultural isolation by exposing the outsider to insider information, or does it create what Jacques Leenhardt calls a "reiterative reality,"[4] confirming the stereotypes the ethnic outsider brings to the text?

Crossing Cultures: Readings for Composition, now in its fourth edition, contains the story "The Loudest Voice" by Jewish writer Grace Paley. After considering responses of some Catholic freshman composition students to this story, it has become apparent to me that such an ethnic narrative can stir up religious animosity. The linchpin appears to be the ability of the reader to accept the "interpretive construct"[5] of the implied author as distinguished from the narrator. When the reader's religious or ethnic passions are incited, the construct fails and s/he refuses to become the ideal implied reader the author desires. In other words, the reader takes the characters to be mouthpieces of the author.

This is not to deny some success to the publishers' claim of "expanding horizons," or a bonding that develops when a reader identifies with an ethnic group outside his/her own through a sense of universality. Occasionally there is a rupture of a response the reader expects to make. Jacques Leenhardt refers to this as the "short-circuit effect,"[6] or a change in the way readers normally try to master innovation by making it conform to what they already think. This effect is comparable to a phenomenon discussed by Lucien Goldmann. Each social group has its own mental structure, that is, feelings, habits of thought, and ways of dealing with the world, which he calls a world view. Ordinarily there is no imbrication of one world view by another, but occasionally there is an exception.

> The work corresponding to the mental structure of some social group can be elaborated in certain (admittedly rare) cases by an individual with very little relationship to this group ... [T]he individual can only push it to a very high degree of coherence and transpose it on a plane of imaginary creation, conceptual thought, etc.[7]

The individual can go outside of her world view only in a theoretical way. However, a rupture with parochialism can occur, precipitating what I will call an interpretive crisis for the reader who involuntarily crosses boundaries, and unexpectedly identifies with a person or situation outside his/her immediate experience.

The Need to Homogenize the Disparate

Before exploring differing reader responses to Paley's story, I want to problematize the way in which universality (appreciation for underlying similarities between different ethnic groups) has been valorized by modernists over polyculturalism (appreciation for difference). As Fredric Jameson puts it, "the process of cultural 'universalization' ... implies the repression of the oppositional voice, and the illusion that there is only one genuine 'culture.'"[8]

In M.H. Abrams collection, *Literature and Belief*, Cleanth Brooks argues that unless we can tap into some sort of essential oneness of humankind, there is no basis for aesthetics at all.

> ...[Y]et there is the danger that our present-day awareness of cultural diversity and the claims of cultural relativism may obscure for us the importance of the basis upon which our participation in literature rests. If man in his essential humanity does not exist, and if his unchanging fundamental oneness does not

> transcend the innumerable differences that set apart individual men and men
> of various cultures and periods of history, then I do not think we can talk
> about poetry at all.[9]

Brooks is granting second class citizenship to cultural diversity in the narrative, making it less important than the "'human' nature that exists within us."[10] There is no attempt to define this alleged essence. What does "essential humanity" actually mean? Brooks implies that the polycultural ethnic narrative, one that celebrates heterogeneity, is not really literature at all.

Douglas Bush's essay in *Literature and Belief* takes the argument one step further; he presumes to speak for the nonbelieving Other. The equation of Christianity with universality is strong. "Few readers, *one imagines*, are untouched - if they read them - by the purity and power of medieval poems, from 'The Dream of the Rood' to 'Quia Amore Langueo.'"[11] Apparently feeling the need for some evidence to support his imaginary information, Bush bolsters his case by quoting the comment of *one* Jewish student, "who, remarking on the very different tradition in which he had grown up, argued that no one who wished to live above the natural level could fail to be moved by Herbert."[12] One wonders if any resistant non-Christian students, apparently subsisting below "the natural level," ever expressed their discomfort with the text.

We can see the elevation of supposed universality over particularity in commentary on Jewish writers as well. Referring to Bernard Malamud, Daniel Walden writes, "In penetrating deeply into the particular, the life that he knew and wanted to understand, he exposed the universal."[13] In an essay on Grace Paley's "Jewish Miniatures," ordinary characters who are imbued with heroicalness, Bonnie Lyons declares, "In Paley's work, as in Olsen's, is the same commitment to one worldly humanity that transcends all distinctions and unites all human beings as human beings."[14] I have encountered some who would disagree with Lyons' reading.

A Reader Response Survey

During my first semester teaching writing at Boston College, a predominantly white institution, I selected the composition reader *Crossing Cultures,* somewhat naively expecting that exposure to the contents would automatically "expand horizons." Students were asked to read Grace Paley's story, "The Loudest Voice,"[15] which is about the responses of Jewish parents when their children are chosen to play the leading roles in the school's Christmas pageant. The school is oblivious to the fact that some Jews might find this offensive.

On the other hand, having grown up with a mother and a grandmother who disliked everybody who was not Jewish, I found the story to be a humorous and accurate representation of *their* prejudices. However, when we discussed the story in my predominantly Catholic class, I laughed alone and finally gave up trying to "explain" the humor to my students. I came away from the class that day feeling disappointed and inadequate as a teacher. The experience brought to mind a statement Tom Newkirk made in regard to teaching narratives. "There is an emotional turbulence and a frequency of failure in my own teaching that I do not see reflected in many accounts, including ones I have written or edited myself."[16] Rather than follow his suggestion to "create [a] forum for telling failure stories," I decided instead to find out what was behind my students' silence.

Influenced by some of the pedagogy of David Bartholomae, Anthony Petrosky, and Mariolina Salvatori[17], I decided to try to "teach" the story again the next semester, but this time have my students, 86% of whom were Catholic, respond to a questionnaire to determine their reactions to specific parts of the text. Similarly, a teacher of freshman composition at Brandeis University had her class, which was 69% Jewish, complete the questionnaire. (See Appendix.)

Before reporting some of the students' responses to "The Loudest Voice," let me describe the story in more depth for the reader who may be unfamiliar with it, acknowledging that my Jewish background both privileges and prejudices my reading of the text. Shirley Abramowitz, a Jewish girl in a heterogeneous elementary school, is chosen to play the voice-over of Jesus in the upcoming Christmas pageant because she has the loudest voice. In fact, all the main characters are played by Jewish children with their Christian peers being given either minor parts or no parts at all. Clara Abramowitz, Shirley's mother, is offended that Jewish children are put in the position of playing out a drama that falls outside of their religious beliefs. Her father, Misha, initially tries to console his wife by catering to her prejudices. After the performance he says, "'Still and all, it was certainly a beautiful affair, you have to admit, introducing us to the beliefs of a different culture.'"[18] To me, these are stock Jewish figures, the bigot and the liberal. In the end of the story, however, Clara defends the roles of the Jewish children as a way of gaining power. "'[The Christian children] got very small voices...You think it's so important they should get in the play?

Christmas...the whole piece of goods...they own it.'"[19] The Christians in the story are stereotyped as people totally insensitive to religious differences. They put up a Christmas tree in the middle of a Jewish community and expect Jewish participation in a Christian event without ever once considering how the Jews would feel. The Christian reader might feel offended by the way s/he is constructed.

As a Jew who grew up in a family so rife with anti-Christian bias that the most frequently repeated word was the epithet "goyim," I shook my head laughing as I recognized Clara Abramowitz's objections to her daughter's role, expressed with just the right Yiddish inflection. In fact, my own mother, whose "Christian name" is also Clara, went to great lengths to transfer me from a largely Catholic school to a Jewish one. My response defines my participation in a certain interpretive community. Co-editor Myrna Knepler, also a Jew, came from the same community. When asked why she selected this story for *Crossing Cultures*, she said, "It's funny. ... There was the feeling as a kid of being involved in all kinds of celebrations, ones which were not mine, without my consent."[20]

Marjorie Godlin Roemer writes, "I fear that even in the most open discussions of texts, teachers often send subtle but firm messages about which readings should be shared, condoned, and supported, and which readings mark the reader as aberrant."[21] When I decided to have my students respond to a questionnaire related to the story, it was because I wanted to learn why they did not "get it." What I learned instead was that, from the perspective of some of them, I was the one who did not get it. I was the aberrant reader. Some were put off, even angered, by the anti-Christian and anti-Arab remarks uttered by the characters. The responses from these students, from Myrna Knepler, and from myself illustrate what Booth, calls "under-distance." "[I]f it is 'under-distanced,' the work becomes too personal and cannot be enjoyed as art."[22] Or, as Bakhtin puts it, "[H]ere we encounter the specific danger inherent in the novelistic zone of contact: we ourselves may actually enter the novel..."[23] Given the fact that religious conflict between Jews and Christians has been going on for thousands of years, I wonder how we could expect anything even approximating an "objective" response to "The Loudest Voice." Yet when I first assigned the story, I was as naive as Myrna Knepler who told me that it "never occurred to [her] that the Christian reader might be offended." In fact, there were four different responses to the story: a sense of universality, a polycultural appreciation of difference, a reinforcement of stereotypes, and feelings of being offended or excluded.

Affirming and Subverting Universality

Elizabeth Odónez and Valerie Lee write that the ethnic narrative can stimulate identification in ethnic outsiders. Odónez argues that, if "properly read and decoded," the ethnic narrative modifies "personal and collective identity,"[24] establishing a cross-cultural bond between reader and character. Lee, an educator who has taught both ethnic and traditional literature to over twelve hundred college students, finds that the "universality" of some ethnic works surprise white student readers who expect it to be parochial.

> They do not expect the experience to touch their lives, little realizing that any well-written work of literature will not demand that they have the exact experiences, but only that they be able to translate those experiences into their own.[25]

If the identification comes as a reversal of expectation, it can cause what I all an interpretive crisis in the reader. In fact, I experienced such a crisis when I read Misha Abramowitz' own defense of universality. "We learn from reading [Christmas] is a holiday from pagan times also, candles, lights, even Chanukah. So we learn it's not altogether Christian."[26] I was initially shocked by the similar ancestry of the Christian and Jewish holidays. I crossed a boundary I had not anticipated.

A sense of universality was evident in the responses to the Paley story from four out of fourteen Boston College students and three out of the sixteen students at Brandeis University. Only one of these three Brandeis readers is Jewish. Here are some excerpts from their responses to the question, "Does this story remind you of anything that happened to you?," followed by their ethnic and religious self-descriptions.

> Having come from another country, I identified with some of the scenes in the story. They resembled the inkling memories of my days in grade school in the States. (Brandeis; Asian; none.)

> I know that persecution because of religion happens. My faith is very important to me, I wouldn't want anyone to change that ... In whatever religion you are in, you must stand up for your faith. Obviously where [Mrs. Abramowitz] had lived before, made her feel suspicious of other religions. She must have felt like she was losing her identity. I can feel for her with this...(Boston College; Russian/Polish; Roman Catholic)

Apparently the Asian student was also forced to participate in practices that were antithetical to his beliefs. Although the Boston College student apparently was never put in such a situation, he allows himself to imagine what it would feel like to have his beliefs threatened. Having read the story, he is able to go outside what Goldmann calls his own world view and conceptually take on the mental structure of the Jew.

Other students translated the experience of the characters to parallel their own but in a way that was decidedly hostile to the Jews.

> The only thing that could be remotely connected to this is that the Music Chairman at my school was Jewish. He frowned upon Christmas music, but we sang it anyway. (Boston College; Irish/Scottish/Welsh; Roman Catholic)

> Before transferring to this class I was with a teacher that wanted the class focus to be solely on the holocaust. I felt that was unfair to me. I could not sit in a class for four months and sympathize with her about something that happened so long ago when my people are dying in the West Bank and Ethnic cleansing is taking place in Bosnia. (Boston College; Arab; Christian)

The first responder gleefully reports defying the Jewish music director and, like the second responder, identifies with Clara Abramowitz in his anger at being forced to participate in something he does not believe in. In subverting the spirit of commonality, the Arabic student makes it clear that he believes there are no lessons of the Holocaust that could be applied to the Palestinians or the Bosnian Muslims. Given the conflicted nature of some of these responses, I would have to say that the story achieved only limited success in eliciting a sense of universality for these non-Jewish readers.

Polyculturalism

The editors of *Crossing Cultures* define a dual polycultural purpose for their anthology.

> [C]ross-cultural subjects ... challenge accepted beliefs by asking students to consider the lives, ideas, aspirations -- and prejudices of people who are different from them. At the same time, reading, and having one's classmates read, selections related to one's own culture is likely to heighten student's self-assurance and cause them to reflect on the meaning of their own experience.[27]

Signs of polyculturalism among the student responses in this survey included: an increase in tolerance, an appreciation of difference, and, for the Jewish students, a recollection of similar experiences. Four students from Boston College and seven from Brandeis University demonstrated such responses.

An excerpt from a Boston College student illustrates what Leenhardt calls the short-circuit effect which "indicates that there is a 'hole' in the checkerwork of meaning ... [T]he text may disturb the pre-established reading scheme and thus destabilize the mental structures of reception."[28] Instead of deriving from the text a confirmation of what the reader already thought prior to exposure to the words on the page, the student experiences a rupture when s/he does not find the anticipated meaning.

> Christmas was always a big deal for my family when I was a kid. I did not think of much but getting presents. *Considering this, it is a change* to think that many people don't recognize Christmas and may even be offended by it. I do remember being very confused when my Jewish friends did not appreciate the end of December as much as my brother and I did. (Boston College; Irish; Roman Catholic) [Emphasis mine]

This student learned something from the story; for the first time, he was able to see that people from a different religious background than his react differently to Christmas. He seems surprised and recognizes that he has experienced a "change."

Most of the polycultural response from Brandeis students came in the form of recollection of personal experiences of being forced to participate in Christian celebrations. As one student put it,

> I recall in 5th grade, I had an argument with an Art teacher because she wanted everyone to make Christmas trees out of construction paper. I refused. I was not trying to be obstinate or close-minded; I just felt it was being imposed on me. (Female; white; Reform Judaism)

The story clearly replicated some of their own religious difficulties in a heterogeneous elementary school. In fact, as indicated earlier, co-editor Myrna Knepler reacted to the Paley story in the same way. "There was a feeling as a kid of being involved in all kinds of celebrations, ones which were not mine, without my consent."

Reinforcement of Stereotypes

Leenhardt writes that the short-circuit effect is a "system of dysfunctioning [which] arises from a failure in the regulating system, which normally tends to master innovation in order to transform it into what is already known, i.e., into a reiterative reality."[29]   For example, in a large scale reader response study in France and Hungary, readers of the ethnic novel imposed schemes on the text to accommodate it to what they were familiar with. French readers disturbed by fragmentation in the Hungarian novel, essentially restructured the novel around a central hero.

In the case of the Paley story, two out of thirty readers created a reiterative reality, indicating a biased perception of Jews.

> I found all the uproar about the Christmas tree to be stupid. Anybody can enjoy Christmas. Why would somebody deliberately downgrade it because he or she doesn't believe in it. People who feel that way have no business being that way. Either ignore people like this or treat them like the close-minded people they are. (Boston College; Indian; ...)

> The little girl gets the main part in the school Xmas play due to her having a loud voice and also being jewish....I thought the mother discriminated a lot against christians, and then she'll wonder why they will discriminate towards jews. (Boston College; English; Church of England)

The first reader is quite belligerent toward the Jews whom he sees as being "close-minded people." He lacks a sense of religious relativism, while expecting the Jews to have precisely what he lacks. In other words, he calls for tolerance and acceptance of Christmas while displaying intolerance toward those who resist his concept of tolerance.

In my reading of the story, Shirley was chosen for the part because of her voice, not because she was "typecast" as a Jew. Jewish children were chosen to play Christians in spite of the fact that they are Jewish. The second student either did not read the text carefully or reacted to it in terms of a strong negative image of Jews. Her statement seems to suggest a stereotype of a group of people who are loud and pushy; any discrimination they feel may very well be a consequence of their own behavior.

Excluding or Offending the Ethnic Outsider

Bonnie Lyons argues that the values in Paley's work stem from "Yiddishkeit," or the folk expression of Jewish culture and beliefs, specifically characterized by an elevation of the ordinary person who is struggling with everyday problems. She finds that Paley's statement "that art is 'on the side of the underdog' ... suggests the humanistic bias of Yiddish and American Jewish literature."[30] Applying Lyons' reading of Paley's work, one could say that for the implied author of "The Loudest Voice," the Jewish schoolchildren are the underdogs, victims of the school officials; this point of view is most sharply represented by Clara Abramowitz. On the other hand, Lyons also argues that a particular form of Yiddishkeit, "the idealistic, socialist version of her own upbringing,"[31] is what resonates most strongly in her work. Misha Abramowitz, whose affirmative statement about learning "the beliefs of a different culture" (65), hints at an international unity. What we have then is not a unified notion of "Yiddishkeit," but a dialogized version, one that re-enacts the struggle between the Maccabeans who wanted to maintain Jewish tradition in the face of Syrian-Greek oppression, and the Hellenist Jews who remained Jewish while adopting Greek ways.

The struggle between the two forces in Paley's story, which I have described as polyculturalism and universality, can have a disruptive affect on the audience. Rather than forcing the reader into the non-choice of "playing out roles dramatized in the text,"[32] the tendentious discourse of "The Loudest Voice" sparks a third option: hostility and the formation of the "mock reader"[33] who refuses to engage with and remains estranged and excluded from the text.

Eight responders from Boston College (50%) and four from Brandeis (25%) felt excluded or offended by passages in the Paley story. Of note is the fact that five students from Boston College and two from Brandeis were offended by the same passages. These come after Clara Abramowitz says, "'I'm surprised to see my neighbors making tra-la-la for Christmas'" (62).

> My father couldn't think of what to say to that. Then he decided: "You're in America! Çlara, you wanted to come here. In Palestine the Arabs would be eating you alive. Europe you had pogroms. Argentina is full of Indians. Here you got Christmas....Some joke, ha?" (62, paragraph 28)

"Very funny, Misha. What is becoming of you? If we came to a new country a long time ago to run away from tyrants, and instead we fall into a creeping pogrom, that our children learn a lot of lies, so what's the joke? Ach, Misha, your idealism is going away. (paragraph 29)

"So is your sense of humor." (paragraph 30)

In my reading, I see that Clara objects to the Christmas play as it represents a "creeping pogrom," that is, an insidious ideological extermination of the Jews. Misha exhibits sang-froid in the face of a cultural challenge. He is attempting to cajole his wife into accepting the play with a benign resignation toward the fate of the Jew in a mixed society, as if to say, "What are you going to do?" The Christian and Jewish students who cited these passages did not take it so lightly.

I'm not sure exactly what the mother means. She says they come to a "creeping pogrom" where the "children learn a lot of lies." Does this mean she is referring to Christmas as a lie? (Boston College; Italian; Catholic)

The father seemed racist about everything except Christmas....What does he mean when he says "Arabs would be eating you alive." Not only that, but so what if "Argentina is full of Indians." I don't see it as being of any significance. (Boston College; Arab; Christian)

I was angry on p.61 paragraph 28-29 when Shirley's mother was too close-minded towards other religions & towards wanting her daughter to participate in a play about the birth of Christ. (Boston College; white/caucasian; Jewish)

[I]f I were Christian and this holiday was very dear to me, then I might be a little offended. (Brandeis; Russian Jew; Judaism)

These responses are emotional and political, the kind of reading that has been called inexperienced and unsophisticated. M.H. Abrams writes,

Most critics and aesthetic philosophers ... hold that, in appreciating literature as literature, the *skilled* reader in some fashion suspends his disbelief so as to go along in imagination with express judgments and doctrines from which he would ordinarily dissent.[34] (emphasis mine).

From Abrams' perspective, such students are not appreciating the story as literature; they are taking it quite literally. They parallel the east Asian reader, who, according to Miner, "in the absence of countervailing evidence, ... presume[s] that poets speak 'in propia persona.'"[35]

The student readers either do not see or do not accept that behind Clara and Misha lies the narrator, the child Shirley Abramowitz, who seems to be deliberately presenting offensive opinions, a live example of socio-cultural heteroglossia among the Jewish community. Further archeology reveals an implied author who may be even more distant from the representation of the characters than the narrator. In this case, the offended readers may be so politically and religiously estranged from the characters, that they may fail to engage with the story as literature. However, given such political or religious differences, should it then follow that such readers are "unskilled" or naive? After all, reading, as Jameson and Bakhtin would argue, is an ideological act.

It is also important to recognize that the nature of the feeling of exclusion varies between the two groups of readers. The Christian readers' rejection of the Jewish discomfort with the Christmas pageant actually duplicates that discomfort, something they do not seem cognizant of. Referring to a student who feels disoriented by certain parts of "The Waste Land," Salvatorini writes, "What, then, prevents her from recognizing that her repeatedly unfulfilled expectations *are* an actualization of the poem?"[36] The same question may be asked of the adverse response of the Christian readers to Paley's text. What is preventing them from realizing that their sense of being confused, troubled, and angry is an actualization of how the Jews in the story feel as a group of religious others asked to uncritically take on the trappings of the dominant culture? Some Christian readers are unable to identify with the Jews in spite of their reciprocal feelings of alienation.

On the other hand, we can see what appears to be an interpretive crisis in the response of the offended Jewish reader; he is compelled to step outside of his interpretive community to take offense on behalf of the Christian reader. He writes, "If I were a Christian ... I might be a little offended." The reader crossed a boundary into another world view, ironically universalizing the feeling of exclusion.

Forty percent of the small sample students who read "The Loudest Voice" in the popular multicultural composition reader, *Crossing Cultures*, were made uncomfortable by it. Co-editor Myrna Knepler believes that this discomfort is a stage of awareness, one that the instructor must help them through so that they come to realize that the antagonism of the Jews to the Christmas pageant is being actualized in their response.

In the end, I do not feel that all the burden of interpretation should be put on either the teacher or the reader. Does the ethnic narrative necessarily become assimilative if, for example, editorial notes clarify the culture's fears? Could Paley have written "The Loudest Voice" in such a way that more Christian readers could hear it? I am amazed at how many of my Catholic students know nothing about pogroms or little, if anything, of the Holocaust. We live in a world that fibrillates daily with ethnic clashes. It is time to select for study and continue to develop the ethnic narrative that valorizes difference while playing the part of the good host(ess) to the outsider. To do so would be to embrace a literary ethic in the service of a social good.

Karen Surman Paley

Works Cited

Abrams, M.H. *Literature and Belief.* New York: Columbia University Press, 1958.

Bakhtin, M.M. *The Dialogic Imagination: Four essays by M.M. Bakhtin.* Ed. Michael Holquist. Austin: University of Texas Press, 1981.

Bartholomae, David and Anthony Petrosky. *Facts, Artifacts and Counterfacts: Theory and Method for a Reading and Writing Course.* Portsmouth, NH: Heinemann, 1986.

Booth, Wayne C. *The Rhetoric of Fiction.* 2nd ed. Chicago: University of Chicago Press, 1983.

Brooks, Cleanth. "Implications of an Organic Theory of Poetry." *Literature and Belief.* Ed. M.H. Abrams. NY: Columbia University Press, 1958. 53-79.

Bush, Douglas. "Tradition and Experience." *Literature and Belief.* Ed. M.H. Abrams. NY: Columbia University Press, 1958. 31-52.

Culler, Jonathan. *On Deconstruction: Theory and Criticism after Structuralism.* Ithaca: Cornell University Press, 1982.

Divakaruni, Chitra, ed. *Multitude: Cross-Cultural Readings for Writers*. New   York: McGraw-
Hill, 1993.

Evans, Faun Bernbach, Barbara Gleason, and Mark Wiley. *Cultural Tapestry: Readings for a
Pluralistic Society*. New York: HarperCollins, 1992.

Goldmann, Lucien. "Introduction to the Problems of the Sociology of the Novel."*Telos,* 18
(Winter 1973-4): 122-135.

Jameson, Fredric. *The Political Unconscious: Narrative as a Socially Symbolic Act*. Ithaca:
Cornell University Press, 1981.

Knepler, Henry, Myrna Knepler, and Kathleen Kane. *Crossing Cultures: Readings for
Composition*. 4th ed. NY: Macmillan, 1994.

Knepler, Myrna. Personal communication. 3 March 94.

Lee, Valerie. "Responses of White Students to Ethnic Literature: One Teacher's Experience."
Reader (Spring 1986): 24-33.

Leenhardt, Jacques. "Toward a Sociology of Reading," in *The Reader in the Text: Essays on
Audience and Interpretation*. Eds. Susan R. Suleiman and Inge Crosman. Princeton:
Princeton University Press, 1980. 205-224.

Lyons, Bonnie. "Grace Paley's Miniatures," *Studies in American Jewish Literature,* 8.1(1989): 26-
33.

Miner, Earl. *Comparative Poetics: An Intercultural Essay on Theories of Literature*. Princeton:
Princeton University Press, 1990.

Newkirk, Thomas. "Silences in Our Teaching Stories: What Do We Leave out and Why?" in
Workshop 4: The Teacher as Researcher. Ed Thomas Newkirk. Portsmouth: Heinemann,
1992. (21-30).

Ordóñez, Elizabeth J. "Narrative Texts by Ethnic Women: Rereading the Past, Reshaping the
Future." *MELUS,* 9.3 (1982): 19-28.

Paley, Grace. "The Loudest Voice," in *Crossing Cultures*. 4th ed. Eds. Henry   Knepler, Myrna
Knepler, and Kathleen Kane. New York: Macmillan, 1994. 60-67.

Notes:

[1] Henry Knepler, Myrna Knepler, and Kathleen Kane, ed., *Crossing Cultures: Readings for
Composition,* 4th ed, (New York: Macmillan, 1994). Marilyn Rye, *Making Cultural Connections:
Readings for Critical Analysis*, (Boston: Bedford, 1994). Faun Bernbach Evans, Barbara Gleason,
and Mark Wiley, *Cultural Tapestry: Readings for a Pluralistic Society.* (New York:

HarperCollins, 1992). Chitra B. Divakaruni, ed., *Multitude: Cross-Cultural Readings for Writers*, (New York: McGraw-Hill, 1993.)

[2] Nancy Shapiro, "Rereading Multicultural Readers: What Definition of Multicultural are We Buying?," at Conference on College Composition and Communication (43rd, Cincinnati, OH, March 19-21, 1992), 1. ED 346 471.

[3] *Ibid.*, 8.

[4] Jacques Leenhardt, "Toward a Sociology of Reading," in *The Reader and the Text: Essays on Audience and Interpretation*, ed., Susan R. Suleiman and Inge Crosman, (Princeton: Princeton University Press, 1980), 224.

[5] Susan R. Suleiman and Inge Crosman, "Introduction," in *The Reader in the Text: Essays on Audience and Interpretation*, ed. Susan R. Suleiman and Inge Crosman, (Princeton: Princeton University Press, 1980), 11.

[6] *Op. cit.*, 221.

[7] Lucien Goldmann, "Introduction to the Problems of the Sociology of the Novel." *Telos*, 18 (Winter 1973-4): 129.

[8] Fredric Jameson, *The Political Unconscious: Narrative as a Socially Symbolic Act*, (Ithaca: Cornell University Press, 1981), 87.

[9] Cleanth Brooks, "Implications of an Organic Theory of Poetry," in *Literature and Belief*, ed. M.H. Abrams, (New York: Colombia University Press, 1958), 70.

[10] *Ibid.*, 70.

[11] Douglas Bush, "Tradition and Experience," in *Literature and Belief*, ed. M.H. Abrams (New York: Colombia University Press, 1958), 39. Emphasis added.

[12] *Ibid.*, 39.

[13] Daniel Walden, "Bernard Malamud, An American Jewish Writer and His Universal Heroes." *Studies in American Jewish Literature* 7.2 (1988): 160.

[14] Bonnie Lyons. "Grace Paley's Miniatures." *Studies in American Jewish Literature* 8.1 (1989):32.

[15] Grace Paley, "The Loudest Voice," in *Crossing Cultures*, 60-67.

[16] Thomas Newkirk, "Silences in Our Teaching Stories: What Do We Leave Out and Why?," in *Workshop 4: The Teacher as Researcher*, ed. Thomas Newkirk (Portsmouth: Heinemann, 1992), 23.

[17] See David Bartholomae and Anthony Petroskey, ed., *Facts, Artifacts and Counterfacts: Theory and Method for a Reading and Writing Course* (Portsmouth: Heinemann, 1986).

[18] Grace Paley, "The Loudest Voice," 65.

[19] *Ibid.*, 65.

[20] Myrna Knepler, telephone conversation with the author, 3 March 1994.

[21] Marjorie Godlin Roemer, "Which Reader's Response?" *College English*, 49.8 (Dec. 1987), 915.

[22] Wayne C. Booth, *The Rhetoric of Fiction*, 2nd ed., (Chicago: University of Chaicgo Press, 1983), 122.

[23] M.M. Bakhtin, *The Dialogic Imagination: Four Essays by M.M. Bakhtin*, ed. Michael Holquist (Austin: University of Texas Press), 32.

[24] Elizabeth J. Ordønez, "Narrative Texts by Ethnic Women: Rereading the Past, Reshaping the Future." *Melus*, 9.3 (1982): 19.

[25] Valerie Lee, "Responses of White Students to Ethnic Literature: One Teacher's

Experience." *Reader* (Spring 1986): 30.

[26] *Op. cit.*, 63.

[27] Henry Knepler, Myrna Knepler, and Kathleen Kane, ed., *Crossing Cultures*, iii.

[28] Jacques Leenhardt, "Toward a Sociology of Reading," 224.

[29] *Ibid.*, 224.

[30] Bonnie Lyons, "Grace Paley's Miniatures," 31.

[31] *Ibid.*, 27.

[32] Jonathan Culler, *On Deconstruction: Theory and Criticism after Structuralism* (Ithaca; Cornell University Press), 81.

[33] Wayne C. Booth, *The Rhetoric of Fiction*, 138.

[34] M.H. Abrams, *Literature and Belief* (New York; Colombia University Press), 1958.

[35] Miner, Earl, *Comparative Poetics: An Intercultural Essay on Theories of Literature*, (Princeton: Princeton University Press, 1990), 30.

[36] Mariolina Salvatori, "Toward a Hermeneutics of Difficulty," in *Audits of Meaning: A Festschrift in Honor of Ann E. Berthoff*, ed. Louise Smith, (Portsmouth: Boynton/Cook, 1988), 90.

2

SAM, WALTER LEE,
AND THE POWERLESS BLACK MALE

At first glance, Sam from Athol Fugard's *"Master Harold"...and the boys* and Walter Lee from Lorraine Hansberry's *A Raisin in the Sun* might seem to have little in common. One is South African, the other American; one does not change, the other grows; one has dignity and presence, the other is immature and self-pitying for much of the play. Nonetheless, there is a basic similarity between the two. They are adult black males whom the white societies around them have attempted to render powerless.

Despite his intelligence and abilities, Sam is held down by apartheid. For years he and Willie were reduced to living in "a gray little room with a cold cement floor," a "wobbly little table," and a bed "propped up on bricks."[1] In fact, the system has left them with so few resources that they cannot even afford sixpence for the jukebox.

In similar fashion, Walter Lee is held down in white America. If Sam has had to share a small, dingy room, the Youngers have been forced to live in a "rat trap," a cramped and overtaxed apartment that has "had to accommodate the living of too many people for too many years."[2] So poor is the family that the Youngers cannot afford the 50 cents that his teacher wants Travis to bring to class.

Moreover, their racist societies afford both Sam and Walter Lee only the most limited prospects for advancement. For many years Sam has done menial labor for Hally's mother with no ostensible improvement in his lot. Indeed, Hally maliciously reminds him of his lowly position, telling him pointblank, "You're only a servant in here, and don't forget it" (53).

Walter Lee is likewise well aware of his subservient status as a chauffeur:

> I open and close car doors all day long. I drive a man around in his limousine and I say, "Yes, sir; no, sir; very good, sir; shall I take the Drive, sir?" Mama, that ain't no kind of job...that ain't nothing at all....Sometimes it's like I can see the future stretched out in front of me....a big, looming blank space -- full of *nothing*. (61)

Not surprisingly, both men resent their predicaments. Sam may of necessity keep his feelings on apartheid largely to himself, but on occasion his attitude becomes clear. For instance, when Hally asks him to name a great "man of magnitude," he unhesitatingly chooses Abraham Lincoln, implying that he longs for liberation. Hally understands this and responds to Sam's choice with, "I might have guessed as much" (20).

Walter Lee is more outspoken and expresses his frustrations time and again. For example, he complains to his wife Ruth, "I'm thirty-five years old; I been married eleven years and I got a boy who sleeps in the living room -- and all I got to give him is stories about how rich white people live" (15). As he tells George Murchison, the situation leaves him feeling like "a volcano" (76).

Interestingly, one way that both men deal with their sense of frustration is by dreaming. Sam nourishes "a dream about a world in which accidents don't happen" (45), a dream that is embodied for him in ballroom dancing. As Sam explains it, dancing is

> beautiful because that is what we want life to be like. But instead,...we're bumping into each other all the time....None of us knows the steps and there's no music playing. And it doesn't stop with us. The whole world is doing it all the time....America has bumped into Russia, England is bumping into India, rich man bumps into poor man....People get hurt in all that bumping, and we're sick and tired of it now....Are we never going to get it right? (46)

In the face of his seemingly hopeless situation, Sam's dream is an act of hope, in which he envisions the world as it ought to be.

Dreams are central to *A Raisin in the Sun* as well. The title itself, taken from Langston Hughes' "Harlem (A Dream Deferred)," proclaims as much. Beneatha, Walter Lee's sister, longs to become a doctor. His mother Lena has always wanted to buy a house and make "a little garden in the back" (28). Joseph Asagai, a Nigerian student, has his dreams about Africa, where he "will teach and work and things will happen" (128); and Walter Lee has his own dream of owning a liquor store, a dream he clings to with fervor and at times desperation.

Their dreams have allowed both Sam and Walter Lee to imagine a better tomorrow despite the oppression they face today. To do so, though, has at times been a challenge, as their social systems have consistently denied them status and power. The two plays in fact use the same metaphor for their societies' attempts at emasculation: their worlds would reduce these grown men to the status of boys.

This reality is implied by the very title of Fugard's drama, in which a white seventeen-year-old is elevated to "master" and the black forty-five-year-olds become "boys." Moreover, Fugard underlines this tragic irony throughout the play. For example, after Hally physically punishes Sam and Willie, he goes on to complain, "How the hell am I supposed to concentrate with the two of you behaving like bloody children!" (38)

Similarly, life in white America has left Walter Lee so emasculated that his own manhood is in jeopardy. Hansberry makes this clear when he faces Karl Lindner, the representative of the Clybourne Park Improvement Association. Walter Lee speaks to this racist "like a small boy, looking down at his shoes and then up at the man" (142). Indeed, so powerless has Walter Lee been rendered that he repeatedly feels the need to assert, "I'm a grown man" (59).

His defensiveness on the topic, though, leads to a major point of distinction. Despite their resemblance, there is a critical difference between Sam and Walter Lee. In both cases, their societies may attempt to strip away their manhood, but one society fails. Apartheid may label Sam a boy, but he is a boy in name only. Even Hally, his primary assailant in the play, looks up to him as a father-figure and feels "a deep and sincere admiration of the man" (46). On the one occasion when Sam is uncharacteristically tempted toward violence, he checks himself, explaining to Hally, "I've got no right to tell you what being a man means if I don't behave like one myself" (59). In the face of all the indignities directed at him, Sam's manhood ultimately remains intact.

On the other hand, if Walter Lee seems defensive about his manhood, there is good reason for it since he truly behaves like a child through much of the play. Hansberry establishes this fact from the start as his wife Ruth awakens their son Travis and then has to do the same for Walter Lee. Next, Travis asks her for 50 cents, after which Walter Lee asks her for 50 cents. Similarly, we watch Travis mope and lash out when he is not given the school money by his mother, and we watch Walter Lee mope and lash out when he is not given the insurance money by *his* mother. Indeed, throughout *Raisin* Walter Lee indulges in adolescent self-pity, voicing the typical teenage complaint that no one understands him. American society has in large part succeeded where South African society has failed. Walter Lee has been emasculated, to the point that Joseph Asagai terms his behavior "childish" (127) and his own sister declares, "that is not a man" (138).

In this regard, Hansberry intended Walter Lee to serve a representative function. She referred to him as "the American ghetto hero," the "representative hero" of "American Negroes,"[3] and she depicts in him behaviors that were widely viewed as resulting from American racism. For example, in 1964, Whitney Young, the Executive Director of the National Urban League, asserted, "the Negro male is made to feel inadequate....To this situation he may react with withdrawal, bitterness toward society, aggression both within the family and racial group, self-hatred, or crime. Or he may seek escape through a number of avenues that help him to lose himself in fantasy."[4]

Walter Lee demonstrates several of these reactions to his powerlessness. If Young speaks of the black male's withdrawal and bitterness, Walter Lee withdraws from both his family and job, failing to appear at work, going out alone at night, and wandering the city aimlessly. He is so filled with anger that George Murchison aptly describes him as "all wacked up with bitterness" (76); and as for avenues of escape that, in Young's words, "help him to lose himself," he turns increasingly to alcohol, leading Ruth to predict he will "drink himself to death" (59). His acute sense of powerlessness is driving him toward self-destruction.

Also of significance is Walter Lee's behavior toward women. If Young talks of "aggression...within the family," Walter Lee berates his mother for not giving him the insurance money, castigates his sister for wanting to go to medical school, and tells his wife that marrying her "was my greatest mistake" (59). Lacking power in the outside world, he attempts to assert it at home, much as Willie in

Fugard's play has a history of battering his girlfriends, first Eunice and now Hilda (7).

Walter Lee even goes so far as to blame black women for the plight of black men in general, declaring, "That is just what is wrong with the colored woman in this world...Don't understand about building their men up and making 'em feel like they somebody. Like they can do something....We one group of men tied to a race of women with small minds!" (16-17) Given his attitude, it is perhaps not surprising to find him accusing his mother rather than society of having "butchered up" his dream (87).

In such passages, Hansberry is touching upon one of the most controversial black issues of the day. If in her words Lena Younger is "the black matriarch incarnate,"[5] some African-Americans were directly charging black mothers with having emasculated their male offspring. For example, William Grier and Price Cobbs, two black psychiatrists, bluntly asserted that the black mother has "come to systematically drive out manliness from her sons." According to them, she must "shape and mold a unique type of man. She must intuitively cut off...his masculine assertiveness and aggression lest these put the boy's life in jeopardy....As a result, black men develop considerable hostility toward black women as the inhibiting instruments of an oppressive system."[6]

By the late sixties such views had in fact led to works like Jimmy Garrett's play *And We Own the Night*. In it the wounded hero Johnny says of his mother, "I'm scared. I can't fight her and the white man too....On the street, in the alley, I'm a fighter. But in my Mama's house I ain't nothin....She's too strong. She about killed my Daddy. Made a nigger out of him." The work ends as Johnny proclaims, "We're...new men, Mama...Not niggers. Black men," after which he shoots her twice in the back[7]. While Garrett's play clearly represents an extreme case, Walter Lee's repeated attempts to blame his situation on the women in his life have their roots in the same sexist thinking.

What is striking is how profoundly different Sam's behavior is from Walter Lee's in this respect. Walter Lee may lash out at women, but Sam does not. Quite the contrary, he actively objects to Willie's mistreatment of his girlfriends (7). Indeed, if Walter Lee in his powerlessness becomes bitter and destructive, Sam's conduct provides a marked contrast. Where Walter Lee is self-pitying and demands that others support him, Sam pities others and is the one they turn to for support.   Where Walter Lee withdraws from his job and family, Sam is a responsible worker and is always there for those he loves, even offering Hally a second chance. Where Walter Lee abuses alcohol like Hally's real father, Sam -- Hally's surrogate father -- does not.

How is one to account for such dissimilar reactions to similar circumstances? Why does one man succumb to society's emasculating forces while the other never does? One possible explanation may lie in the differing nature of the two men's dreams.

Walter Lee's dream is a thoroughly materialistic one. His goal is to rise to the economic status of a Mr. Murchison, who is about to buy a large hotel (75), or a Charlie Atkins, whose dry-cleaning business grosses $100,000 a year (13). The fact that Walter Lee's dream is of financial gain, though, puts him in a vulnerable position. Society need only deny him the material means to fulfill his aspirations, and his dream will collapse.

That is of course exactly what American racism does to Walter Lee and other blacks as it imprisons them in poverty. Hansberry herself estimated that the "comfortable" black middle class of her day was at most "five to six percent of our people, and they are atypical of the representative experience of Negroes in this country."[8]   Indeed, for every Charlie Atkins, there are many more Walter Lee Youngers, who work as chauffeurs, whose fathers were laborers, whose wives and mothers do "domestic work in people's kitchens" (141). Without the necessary resources, Walter Lee's dream is readily blocked, and the result is the fury and frustration expressed in the play's epigraph:

> What happens to a dream deferred?
> Does it dry up
> Like a raisin in the sun?
> Or fester like a sore --
> And then run?
> Does it stink like rotten meat?
> Or crust and sugar over --
> Like a syrupy sweet?
>
> Maybe it just sags
> Like a heavy load.
>
> *Or does it explode?*

However, Walter Lee is vulnerable to society at a deeper level as well. His dream of finding happiness through the gaining of wealth is, after all, not original. Rather, Walter Lee has simply embraced the classic American dream and made it his own. Growing up in America, he has accepted his nation's self-proclaimed image as the land of opportunity and believes so firmly in its capitalistic preachings that at one point he flatly declares, "money is life" (61). Thus, his dream is in many ways an endorsement of American values. He does not want to change society; he wants to enter it.

In short, Walter Lee's dream expresses not merely his faith in his own future but his faith in his country and its ways. Consequently, when American rhetoric is undercut by American racism, when its fabled door of opportunity proves to be locked, the reality undermines not simply his dream but his system of beliefs. It is appropriate that his hopes are literally destroyed by a man he had trusted, Willy Harris, who betrays that trust, for in a larger sense his hopes have been destroyed by a country he had believed in, the United States, that betrays that belief.

If his trust was in American values, the betrayal strips him of both trust and values as he sinks into despondency. As he tells his family,

> I laid in there on my back today...and I figured it out. Life just like it is. Who gets and who don't get....it's all divided up....Between the takers and the "tooken."...People like Willy Harris, they don't never got "tooken." And you know why the rest of us do? 'Cause we all mixed up. Mixed up bad. We get to looking 'round for the right and the wrong; and we worry about it and cry about it and stay up nights trying to figure out 'bout the wrong and the right of things...And all the time, man, them takers is out there operating, just taking and taking. (135)

He has gone from dreamer to cynic, from hope to despair.

With Sam, the situation is entirely different. Where Walter Lee's dream is one of economic success, Sam's is one of political idealism. He envisions a world transformed by a "man of magnitude" (18). Thus, when Hally asks Sam if all we can do is dream "about the way it should be," Sam responds, "it starts with that. Without the dream we won't know what we're going for. And anyway I reckon there are a few people who have got past just dreaming about it and are trying for something real. Remember that thing we read once in the paper about the Mahatma Gandhi?" (46-47)

Unlike Walter Lee's, Sam's is not a dream of financial progress for himself but of social progress for all. Consequently, apartheid may deprive him of material goods, but that does not deprive him of his dream. In fact, it confirms it. Since his dream is rooted not in a belief in his society but in a repudiation of it, the very obstacles the system puts in his way merely prove the need for his vision of change. It is no coincidence that after Hally's racist attacks have run their course, the play ends with a final reassertion of the dream as Sam and Willie dance. The events of the day have simply made the urgency of it all the more apparent.

As a result, where Walter Lee's dream leaves him vulnerable to society, Sam's gives him strength in the face of it. Much like the kite that Sam built to make Hally "look up" from despair (58), his dream of a better tomorrow allows Sam to look up and go on. Walter Lee's dream may threaten to destroy him, but Sam's helps to sustain him.

Interestingly, the difference between the two types of dreams is incorporated into *Raisin* itself. In being a materialist, Walter Lee views himself as a realist. This is clear in his reaction to Mama's criticism of his belief that "money is life." When she comments, "Once upon a time freedom used to be life....I guess the world really do change," he counters with, "No -- it was always money....We just didn't know about it" (61). Walter Lee sees himself as the man who understands "what counts in this world" (135), who knows that "don't *nothing* happen for you in the world 'less you pay somebody off" (15).

On the other hand, Joseph Asagai, the African student in the play, identifies himself not as a realist but as an idealist. When Beneatha at her lowest point asserts that there is no progress, that all we do is march around in a circle, he disagrees: "It isn't a circle -- it is simply a long line...that reaches into infinity....And it is very odd but those who see the changes are called 'idealists' -- and those who cannot...they are the 'realists'" (127).

Like Sam, Asagai is an idealist who "dreams of the future" (126), and his too is a vision of political change. It is a dream that, like Sam's, can sustain him despite the worst that the world can do. As he tells Beneatha,

> I will teach and work and things will happen, slowly and swiftly. At times it will seem that nothing changes at all....Retrogression even. Guns, murder, revolution. And I even will have moments when I wonder if the quiet was not

> better than all that death and hatred. But I will look about my village at the
> illiteracy and disease and ignorance and I will not wonder long. (128)

The idealist's vision is essentially an act of faith in the future, a spiritual belief in the possibility of progress. Indeed, Asagai calls it the "religion of doing what is necessary in the world" (127).

It is not accidental that Hansberry has the spiritual dreamer be a Nigerian while the materialist is a black American, for she saw materialism as a very real African-American problem. Two weeks before the Broadway opening of *Raisin*, she posed this question at a conference of black writers:

> What are the sores within our people that bear exposure and examination? I
> say that foremost are the villainous and often ridiculous money values that
> spill over from the dominant culture and often make us ludicrous in pursuit of
> that which has its own inherently ludicrous nature: acquisition for the sake of
> acquisition. The desire for the possession of "things" has rapidly replaced
> among too many of us the impulse for the possession of ourselves, for
> freedom.[9]

Having accepted the "money values" of the larger society, Walter Lee does indeed lack "possession" of himself.   He defines himself and his stature not by internal but by external standards, namely, by the materialistic criteria of American culture. He thinks that wealth and assets are the measure of a man, as becomes obvious when he attempts to justify taking Lindner's money: "Hell, yes, I want me some yachts someday! Yes, I want to hang some real pearls 'round my wife's neck....I tell you I am a *man* -- and I think my wife should wear some pearls in this world!....Going to feel fine...a man" (137-38).

Walter Lee believes that manhood and dignity are commodities to be bought, not qualities to be earned. This gives society yet another hold over him. If money is truly the gauge of a person's worth, then by withholding money society can render the person worthless. By blocking Walter Lee's materialistic aspirations, it can destroy not only his dream but his very identity as a man. It therefore makes perfect sense that we find him acting childishly through much of the play. If society wishes to render him a "boy," he has given it the power to do so. In playing by society's rules, Walter Lee has effectively surrendered control of his life. He has lost his freedom.

Sam, on the other hand, may be subject to a still more repressive system than is Walter Lee, but he nonetheless retains possession of himself. He in fact exemplifies what Brian Crow terms Fugard's "existential belief in the ultimate freedom of even the most oppressed individual."[10] According to existentialism, the conditions society imposes on us do not so much take away our freedom as provide the framework within which that freedom can unfold. Society may attempt to dictate our actions, but in the final analysis we make our own choices. Thus, in a passage in his *Notebooks*, Fugard praises Camus' "man who doesn't subscribe. The man who does not contribute the authority of his consent, to social sanction. Something is...surrendered with that subscription....What is it? It is defined by the Christian ethic...which can only exist on the basis of complete moral freedom."[11]

Walter Lee has given up his freedom. He has ceded possession of himself to society and its values. On the other hand, Sam may live under a virulently racist regime which does its best to restrict him, but his soul is still his own. His self-definition is no more dependent on society's rewards than is his dream, and that fact allows him to preserve his manhood and dignity despite the worst that Hally can do. Indeed, it is his very inability to shake Sam's quiet strength that infuriates Hally in their confrontation and drives him to escalate his attacks.

Ironically, though, the person whose manhood is undercut by Hally's racist assault is not Sam but Hally. If Walter Lee mistakenly thinks he can gain stature through the power money bestows, Hally mistakenly thinks he can do so through the power apartheid gives him. In point of fact, however, all his attack does is to demonstrate that he is an immature "little boy....Little *white* boy. Long trousers now, but he's still little boy" (57). While Walter Lee may suffer from a sense of powerlessness, at the end of *"Master Harold"* it is not Sam but Hally who makes the "helpless gesture" (59).

Apartheid in *"Master Harold"* ultimately emasculates the black servant less than it does the white boss, with Fugard showing that racism may do fully as much spiritual damage to its practitioners as to its victims. It is not the target of racism who forfeits his manhood but its enforcer.

Sam, the visionary dreamer, is at his core Camus' "man who doesn't subscribe," and he finally urges his would-be master to become one as well. In his last words to Hally, Sam speaks of the whites-only bench that separated them years before: "there's one thing you know. You don't *have* to sit up there by yourself. You know what that bench means now, and you can leave it any time you choose. All you've got to do is stand up and walk away" (59-60). In Sam's view, one has the freedom to walk away spiritually if not physically and so to maintain one's dignity in the face of a racist system.

It is, on the other hand, exactly his freedom and dignity that Walter Lee will utterly and irredeemably surrender if he takes Lindner's money, money that in Mama's words is a way "of telling us we wasn't fit to walk the earth" (137). In assenting to the payment, he will be accepting not merely American materialism but American racism. He will become a collaborator in the system, as Hally is and Sam is not. He will be agreeing to its terms and playing its game.

This becomes brutally clear when a frenzied Walter Lee, showing his family how he will behave with Lindner, begins groveling and "wringing his hands in [a] profoundly anguished imitation" of the servile black stereotype. Sam may have been appalled when Hally demanded he call him "master," but Walter Lee of his own volition speaks the words "Captain, Mistuh, Bossman....Great White Father, just gi' ussen de money, fo' God's sake, and we's ain't gwine come out deh and dirty up yo' white folks neighborhood" (138).

However, at the last possible moment, with his entire family looking on, Walter Lee finds that he cannot do it. He tells Lindner pointblank, "We don't want your money" (142), and in doing so, he rejects the racist and materialistic system. He may previously have believed that self-esteem came from wealth, but he now understands otherwise. Though his family lacks money, he sees that they have "a lot of pride" (142), a pride that he at long last shares. Ironically, it is by turning his back on the money that he thought would give him self-respect that he gains self-respect.

Walter Lee exercises his freedom to choose. He becomes the "man who doesn't subscribe" and in the process liberates himself from his society's emasculating power. He may have approached Lindner "like a small boy, passing the back of his sleeve across his mouth from time to time" (140-41). He leaves him, though, having "come into his manhood" (145), as his materialistic dream is replaced with a worthier one. In Hansberry's words, "he has finally reached out in his tiny moment and caught that sweet essence which is human dignity, and it shines like the old star-touched dream that it is in his eyes."[12]

It is significant, too, that at this very moment he expresses his pride in his sister Beneatha, who is "going to be a doctor" (142). Earlier, he had blamed his powerlessness on his wife, mother, and sister, as much as on society as a whole. Faced with his misery, even Mama seemed willing to entertain the possibility that she bore some responsibility for his plight. Thus, in turning over the insurance money to him, she said, "I've helped do it to you, haven't I, son?....I been doing to you what the rest of the world been doing to you....I'm telling you to be the head of this family from now on" (93-94).

However, Hansberry herself termed the idea of the castrating black woman a "legend"[13] and declared the tradition of strong African-American females to be "a *great* thing."[14] In point of fact, the play provides her own answer to the question of these women's guilt. Mama may entrust Walter Lee with the money in an effort to empower him, but her gesture has the opposite effect as he proceeds to lose it all. The real emasculators of black men are not their mothers and wives and sisters but society at large. The real enemy of black men is not black women but the system that oppresses them both. It is this that Walter Lee finally understands when he rejects the Clybourne Park Improvement Association's money, embraces the women in his life, and comes into his own as a man.

The endings of both plays are problematic but hopeful. As *"Master Harold"* concludes, Sam tries one last time to turn a fragment of his dream into reality. He extends to Hally a second chance, offering to "fly another kite" (59) and reminding him that he has the freedom to choose. Like Walter Lee, Hally can remain a boy and accept the rules of a racist society that demeans him as well as Sam, or he can come of age. Whether Hally has learned his lesson, though, we cannot tell. Indeed, the confused young man exits the play saying, "I don't know. I don't know anything anymore" (59).

However, at least one person has learned from the day's events. In an effort to comfort his friend, Willie promises to stop abusing his girlfriend and endorses Sam's utopian vision of life as a ballroom. "Let's dream," he says, and the two men dance together in a final display of harmony as the jukebox shines in "a spectrum of soft, romantic colors" (60). Sam had earlier defined "romance" as a story with a happy ending (5), and this concluding image leads one to hope against hope that there may yet be a happy ending for Sam and Hally and for South Africa.[15]

When he decides to move into Clybourne Park, Walter Lee, too, asserts hope for the future. Again, we do not know what lies ahead, as the Youngers leave for their new home in a hostile and racist community that does not want them. Neither play assures us that all will be well; but in choosing to reject racism and stand up for human dignity, Sam and Walter Lee have ultimately confirmed their power and manhood in the face of societies that would strip them of both.

Charles Trainor

Notes

[1] Athol Fugard, *"Master Harold"...and the boys* (New York: Viking Penguin, 1984), 26. All subsequent references to this edition will be made within the text.

[2] Lorraine Hansberry, *A Raisin in the Sun* (New York: Random House, 1959), 28, 3. All subsequent references to this edition will be made within the text.

[3] Lorraine Hansberry, "An Author's Reflections: Willy Loman, Walter Younger, and He   Who Must Live," *The Village Voice Reader*, eds. Daniel Wolf and Edwin Fancher (Garden City, N.Y.: Doubleday, 1962), 198-99.

[4] Whitney M. Young, Jr., *To Be Equal* (New York: McGraw-Hill, 1964), 174.

[5] Lorraine Hansberry, "Playwrighting: Creative Constructiveness," *Annals of sychotherapy* 5 (1964): 14.

[6] William H. Grier and Price M. Cobbs, *Black Rage* (New York: Basic Books, 1968), 4, 62-63.

[7] Jimmy Garrett, *And We Own the Night, Tulane Drama Review* 12 (Summer 1968): 3-64, 69.

[8] Lorraine Hansberry, "Make New Sounds: Studs Terkel Interviews Lorraine ansberry," *American Theatre* 1 (November 1984): 7.

[9] Lorraine Hansberry, "The Negro Writer and His Roots: Toward a New Romanticism," *The Black Scholar* 12 (March-April 1981): 8-9.

[10] Brian Crow, "Athol Fugard," *Post-Colonial English Drama: Commonwealth rama Since 1960*, ed. Bruce King (New York: St. Martin's, 1992), 160.

[11] Athol Fugard, *Notebooks: 1960-1977* (New York: Theatre Communications Group,1984), 49.

[12] "An Author's Reflections," 199.

[13] Lorraine Hansberry, "This Complex of Womanhood," *Ebony*, August 1960: 15.

[14] Quoted in Steven R. Carter, *Hansberry's Drama: Commitment amid Complexity* (Urbana, Il.: University of Illinois, 1991), 53.

[15] For a discussion of romance elements in the play, see John O. Jordan, "Life in the Theatre: Autobiography, Politics, and Romance in *'Master Harold'...and the boys*," *Twentieth-Century Literature: A Scholarly and Critical Journal* 39 (Winter 1993): 461-472.

3.

WILLA CATHER'S AMERICA,
A NATION OF NATIONS

From the cultural and ethnic point of view, it is hard to find a roomier America in American literature than the one presented by Willa Cather in her novels and short stories, though they ostensibly deal with, for the most part, life on one small region of the countryside--Nebraska. In her works, Americans, the descendants of the early settlers, share the land with the more recent immigrants belonging to several nationalities and cultures: Swedish, Norwegian, Danish, Hungarian, Polish, Austrian, Czech, German, Bohemian, Italian, French, Irish, Mexican, Russian, Japanese, and so on. None of these groups feels any strong urge either to shun its cultural ways, or desperately cling to them, or proudly celebrate them. Ethnicity comes naturally to the people of all groups, and, as such, they carry it quietly without drawing envy, jealousy, or suspicion. A Cather specialist may protest that this gives a rosier picture than the one Cather actually presents, and cite instances from her novels of mutual prejudices between ethnic groups. Cather is, indeed, too realistic to ignore these prejudices, but she does not see them creating any serious disturbances. Willa Cather's America, a composite of nations, enjoys an ethnic harmony enviable anywhere in the world today. Like any other writer's picture of reality, Cather's is, it may be mentioned, an artistic representation of the world, as she saw it, with no mean historical significance.

The biographical studies by Edith Lewis, E. K. Brown, Phyllis Robinson, Stanley T. Williams, and others show Cather's interest in foreign cultures from her childhood days in Catherton and Red Cloud. In Cather scholarship, a frequent topic of discussion is her immigrant experience. In her excellent bibliography *Willa Cather: A Reference Guide*, Marilyn Arnold lists as many as thirty-eight items under "Immigrant, immigrants in Cather's experience and writing" in the Subject Index. Depending on their interest in a particular foreign culture, Cather scholars elucidate one ethnic culture or other present in her works. James Woodress has, for instance, made an extensive study of the French element in Cather's fiction. What has not received sufficient attention is the fact that Cather presents different ethnic groups in contact and that she gives a picture of a harmonious, multi-ethnic American society. Indeed, Cather's presentation of immigrants in her short stories and novels goes with her vision of America as a nation of nations.

The story "Flavia and her Artists" in Willa Cather's book *The Troll Garden* (1905) neatly illustrates her many-in-one America. The assembly at Flavia's house at Tarrytown is a beautiful symbolic representation of the country's ethnic mosaic. A flavor of the varied American society can be easily had from the names of persons of different European nationalities who have gathered at Flavia's house in Tarrytown: M. Emile Roux, Jules Martel, Alcee Buisson; Professor Herr Schotte and Frau Lichtenfeld; Signor Donati; Ivan Schemetzkin and Restzhoff. Though six different languages can be heard spoken in the servants' quarters producing a chaotic situation there, Flavia's honored guests all speak English and the differences in their cultural background hardly gives rise to any problems.

It is true that the gathering in Tarrytown includes foreigners who have come in response to Flavia's special invitation. It can be argued that a stray meeting like this organized by her cannot be taken to represent American social reality in any serious way. M. Roux, for example, hails from Paris. It may be safe to infer that Frau Lichetenfeld lives and writes in Germany. As for others, it is difficult to say for certain whether they are visitors or permanent residents of the country. Taking into account everything, the overall picture one gets from the story is of a country where there is a good deal of mixing and mingling of diverse nationalities and cultures.

Such an international setting provides an ideal situation to show how cultural differences give rise to conflicts between individuals and groups. Willa Cather's story is, however, not one that deals with inter-cultural conflict. Roux's vitriolic attack on the Advanced American Woman is not inspired by cultural prejudices, nor are Arthur Hamilton's biting remarks on Roux and his ilk. Their attacks are directed towards common human weaknesses such as egoism, vanity, snobbery, ingratitude, etc. as exhibited by particular individuals. Willa Cather's primary interest is the human being and his/her greatness, his/her smallness. Though multi-cultural in setting with a potential background for a story of cultural conflict,

Willa Cather turns the focus of her attention to the delineation of human nature so much so that she may even give an impression of being indifferent to ethnic differences of people.

While Willa Cather's American West, the setting of most of her stories and novels, is almost entirely populated by "foreigners," as they are generally referred to, the first, the second and the third generation immigrants. Yet bad feelings or fights between the ethnic groups are, if not altogether absent, are rarely to be witnessed in these works. Half a dozen or so European nationalities, for example, inhabit the Divide in *O Pioneers!* (1913). They live in easy reach of one another, though sometimes they live in groups in separate, isolated pockets. The Bergsons, the Swedes, have, for their neighbors, a Bohemian couple, Marie and Frank Sabata, and, before the Sabbatas moved in, a German family lived on the farm, Carl Linstrum and his parents. The French country lies not too far away from where the Bergsons live. Ivar, the Norwegian, and half a dozen Russian families live across the county line. During her prosperous days, Alexandra Bergson had in her employment Swedish maids and farmhands, Ivar, the Norwegian, and Barry Flinn, the Irishman. The settlers face the hostility of the land, but there is no group hostility of any kind on the Divide.

Willa Cather does not present the foreigners in *O Pioneers!* as one big mass of humanity. She is careful to differentiate the groups, one from the other. References to the peculiarities of their physical features, dress, speech, temperament, manners, and beliefs are interspersed throughout the book. They occur in many ways in many contexts and serve many purposes. It will be seen that most of them express appreciation of one of group for the other, as, for example, when Alexandra Bergson says that the Bohemians "certainly know how to make more kinds of bread than any other people in the world" (194). If a reference is made to a certain peculiarity with a humorous intention, the target group is often the speaker's own, as when Alexandra remarks, "Now that I think of it, most of my girls have married men they were afraid of. I believe there is a good deal of the cow in most Swedish girls.... We're a terribly practical people, and I guess we think a cross man makes a good manager" (228- 29).

The foreign settlers on Willa Cather's Divide are sometimes shown to yield to the pressure of the Americanizing process. For example, Alexandra's brother Lou and his wife Annie speak mostly English and only sometimes Swedish at home. When she happens to speak Swedish, Annie is "almost as much afraid of being 'caught' at it as ever her mother was being caught barefoot" (99). Oscar, Alexandra's second brother, "still has a thick accent, but Lou speaks like anybody from Iowa" (99). Oscar's children "do not understand a word of Swedish" (99).

Such examples of acculturation are not numerous in *O Pioneers!* But acculturation is also no guarantee of a total surrender of one's cultural identity. Even though Emil, Alexandra's youngest brother, has, as a student at the University of Nebraska, come under the influence of the outside world and is greatly changed in his outward behavior, Alexandra notices that he is basically a Swede. Speaking to Carl Linstrum, she says, "It's curious, too; on the outside Emil is just like an American boy,--he graduated from the State University in June, you know,--but underneath he is more Swedish than any of us. Sometimes, he is so like father that he frightens me; he is so violent in his feelings like that" (117).

O Pioneers! contains a long and interesting dialogue between Alexandra and Ivar, which must have been intended by the author to defend diversity against forces of acculturation. Being different from the rest of the people, Ivar fears that he will be taken for a crank and sent to an asylum. In the dialogue he pleads with his employer to bear with him. After patiently listening to his many imaginary woes, Alexandra speaks to him soothingly:

> "There is a great deal in what you say, Ivar. Like as not they will be wanting to take me to Hastings because I have built a silo; and then I may take you with me. But at present I need you here. Only don't come to me again telling me what people say. Let people go on talking as they like, and we will go on living as we think best. You have been with me now for twelve years, and I have gone to you for advice oftener than I have ever gone to any one. That ought to satisfy you." (94)

Willa Cather seems to be speaking here through Alexandra and expressing her own conviction that one has a right to live as one thinks best whatever others may say. In her America nobody is required to conform to somebody else's ideal except his or her own, and mutual sympathy, understanding, and cordiality reign supreme.

Against this setting of ethnic diversity, Willa Cather narrates the moving story of Alexandra's life. After the death of her father, she, being the eldest member of the family, is called upon to take care of the farm and bring up her brothers. Ignoring her own life and future, she struggles hard to tame the wild land and help her brothers. When success crowns her efforts, she is already in her late thirties, past all hopes of finding any true happiness in her own life. When her childhood friend Carl Linstrum comes and proposes to marry her, she is prevented from marrying him by her own brothers for fear of losing her share of the property. She has no knowledge that her youngest brother, on whom she has built great hopes, is in love with Marie Sabata, the neighbor's wife. She comes to know about it to her great shock after both he and Marie are killed by the husband. Ignoring her personal loss and grief, she meets Frank Sabata in prison and promises to do everything she can to get him out of it. Characters in *O Pioneers!* belong to different nationalities, but Willa Cather's themes are family obligations, commitment to land, struggle and sacrifice, strong will and resolute determination, love, loss, grief, reconciliation, etc. In respect of these matters she seems to believe that all human beings are alike. In any case, Cather's growing concern for ethnicity becomes quite evident when her ethnics in the novel are compared with those in "Flavia and Her Artists."

In a similar manner *The Song of the Lark* (1915) and *My Antonia* (1918) are also set in the American West and possess multi-ethnic background. In an alien and hostile environment, with no help coming from any quarter, the poor and the destitute immigrants fall back upon the virtues and strengths of their own national character and survive. They not only survive but also endure and achieve distinction. Mrs. Kohler's garden in the sand valley in Moonstone, Colorado, in *The Song of the Lark* speaks volumes about the power of the German spirit to find expression in America: "Beside that sand gulch, she had tried to reproduce a bit of her own village in the Rhine valley" (23). About Mrs. Kohler's countrymen, the narrator says:

> There is hardly a German family in the most arid parts of Utah, New Mexico, Arizona, but has its oleander trees. However loutish the American-born sons of the family may be, there was never one who refused to give his muscle to the back-breaking task of getting those tubbed trees down into the cellar in the fall and up into the sunlight in the spring. They may strive to avert the day, but they grapple with the tub at last. (26)

The Germans in *The Song of the Lark* live peacefully with the Japanese as well as the people of European nationalities including the Hungarians, Austrians, and the Poles, each made of some special stuff, like the Germans. Talking to Thea Kronborg, the heroine of the novel, Dr. Archie says, for example, "Oh a Swede can make good anywhere, at anything! You've got that in your favor, miss..." (83). Responding to Dr. Archie, Thea admits her special constitution, but is modest in her claims: "Yes, I used to be ashamed of being a Swede, but I'm not any more.

Swedes are kind of common, but I think it's better to be *something*" (83). Thea's great- great grandfather had married a Norwegian woman, and the novelist makes a painstaking effort to reveal the Norwegian strain in Thea's character and actions. The novel narrates how the land nurtures the musical talent of Thea, the daughter of an immigrant family, and gives her a song never sung before. People of different nationalities come and settle in Willa Cather's country, where there are no boundaries, walls, or curtains, and where the national talents of each one are nurtured and developed to sing the song of all humanity.

Similarly, in the thickly laid ethnic mosaic of *My Antonia*, Willa Cather traces the history of a Bohemian girl, Antonia, from her childhood and arrival on a farm near Black Hawk, Nebraska, to her life as a young woman in town and her seduction and betrayal there, and her final return to the farm where she marries and raises a large family. Back on the farm, Antonia engages herself in hard work and undergoes a process of deculturation of American influences, including the use of English language. Compared to her friends, who have made it in the outside world, Antonia's life may appear to be a failure. To Jim, the Swedish narrator, Antonia is, however, a special person:

> She lent herself to immemorial human attitudes which we recognize by instinct as universal and true. I had not been mistaken. She was a battered woman now, not a lovely girl; but she still had that something which fires the imagination, could still stop one's breath for a moment by a look or gesture that somehow revealed the meaning in common things. She had only to stand in the orchard, to put her hand on a little crab tree and look up at the apples, to make you feel the goodness of planting and tending and harvesting at last. All the strong things of her heart came out in her body, that had been so tireless in serving generous emotions.

> It was no wonder that her sons stood tall and straight. She was a rich mine of life, like the founders of early races. (398)

In Willa Cather's America , an ethnic can thus lend himself or herself to "immemorial human attitudes," "universal and true." It is, therefore, no surprise that people of so many different nationalities have been able to live there in harmony. Commenting on Willa Cather's treatment of European settlers in *O Pioneers, The Song of the Lark,* and *My Antonia*, David Daiches perceptively writes, "Here are no facile studies of children of immigrants being educated or absorbed into "Americanism": Miss Cather knew that Americanism is Europeanism meeting the challenge of a new environment in its own terms" (18).

If during World War I the age-old cordial relationships between German immigrants and others suffer some jolts in the country, Willa Cather shows in *One of Ours* how good sense and solidarity prevails over antagonistic feelings. The protagonist Claude Wheeler whose ideal of a family is represented by the Erlichs' is pained and disappointed by the German aggression against the French, but his mother reminds him that "Yet we have had so many German neighbors, and never one that wasn't kind and helpful" (170). Mahailey, the maidservant, is at a loss over German brutality. She wonders "how comes it all them Germans is such ugly lookin' people? The Yoeders and the German folks round here ain't ugly lookin'." Claude puts her off indulgently, saying, "Maybe it's the ugly ones that are doing the fighting, and ones at home are nice, like our neighbors" (215). When Mrs. Voight, the German proprietress of a railroad restaurant is harassed by some boys, Claude immediately goes to her help. One of the soldiers sailing with Claude to fight the Germans is a German American, Fritz Tannhauser, who, when asked his name, usually said that he was Dennis and of Irish descent. Claude dies fighting the Germans with a dear German American by his side. Cather demonstrates how differences and conflicts are resolved by an appeal to sanity and good sense in her presentation of the trial of two Germans, Mr. Troilus Oberlies and Mr. August Yoeder, for their defamatory remarks against the American government. Whatever the ethnic affiliation, a person can easily find a place in Willa Cather's America, as long as he/she shows a consideration for the feelings of the neighbors, something without which no civilized society is anywhere possible.

An author today is often judged on the basis of the race to which he/she belongs, and Willa Cather is no exception. Critics such as Bernice Slote and Mike Fischer have argued that Willa Cather is conditioned to a very large extent by the Eurocentric cultural assumptions of her time. With specific reference to *Death Comes for the Archbishop* (1927) E. A. Mares has criticized Willa Cather at length on similar lines. Indeed, such interpretations can easily be supported by isolating statements like the one below, which is an extract taken from the letter of the French protagonist Archbishop Latour to his brother:

> ...All day I am an American in speech and thought--yes, in heart, too. The kindness of the American traders, and especially of the military officers at the Fort, commands more than a superficial loyalty. I mean to help the officers at their task here. I can assist them more than they realize. The Church can do more than the Fort to make these poor Mexicans 'good Americans.' And it is for the people's good; there is no other way in which they can better their condition. (35)

Father Latour's prolonged battle with the Mexican clergy, who were opposed to the American occupation of the land heralding the gradual loss of their own control over it, may have also given further grounds for critics to attribute a pro-American bias to the author. However, the novel taken in its totality gives little room for limiting criticism of the kind.

While giving an account of the way two French missionaries, Archbishop Jean Marie Latour and Father Joseph Vaillant, travel to the most inaccessible land of New Mexico, recently annexed to the United States, and the way they rejuvenate the religion that had lost its meaning and significance in the hands of a corrupt clergy, *Death Comes for the Archbishop* presents a beautiful drama of cross-cultural encounter. In the course of the novel, Willa Cather describes the bitterness and animosity of the local inhabitants, Mexicans and Indians, towards Americans, and towards each other. If hostile feelings were widespread, it would be, however, unfair to make Willa Cather a secret sharer of these feelings, particularly when she has, in novel after novel, shown her great respect for different ethnic groups. Perhaps, she underplayed the resentments existing between these groups in her earlier novels. Though she delineates them now, she shows no erosion of her faith in love and understanding. She dwells mostly on the themes of brotherhood and love in *Death Comes for the Archbishop*--on how the two missionaries win the people over by the goodness and purity of their heart. As the two priests complete their mission, different ethnic groups reconcile and quietly settle down to live their different lives. Clearly, behind *Death Comes for the Archbishop* lies Willa Cather's vision of America as a nation of nations. No better embodiment of that vision can, perhaps, be found anywhere else in American literature.

A close analysis of *Death Comes for the Archbishop* will, however, reveal that nowhere in the novel does Archbishop Latour attempt, either in word or deed, to make "good Americans" of Mexicans or Indians, if that phrase is taken to mean conformity or loyalty to ideas and values of a nation other than those held by Mexicans or Indians. With ample evidence in the present novel, as also in other novels and short stories, of Willa Cather's equal love and respect for all cultures, the charge against her of the so-called American bias does not stand under close scrutiny. She makes the foreigners speak for themselves, construct their own identity, and makes the reader appreciate their "differences." Not done from any privileged point of view, Cather's portrayals do not deny subjectivity to the foreigners, the "Others." What follows is an attempt to elucidate Willa Cather's decentered outlook on the subject of ethnicity by reference to the novel and find a proper definition of a good American in Cather's vocabulary.

Notwithstanding what Father Latour says about himself, Cather portrays him not as a political agent, but as a priest, first and last, loyal only to the Church. She advances this view of his character, right from the start, in the "Prologue," where she describes how the interest of the Church was uppermost in the mind of Father Ferrand, the American Bishop visiting Rome with the name of Father Latour for the vicarate of New Mexico. When Father Ferrand meets Cardinal Garcia Maria de Allende at Rome to persuade the Cardinal to put in a special word to the Provincial Council for Father Latour's appointment to the vicarate of New Mexico, the Bishop dwells on at length why this country, newly annexed to the United States, is so important to the Church and how Father Latour is the best person for the job.

Parallel to Willa Cather's life of dedication to her literary vocation, Father Latour devotes his entire life to the work of the Church. Assisted by his vicar, Father Joseph Vaillant, he brings about a rejuvenation of the Church in the southwest. In all his dealings with local Mexicans and Indians, no interest other than religion ever enters Father Latour's mind.

At the house of Benito in the Spanish settlement of Hidden Water on his way back to Santa Fe from Durango, Father Latour's conduct bespeaks of him as an ideal figure of a priest. The priest in him makes him happy to note the bareness, simplicity, and comeliness of Benito's place, and feel "a kind of peace about it" (23). Sitting with Benito's family, he finds himself "very much at home" (23), and everything agreeable--their manners, their voices, the way they knelt on the floor beside the table when he said grace before meat, the holy images on the shelf over the fireplace, and the simple story of their lives. The statement of the grandfather of the family that the Blessed Virgin must have led the Bishop from his path and brought him there to baptize the children and to sanctify the marriages might not have sounded untrue to Father Latour, though no record of his reaction is given in the context. We are told that Father Latour had expected to make a dry camp in the wilderness, and to sleep under a juniper tree, like the Prophet, tormented by thirst, but he found a place to sleep "in comfort and safety, with love for his fellow creatures flowing like peace about his heart" (27).

When Jose, the elder grandson, expresses his strong antipathy towards the Americans, Father Latour does try to soften his feelings, but he does not defend his "clients" with any unseemly vehemence as one would expect a political campaigner to do. Jose remarks, "They say at Albuquerque that now that we are all Americans, but that is not true, Padre. I will never be an American. They are infidels" (25). He goes on to add, "They destroyed our churches when they were fighting us, and stabled their horses in them. And now they will take our religion away from us. We want our own ways and our own religion" (25). All that Father Latour does is to tell him that, speaking from his experience of living with Americans for ten years, there are many devout Catholics among them and that he had friendly relations with Protestants in Ohio. However, he notes that it is no use to try to change their mind because "they had not room in their minds for two ideas: there was one Church, and the rest of the world was infidel" (25).

No American bias can be attributed with fairness and justice to Willa Cather when she allows Mexicans to freely express their anti-American sentiments, as in the scene relating to Jose. One can indeed see her taking a strong critical attitude towards Americans in the episodes concerning Magdalena and Sada. Magdalena, a poor Mexican woman, marries Buck Scales, an American, in the hope of coming up in the world, but she comes to receive savage treatment from him and becomes a mute witness to his murders of innocent passers-by, who approach him for shelter. Father Latour and Father Vaillant narrowly escape death, thanks to Magdalena's quick and timely warning, and, in their turn, they save Magdalena from Buck Scales. Similarly, the story of Sada, a Mexican slave woman in an American family, brings little credit to Americans. Being Protestants and hostile to the Roman Church, Sada's masters do not allow her to go to Mass or receive the visits of a priest. After nineteen long years, she is able to escape one cold night and come to church to pray. If anything, the stories of these two women are a damning indictment of white America, and it is difficult to imagine a writer with an American bias penning such stories.

As Father Latour's prolonged battle with the clergy, which might give grounds for a critic to see a pro-American bias in Cather, it may be noted that Father Latour's battle is directed towards the defiant and the corrupt among the Mexican clergy and not towards the Mexican clergy as a whole and not towards the Mexican people in any way. All along the running battle with the clergy, Father Latour shows great tact and restraint, and is extremely careful not to estrange the Mexican population. When Father Vaillant is impatient for the removal of Father Martinez of Taos, he calmly replies, "I do not wish to lose the Parish of Taos in order to punish its priest, my friend..." (158). In an encounter with Martinez, he says that "he had not come to deprive the people of their religion, but that he would be compelled to discipline some of the priests of their parishes if they did not change their way of life" (148).

Willa Cather makes use of every opportunity to show how the piety and simplicity of the Mexican people deeply affect those who come into contact with them. Father Latour and Father Vaillant listen to the story of Our Lady of Guadeloupe with rapt attention as Father Escolostico Herrera, a native priest from the Indian mission of Santa Clara, narrates it. Deeply stirred by the priest's recital of the story of visitation of the Mother of God to a poor neophyte, Father Vaillant exclaims:

> "What a priceless thing for the poor converts of a savage country!" he exclaimed, wiping his glasses, which were clouded by his strong feeling. "All these poor Catholics who have been so long without instruction have at least the reassurance of that visitation. It is a household word with them that their Blessed Mother revealed herself in their own country, to a poor convert. Doctrine is well enough for the wise, Jean; but the miracle is something we can hold in our hands and love." (50)

In another context, Father Vaillant says:

> "The more I work with the Mexicans, the more I believe it was people like them our Saviour bore in mind when He said, *Unless ye become as little children*. He was thinking of people who are not clever in the things of this world, whose minds are not upon gain and wordly advancement. These poor Christians are not thrifty like our country people at home; they have no veneration for property, no sense of material values ...." (206)

And he goes on to confess:

> " ... none of our new priests understand those poor natures as I do. I have almost become a Mexican! I have learned to like *chili colorado* and mutton fat. Their foolish ways no longer offend me, their very faults are dear to me. I am *their man!*" (208)

Lacking Father Vaillant's warmth and feeling, Father Latour can only envy his friend's spiritual progress. Whether he likes it or not, the reverse of what he originally planned or intended takes place--the Mexicanization of the American-- really, a Frenchman in this particular context, but from the point of view of Mexicans all non-Spanish European settlers in the land are Americans--instead of the other way round. In any case, Cather presents Mexicans as a people rich in character and presents them in a way that nobody would wish them to be different from what they are.

In her presentation of Indians, Cather goes a step further and artistically conveys that, no matter how strongly one wished or tried, Indians also cannot be separated from their own beliefs and values. Father Latour succeeds in winning over the people, alienated by their Spanish rulers and priests, but he clearly sees no possibility of any interaction between Indians and white Americans at the deeper levels. Though Jacinto, an Indian youth, becomes Father Latour's trusted friend, and each admires the personal qualities of the other, they cannot communicate their deepest thoughts and feelings. Looking at the rock of Acoma, the home of the Acoma tribe, Bishop Latour notes how no power on earth could dispossess these people of their faith. The rocklike faith in the case takes a strange literal character-- "they had their idea in substance. They actually lived upon their Rock; were born upon it and died upon it" (99). During a service at Acoma, Father Latour naturally finds it hard to go through the Mass, a ceremony so foreign to the people. Compared to the changes taking place through centuries in his own part of the world, the Acomas "had been fixed, increasing neither in numbers nor desires, rock-turtles on their rock. Something reptilian he felt here, something that had endured by immobility, a kind of life out of reach, like the crustaceans in their armor" (104).

Like the Marabar caves in E. M. Forster's *A Passage to India*, Jacinto's cave in *Death Comes for the Archbishop* serves to show how the modern civilized world is totally unequipped to deal with an ancient culture and how it woefully betrays utter incomprehension and confusion when brought into a close contact with such a culture. On a journey through the Pecos mountains, Jacinto leads Father Latour to an abandoned sacred cave to take shelter from a sudden snowstorm. On entry into the cave, Father Latour was struck by "a reluctance, an extreme distaste for the place" (129). He found the air and odor terribly disagreeable, and felt dizzy by an extraordinary humming vibration like "a bee of hives, like a heavy roll of distant drums" (131). Added to all this, he found Jacinto's behavior there puzzling. The Bishop kept his promise to Jacinto not to speak about the cave to anyone, but his mind turned to it "always with a shudder of repugnance quite unjustified by anything he had experienced there." The cave had saved his life, but "he remembered it with horror. No tales wonder, he told himself, would ever tempt him into a cavern hereafter" (135). Thinking about the ceremonial cave and Jacinto's puzzling behavior, Father Latour felt inclined to believe some of the unpleasant stories he had heard about Pecos religion. He was totally convinced that "neither the white man nor the Mexicans in Santa Fe understood anything about Indian beliefs or the workings of the Indian mind" (136). A white trader quite knowledgeable about the Pecos Indians, tells Father Latour "No white man knows anything about Indian religion...." "The things they value most," he observes, "are worth nothing to us. They've got their own superstitions, and their minds will go round and round in the same old ruts till Judgment Day." He tells Father Latour that "he might make good Catholics among the Indians, but he would never separate them from their own beliefs" (138).

In her portrayal of Indians, Cather clearly suggests that the people possess a strong inner spirit and character which cannot be touched or changed under whatever circumstances. She also presents many Indian scenes, situations, and character sketches which are full of appreciation. None of the fine qualities of Indians are lost on Father Latour. Indians fare better than Europeans in a number of respects in his assessment, especially in their worshipful attitude towards Nature.

Embodying the feelings of Willa Cather, Father Latour loves and respects Indians. In the war between Navajos and the American government, his sympathies lie fully with the Navajos. He is terribly sorry over the government's decision to forcefully remove the Navajos from their land: "The expulsion of the Navajos from their country, which had been theirs no man knew how long, had seemed to him an injustice that cried to heaven" (296). When Eusabio comes to Father Latour requesting him to meet Manuelito, the bravest of the Navajo chiefs who refused to surrender to the conquering army, he, as a lover of justice, agrees to a meeting, although he knows that it is indiscreet to meet an outlawed Chief. Father Latour explains to Manuelito why he cannot, as a Catholic priest in a Protestant country, intervene in the conflict in behalf of the Navajos. Naturally, when the government realizes its mistake and restores the land to the Navajos, Father Latour feels very happy. He says to Bernard, a priest, "I have lived to see two great wrongs righted; I have seen the end of black slavery, and I have seen the Navajos restored to their own country" (295). Again, he repeats: "God has been very good to let me live to see a happy issue to those old wrongs. I do not believe, as I once did, that the Indian will perish. I believe that God will preserve him" (301).

In Cather's America, God will preserve the Indian, as well as the Mexican. The narrator reports once, "Father Latour often said that his diocese changed little except in boundaries. The Mexicans were always Mexicans, the Indians always Indians" (288). According to Cather, none of them--either the Indian, or the Mexican, or anyone else--will be required to surrender his or her identity to be an American proper. In her definition, an American is a person who holds ethnicity in the highest regard, not only his own, but also of others. This being the case, it is unfair to accuse her of placing one group above another, least of all of making good Americans of people belonging to different ethnic groups by calling upon them to adopt the ways and values of the dominant mainstream American culture.

If Willa Cather criticizes any group, it is white America, a fact which should put to rest the criticism that she allows the culture to which she is born affect her treatment of Mexicans and Indians. In addition to the instances of Cather's critical stand already cited, frequent sharp and unflattering references to white America may be found scattered throughout the book. What most emphatically clears Cather of any American bias is that her protagonist Father Latour, for all his avowed championship of America, himself remains a Frenchman to the end in taste, manners, values, and beliefs. What a finer memorial than the Cathedral at Santa Fe done in Midi Romanesque style could he leave behind to testify his undying love and attachment to France which gave him birth? What better setting and story could Willa Cather have chosen to project her vision of a multi-ethnic America, where a person could erect his/her own cathedral, kiva, synagogue, temple, or mosque according to his/her own deep yearning for beauty, truth, and meaning in life?

Taking a quick, overall view of Cather's works discussed above, one notices an interesting development of Cather's concern for ethnicity. The relatively vague visualization and presentation of a conglomerate of cultural backgrounds in "Flavia and Her Artists" is followed by a vivid delineation of distinct groups in *O Pioneers!* and of their harmonious ways of living, showing an increased appreciation of ethnicity. This appreciation grows from novel to novel. finding its finest and most delicate expression in *Death Comes for the Archbishop* in which Cather presents distinct ethnic groups, all eventually settling down to a life of peaceful coexistence.

Much before the emergence of ethnic awareness among people of different national, cultural, and racial groups in America, Willa Cather saw ethnicity as something positive, a stimulus for finer living. If the recent growth of ethnic consciousness is accompanied by a certain narrowing of human sympathies, race and ideology seldom interfere with the dictates of the heart of Willa Cather's characters. Whatever side they belong, Cather's characters behave in a way that would bring credit to them, first and last, as human beings. In her last novel *Sapphira and Her Slave Girl,* for example, the daughter, aided by her father, helps her own mother's slave to escape to freedom. A Black minister of the Gospel to whom Mrs. Blake brings Nancy, the slave girl, says, while parting, "An' you, lady, the Lawd will sho'ly bless you. Fo' He said Hisself: Blessed is the merciful" (239).

Contrary to the melting-pot theory of American society put forward by various historians according to which immigrants to the country abandon their separate national and cultural identities to form a monolithic American society, Willa Cather's nations lose none of their nationhood while they make a nation together. Cather has given us an America that fits so well with the common description of it as a nation of nations. She has expressed herself strongly against standardization of life and art. In fact, in a talk on "Standardization and Art" to the Fine Arts Society, Nebraska, 1921, she was critical of the "work of overzealous patriots who implant into the foreign minds a distaste for all they have brought from their own country." She warned that one hundred per cent American would be a deaf-mute. What fascinated Cather most was the strenuous efforts made by the immigrants to hold on to their different national and cultural ways in an alien land. Apropos *Shadows on the Rock*, a story of the first French settlers in Quebec, Canada, Willa Cather wrote: "Those people brought a kind of French culture there and somehow kept it alive on that rock, sheltered it and on occasion died for it, as if it really were a sacred fire--..." (16). To Cather each of the ethnic cultures in American society is "a sacred fire" and must be kept burning, or "a sacred spot," to use another phrase of hers occurring in a similar context from her novel *The Professor's House* (221). Cather took the high road to pluralism, whereas, perhaps, her country itself eventually arrived by taking a long, rough, and tortuous route, and arrived there fumbling and panting. All's well that ends well!

Noting the ease and comfort ushered in by the machine and electronic age and Willa Cather's yearning for old, cherished things she had known and her refusal to accept change, Leon Edel makes the following confession in his fine lecture "Willa Cather: The Paradox of Success":

> I must confess to a certain constraint in speaking to you of Willa Cather now, on the periphery of the 1960's--constraint because we have moved so far away from her world. It is gone, gone as if it had never existed, save for the fact that it does exist in some of the best pages of her writing. To use an exaggerated

image, I would say that to talk of Miss Cather's world is a little like trying to extol the Stone Age to a Renaissance man. (2)

If one looks at Willa Cather's works from the perspective of the present study, one sees that, far from moving away from her world, the country has moved/is moving towards it.

S. Krishnamoorthy Aithal

Notes

Arnold, Marilyn. *Willa Cather: A Reference Guide*. Boston: G. K Hall & Co., 1986.

Brown, E. K. *Willa Cather: A Critical Biography*. New York: Alfred A. Knopf, 1953.

Cather, Willa. *Death Comes for the Archbishop*. New York: Alfred A. Knopf, 1927.

_____. *My Antonia*. Boston & New York: Houghton Mifflin Company, 1918.

_____. *One of Ours*. New York: Alfred A. Knopf, 1922.

_____. "On *Shadows on the Rock*." *On Writing*. New York: Alfred A. Knopf, 1949. Originally appeared in *The Saturday Review of Literature*. October 17, 1931.

_____. *O Pioneers!* Boston & New York: Houghton Mifflin Company, 1913.

_____. *The Professor's House*. New York: Alfred A. Knopf, 1925.

_____. *Sapphira and the Slave Girl*. New York: Alfred A. Knopf, 1940.

_____. *The Song of the Lark*. Boston & New York: Houghton Mifflin Co., 1915.

_____. *The Troll Garden*. New York: McClure, Phillips & Co., 1905.

Daiches, David. *Willa Cather: A Critical Introduction*. Ithaca, NY: Cornell UP, 1951.

Edel, Leon. *Willa Cather: The Paradox of Success*. A lecture delivered under the auspices of the Gertrude Clarke Whitall Poetry and Literature Fund. Washington: Library of Congress, 1960.

Fischer, Mike. "Pastoralism and Its Discontents: Willa Cather and the Burden of Imperialism." *Mosaic*, 23 (1990): 31- 44.

Lewis, Edith. *Willa Cather Living: A Personal Record.* New York: Alfred A. Knopf, 1953.

Mares, E. A. ed. *Padre Martinez: New Perspectives from Taos.* Taos: Millicent Rogers Museum, 1988.

Robinson, Phyllis C. *Willa: The Life of Willa Cather.* New York: Doubleday & Company, Inc., 1983.

Slote, Bernice. "Willa Cather and Plains Culture." *Vision and Refuge: Essays on the Literature of the Great Plains.* Ed. Virginia Faulkner with Frederic C. Luebke. Lincoln: U of Nebraska P., 1982. 93- 105.

Williams, Stanley T. "Introduction." *One of Ours* by Willa Cather. New York: Alfred A. Knopf, 1926.

Woodress, James. *Willa Cather: A Literary Life.* Lincoln: U of Nebraska P, 1987.

_____. "Willa Cather and Alphonse Daudet." mss.

_____. "France in the Life and Work of Willa Cather." *Confluences Americaines: Melanges en l'honeur de Maurice Gonnaud.* Yves Carlet & Michel Granger, eds. Nancy: Presses Universitaries de Nancy, 1990. 91- 102.

4.

SPEAKING THROUGH SILENCES:
ETHNICITY IN THE WRITINGS OF ITALIAN/AMERICAN WOMEN

> It's not easy being an angry poet
> when you come from a culture
> whose most profound statement of anger
> is silence.
> > (Rose Romano, "Mutt Bitch")

> Remember me, Ladies,
> the silent one?
> I have found my voice
> and my rage will blow
> your house down.
> > (Maria Mazziotti Gillan, "Public School No. 18,
> Paterson, New Jersey")

The force of acculturation in the United States pressures authors of ethnically and culturally marginalized groups to learn to speak the language of the dominant, Anglo-centric culture, to adhere to its aesthetics, even to mold their art within its parameters[1]. Being an immigrant means to be an outcast in more ways than one: cut off from the culture of consent *and* from the culture of descent, which is reduced to a ghost culture in the new country, immigrants typically occupy a marginal position within the culture of origin prior to emigration. To argue that emigration "forces a disintegration of self, culture, and society," and to posit an integration of such elements prior to emigration[2], though, would mean to ignore the factors that triggered departure from the country of origin (Ostendorf 577). In other words, the sense of loss and separation pre-exists emigration, and immigration, rather than healing the fracture between self and culture, re-enacts the drama of separation and marginalization[3]. Various forms of economic, social, and political subjection suffered in the country of origin constitute the baggage that immigrants carry with them to the new country, where the very conditions they escaped from are often replicated. The literature produced by immigrants and their children articulates' the struggle to extricate oneself from the constraints of such conditions.

The self-silencing that acculturation entails resonates in language, cleansing it of ethnic ties. Lack of recognition generates a perception, both external and internal, of cultural invisibility[4]. Italian/American literature articulates the struggle of a culture caught between assimilation and exclusion[5]. As the poet Rose Romano argues, because Italian Americans can "hide" (*Wop* 35), by camouflaging--or even rejecting--their ethnic identity, they can assimilate into the mainstream, but at the cost of losing cultural identity and internalizing self-hatred. Ethnicity is characteristically expressed--and repressed--in traditional and culturally acceptable Italian/American narratives, as evidenced by the popularity of authors like Mario Puzo and Gay Talese and directors like Francis Ford Coppola and Martin Scorsese[6]. For Italian/American authors it is imperative to rethink the ways in which ethnicity can be represented in order to defy the stultified images of their ethnicity pervasive in mainstream American culture.[7] The literature of many Italian/American authors simultaneously verbalizes and silences ethnicity. This kind of writing, in which a thinly disguised accent reveals ethnic identity, dramatizes the cultural conflicts at the heart of the experience of hyphenation.[8]

The effort to articulate one's own ethnic voice and to construct narratives that claim a position of agency for members of immigrant communities is further complicated when an author must also transcend the cultural limitations linked to gender and sexual identities. She may translate her dual foreignness into a language that is acquiescent and rebellious at once.[9] Discussing Helen Barolini's autobiographical project, Fred L. Gardaphé argues that the autobiographies of Italian/American women are characterized by "an intense politicization of the self" (20) which, in Barolini's work, translates into a continuous effort to achieve both self-legitimization and the legitimization of an Italian/American female literary tradition.[10]

Indeed, many Italian/American women writers root their self-exploration in a relentless analysis of the place occupied by Italian/American ethnicity in American culture. In her essay "An Italian American Woman Speaks Out" (1980), Tina De Rosa laments the isolation rooted in a deeply internalized perception of her culture of origin as an aberration from the standard of American middle-class life. Similarly, in her memoir, *Vertigo* (1996), Louise DeSalvo continues the exploration of Italian/American women's identity which she had begun in her novel *Casting Off* (1987), defying pious and stultifying images of Italian/American womanhood. In *Casting Off*, De Salvo had encoded Italian/American identity in the Irish surnames of her characters, thus articulating the silence enforced by a culture that does not allow for Italian/American characters who break away from the stereotypes inculcated by films such as *The Godfather* and *Moonstruck*.[11] In her poem "Public School No. 18, Paterson, New Jersey," Maria Mazziotti Gillan writes of the teachers who, "without words," tell the young speaker "to be ashamed" of being Italian and "to hate" herself (*Where I Come From* 12-13). She recalls the Psychology professor who had told her that she reminded "him of the Mafia leader/on the cover of *Time* magazine" (*Where I Come From* 13). The speaker of "Growing Up Italian" remembers: "In kindergarten, English words fell on me,/thick and sharp as hail. I grew silent,/the Italian word balanced on the edge/of my tongue and the English word, lost/during the first moment/of every question" (*Where I Come From* 54). Gillan thus interrogates American culture's tolerance for Italian Americans. But like the speaker of "Public School No. 18, Paterson, New Jersey," Gillan and other Italian/American women writers have found the strength and the words to blow down the house of those who silenced them.

* * *

The work of Agnes Rossi, a writer of Italian *and* Irish ancestry, illustrates the kind of negotiations between cultural/ethnic identities undertaken by Italian/American women. Rossi's ambivalent treatment of her Italian background contrasts with a more direct and less complicated approach to her Irish ancestry in *Split Skirt* and, especially, in her unpublished novel, *Fancy*, set in Ireland and the United States. Rossi's narratives bear directly upon questions of ethnic (self-) representation and identity politics, and capture notions of ethnic identity in post-modernity, in which ethnicity eschews static demarcations. Existing on the margins, postmodern ethnicity evokes the elusively defined borders of trans-nationality, migrancy, and homelessness.[12] Rossi's authorial development epitomizes the simultaneity of acceptance and denial of Italian ethnicity, suggesting an ongoing conflict that fuels her creative process. Her first book, *Athletes and Artists: Stories* (1987), silences the ethnic voice, while the protagonist of *The Quick* (1992) is identified through her name as an Italian American. The younger protagonist of Rossi's novel, *Split Skirt* (1994), is, like her author, of Italian and Irish descent, but the only explicit mention of her ethnicity "didn't survive the final edit." [13]

The disappearance of this reference evidences the suppression of the ethnic voice. [14] The editing process that unwittingly cancels traces of ethnicity functions as a form of self-censorship, one that is analogous to the hiding of the speaker of Gillan's "Public School No. 18, Paterson, New Jersey." "My face wants to hide," she confesses, juxtaposing her chattering voice at home, where her words are "smooth" in her "mouth," to her silence in school where she "grope[s] for the right English/words, fear[ing] the Italian word/will sprout from . . . [her] mouth like a rose" (*Where I Come From* 12). [15]

For contemporary writers such as Agnes Rossi, Rita Ciresi, and Cris Mazza, the Italian word often remains unspoken, or is erased. The characters in Ciresi's *Mother Rocket* represent a wide ethnic spectrum because, as Joshua Fausty argues, the author "infuses her ambivalent sense of her own cultural identity into her characters, linking her quest for ethnic/authorial self-definition to their multicultural identities" (204). Mazza, whose experimental fiction escapes simple classification, creates a character, in *Your Name Here   *, in search of her identity with no secure knowledge even of her name. [16] And the protagonist of Renèe Manfredi's novel *Running Away with Frannie*, when asked by his traveling companion, "Who are you again?", answers: "I'm not sure." For characters *and* their authors, living in a post-melting pot and post-white ethnic revival American culture, ethnic identity cannot be traded in for the promise of an American narrative of success; at the same time, the nostalgic evocation of the motherland no longer represents an option for third- or fourth-generation writers. [17]

Ethnic boundaries intersect in a postmodern world struggling to create viable methods for cultural identification and connection. Accordingly, Rossi's characters suffer from cultural displacement and psychological detachment, translated either into a third-person narrative, as in many of her stories--a seemingly uninvolved and isolated voice acting as a mere recorder of events--or into a detached first-person narrative such as that of Marie Russo, the protagonist of *The Quick*, whose last name strikingly resembles the author's. Marie's narrative articulates a disjunction between story and self which in turn mirrors a fracture between self and community. Rossi thus inscribes her own fractures in her characters' ambivalent choices and fragmented identities. As an Italian/American author, Rossi faces the difficulties of entering a literary market that, for the most part, perpetuates stereotypical and folkloric representations of her ethnicity.[18] Commenting on the lack of recognition for Italian/American authors, Gardaphé rightly calls Italian/American writers "cultural immigrants" on the "American literary scene" ("Third Generation," 72). [19]

As a woman author, Rossi must also confront a cultural background--Italian/American--historically hostile to female artistry and scarcely populated by feminine voices that might enable the emerging author to place herself confidently within a literary tradition. [20] As an Irish/Italian/American author writing two decades after the white ethnic revival, she negotiates between ethnic identities, crossing and blending cultural worlds that jar against each other, simultaneously attempting to establish the subject position from which she writes and to avoid the entrapment which speaking solely from that position would entail. [21]

Privileging memory, Rossi's novella *The Quick* strives to narrate an Italian/American story through a narrative in which, ironically, ethnicity goes unnamed. Scattered traces of ethnicity surface in the narrative to create the space in which this author inscribes her ethnic voice. This novella speaks with an accent, ever so slight, yet unquestionably present. The Italian/American background of the narrator, Marie Russo from Paterson, New Jersey, emerges obliquely, and neither the author nor the narrator give it much emphasis. Indeed Marie demonstrates very little awareness of her ethnic roots. [22]

After a terrible fight with her father during which her mother's china shatters, however, Marie remembers that her mother's cabinet contained the "flowered vase" her "father's relatives sent from Italy." "Chris and I," she remarks, "never considered ourselves related to my parents' relatives, especially the ones we never saw, the ones who were just blue airmail letters that lay around the house for a while and then were gone" (85). The relatives are metonymically identified at first with the "vase," and then with the "blue airmail letters," that, like the character's ethnicity, have seemingly disappeared. Thus Marie internalizes the very invisibility of her ethnicity. Her inability to connect with her ethnicity may lie at the core of her psychological and cultural displacement.

In all her relationships, with the exception of her friendship with Phyllis, an older fellow worker, she experiences a discomfort that makes her acutely aware of the contrived quality of her cultural roles as daughter, sister, girlfriend, college graduate, teacher, wife, and mother. After accepting these roles, however, she eventually rejects them all. Moving into an empty and "shabby" apartment (57), she asserts her need for a blank space, devoid of cultural scripts, in which, abandoning herself to the seduction of emptiness, she can plunge into her past and begin to remember and tell. Marie Russo's storytelling, like Rossi's, acknowledges loss and despair with utter honesty, and claims the need for the storyteller to connect with the past, without being weighed down by it, in order to forge her voice.

Rossi confers a unique sense of unity on the complex narrative of her novella through the somewhat monotonous voice of its narrator, a seemingly detached commentator. The narrative opens in the present and then unfolds in a spiral of memories that the narrator weaves in and out of the present. Rossi's reliance on memory and storytelling connects *The Quick* to the traditions of the *bildungsroman*, *kunstlerroman* and memoir. But Rossi challenges the conventions of these genres by telling a story of failed development and failed artistic emergence, and by seemingly depriving her fictional memoir of direction and cohesion. Disrupting narrative continuity, the plot recapitulates Marie's life, a life punctuated by attempts at self-assertion as well as self-erasure: she remembers she could have "made a life" for herself, but she "didn't want to" (70). Ultimately, Marie's life story articulates a fracture between the narrator and her narrative: she disclaims any connection with her narrative subject, just as she disclaims her connection with her Italian relatives. By consolidating the intricate and seemingly disjointed narrative of *The Quick* around loss--loss of people, hopes, opportunities for self-realization--Rossi obliquely expresses her concern with the dying ethnicity of her characters. The vanishing of the ethnic identity is rendered through abrupt narrative shifts, textual fractures and narrative gaps as well as lack of narrative unity or final closure.

The link between Marie's ethnicity and her self-definition is expressed through her longing for a place that feels like "home," the very longing that leads her to go home after quitting her job: "I'd been away long enough to dream up a romantic notion of home as a safe place where I'd be able to get my bearings" (29). For Marie, the search for a "home" begins when, as a twelve year old, she glues a lock on the door of her room--but the glue gives out, "with no fight at all," when her father, completely unaware, pushes it open (63). His violence and ruthlessness haunt Marie's childhood and adolescence: "I knew then that my father would always crash through, without even meaning to, and, worse, without even knowing he'd crashed through" (64). This realization captures the sense of displacement and loss characterizing Marie's self-perception. The search for a home takes her to disparate places, such as Woolworth's, Phyllis' home, the burnt house of the Metuchens, the house where she lives during her marriage to Ralph, and finally the empty apartment where she begins to tell her story. The search articulates Marie's attempt to negotiate between self-definition and cultural definitions. Rejecting romanticized notions of home, Rossi chooses not to resolve Marie's conflicts and does not offer epiphanies that will transform her characters' lives.

Rossi's concern with social outcasts is not limited to *The Quick*. Marginal figures--truck drivers, waitresses, jobless men and women, ex-drug addicts, failed artists--populate *Athletes and Artists* and the stories in *The Quick*. These figures live on the borders, existing at such a distance from mainstream culture that often, its myths do not appeal to them. At the same time, they also appear to be cut off from the culture of descent. Marie's inability to mourn the loss of her ethnicity is bound up with the fact that she identifies it with the patriarchal ideology dominant in her parents' household. Marie's relentless remembering and her interpellation of her audience--"I want to tell you some of the things Phyllis told me that summer but I don't want to have to go on and one [sic] about what color blouse she was wearing when she said a particular thing" (58)--radically contrast her with her mother, who lives in silent expectation of her father's explosions.

In Josephine Gattuso Hendin's novel, *The Right Thing To Do*, the daughter realizes that she is "everything" to her father and that "he could only deal with losing her by controlling her life, so that whatever happened to her would show his mark" (32). It is this paternal mark that Marie tries to escape, often to no avail. The voicelessness and passivity of the maternal figure, however, pose a more pernicious threat to the daughter's self-definition than does the father's physical and psychological abuse.

Gianna Patriarca, an Italian/Canadian writer, powerfully depicts the heritage of maternal silence in poems such as "Italian Women," "My Birth," and "Daughter." The speakers of these poems must face the haunting image of women who "wrap their souls/around their children/and serve their own hearts/in a meal

they never/share" (9). Women writers of Italian ancestry have to fight both the
culture that marginalizes their ethnicity and the ethnicity that silences their gender.

If Marie is, on the one hand, capable of rejecting the model of femininity
offered by her mother, then, on the other hand, she lacks the tools to fashion a new
role for herself. Marie's failed attempt to reconcile her desire for a "conventional
life" with her wish to be "eccentric within that life" (69) parallels her inability to
bridge the gap between two cultures, mainstream American culture and
Italian/American culture. While the seductiveness of American mythology leads
Marie to adopt it--she dreams of a "Cape Cod house" (70)--she is also capable of
realizing that the "shabby" apartment she moves into after the divorce feels more
"like home than the house with three bathrooms ever" did (57). On the other hand,
her relationship to Italian ethnicity is confused, repressed both in Marie's life and
in the text, emerging occasionally, but never enough to provide the opportunity for
confrontation or resolution. In Rossi's novella, Italian/American ethnicity is
represented as a ghost culture that the narrative vainly tries to evoke: it emerges
infrequently, embodied in lost airmail letters or broken china.

Marie's account of her life as a series of scattered and seemingly disconnected
episodes parallels her representation of her ethnicity as an accumulation of tokens.
Italian art and religion are represented by a dwarfed "six-inch bust of Verdi," and a
"plate" with the grotesque face of "the sixties pope," John XXIII, "the one with the
little round head that looked like a newborn baby" (85). This satirically reductive
image both reifies and infantilizes religion. Consequently, the objectification of
Marie's cultural heritage is reflected in her detachment from her life, a life made up
of broken pieces, like the shattered china in her mother's cabinet. "I never heard a
louder noise inside" (82), Marie recalls: the failure to establish a clear referent for
"inside" creates a syntactical ambiguity that collapses the "inside" of the house and
the china cabinet and Marie's "inside." The china cabinet, with its old souvenirs
and its rarely used dishes, functions as the repository of her ethnic past,
inaccessible and now reduced to useless shards and splinters. The grotesque
souvenirs, fragmented and commodified versions of Italian culture, parallel the
phony cultural roles available to Marie. These codified cultural artifacts mirror the
cultures that have produced them. While walking up and down the aisles of
Woolworth's, where she spends "a good part" of her Saturday afternoons,
"wandering amidst water pistols and perspiration shields and brands of cold cream
nobody ever heard of" (53), Marie meets a friend who introduces her to Ralph, her
future husband. As a synecdoche for a culturally impoverished society, the store

that provides Marie with a husband represents the American alternative to the Italian souvenirs, capsules of a culture that neither Marie nor her parents ever experienced directly.

Marie "feels at home" at Woolworth's, a place where she can meditate (53). This grotesque image of meditation in Woolworth's is reminiscent of the "house with a supermarket-style door" (17) that Marie describes at the very opening of the novella as she begins reflecting on her past. Her cultural landscape is an assemblage of odds and ends from both Italian and American mythologies, all of which stifle her confused but emerging sense of selfhood. The narrative translates Marie's dissociation as detachment: only by identifying the sources of her dissociation can Marie experience her speech and her stories as her own. Molding her scattered memories of loneliness, loss, and death into a story becomes a self-created rite of passage for a woman who "felt like an impostor" (57) in the conventional life she had seemingly chosen for herself.

Helen Barolini writes that both of her parents,

> children of immigrants, passed on to their children conflicted feelings about
> their origins. In striving to get past the old generation they severed themselves
> too drastically from it; their lives became all in the foreground, without depth
> or ties to the past, all a surface of American success. ("Becoming a Literary
> Person" 263)

Marie's father's vaguely defined dreams of success, and his hope to attain vicariously, through his daughter, the education that would guarantee him access to mainstream society, are juxtaposed to Marie's rejection of success viewed as social recognition. Although Marie is not seduced by her father's dreams, she is unable to free herself from the cultural constraints linked primarily to her mother's passivity and to her father's expectations of success and dread of social failure. Moreover, she inherits from her parents a longing that can never be satisfied, a sense of cultural emptiness that can never be filled. By the end of the novella, Marie has not glued together the broken china, but she has at least started piecing together the fragments of her life. While her storytelling signals her emergence as a narrator, as a character she can not fashion her story or her part. As a first-person narrator, however, Marie becomes a producer of discourse--written discourse--and thus reverses her positions as a woman within Italian/American culture[23] and as an Italian/American within American culture. Rossi legitimizes Italian/American culture by creating it as a literary experience. Not only does her novella express a search for cultural legitimization, it also questions the forces that legitimize (or de-legitimize) cultural experiences.

* * *

In *The Quick* Rossi explored dialogic possibilities through Marie Russo's conversation with the reader. Rossi's implied audience in *The Quick*, however, differs greatly from the silent patriarchal "God" who motivates Celie's epistolary narrative in Alice Walker's *The Color Purple*. Marie wills into existence this elusive reader/listener, recognizing the necessity of an other who will listen. At the same time, the text of *The Quick* never produces a responsive voice such as Nettie's. Phyllis, the older woman with whom she establishes a relationship that defies the norms prescribed by Marie's social and cultural milieu, never plays a role as active as Phoeby's, Janie's friend and sympathetic audience in Zora Neale Hurston's *Their Eyes Were Watching God*. Walker's and Hurston's engagement in a literary exchange in which they act as each other's audience, but also as precursor/mother/sister/discoverer, translates into the epistolary relationship between Celie and Nettie, anticipated by the relationship between Janie and Phoeby. In contrast, the absence of a female interlocutor in *The Quick* reflects Rossi's lack of a literary community. If, as Barolini argues, Italian/American women authors "write out of the void" ("Becoming a Literary Person" 263), with no community to nurture their voices and no space to legitimize their stories, then Rossi's fiction articulates the search for a community of women to validate authorial speech.[24]

Such a search prompts the narrative structure of *Split Skirt*. In her first novel, *Split Skirt* (1994), Rossi draws upon and yet departs from the tradition of dialogic, communal ethnic narratives exemplified by such works as Alice Walker's *The Color Purple*, Cristina Garcia's *Dreaming in Cuban*, and Amy Tan *The Joy Luck Club* and *The Kitchen God's Wife*, in which the ethnicity of the author legitimizes the credibility of the narrative and establishes a relationship between character and author based on ethnic identity.[25] *Split Skirt* centers around the encounter between two married women, Rita and Mrs. Tyler, respectively of Italian/Irish and Irish descent. They meet in a place one might think unlikely to foster friendship, the Bergen County jail in New Jersey, in which they spend three days, Rita for drunk driving and possession of cocaine, and Mrs. Tyler for one of her escapades as a seemingly incurable kleptomaniac. While the narrative of *Split Skirt* overtly recognizes Mrs. Tyler's Irishness, it withholds Rita's Italian background. The names by which the characters refer to and address each other, Mrs. Tyler and Rita, act as age and class markers: Rita is a lower-middle-class, street-smart twenty-seven year old, while Mrs. Tyler is a sophisticated upper-middle-class woman in her fifties (though through her confessional narrative she retrieves her working-class origins).

Mrs. Tyler's ethnic self-revelation is instrumental in her self-presentation and in shaping Rita's perception of her. Mrs. Tyler generously informs Rita, and the reader, that she has no doubts about her origins--like her mother, she is Irish, a "Brennan" (157)--but Rita never mentions her own last name, thus preventing easy ethnic identification.[26] William Boelhower argues that "by discovering the self implicit in the surname, one produces an ethnic seeing and understands himself as a social, an ethnic, subject" (81). The issue of naming has been of particular relevance to many Italian/American women writers who, assuming their husbands' names, have surrendered the most immediate sign of ethnic identification. [27]

The absence of Rita's name, then, "produces" ethnic invisibility. Italian/American ethnicity surfaces, though, when Mrs. Tyler tells Rita about Judy Gennaro, her long-lost "best" friend, the only one she ever had (159). She quotes the reaction of her husband, John, after hearing screams coming from the Gennaros' house, where Judy is repeatedly the victim of her husband's violence: "goddamn Italians" (159). John's comment, which reproduces the common stereotype of Italian/American men as wife-beaters, represents the only direct reference to Italians in the book. When Judy first appears, Mrs. Tyler refers only obliquely to her background: she is "Mediterranean" (157). She never specifies her ethnicity. Moreover, John's remark does not elicit further elaboration on Mrs. Tyler's part or a response from Rita: Mrs. Tyler acts as if she is unaware of Rita's ethnic background, which is not surprising since Rita herself seems to have erased ethnic memory. Rossi inscribes her ethnic autobiographical narrative in a text which does not advertise itself as either a multicultural novel or an Italian/American novel. Nevertheless, it is noteworthy that in *Split Skirt* the two women who act as Mrs. Tyler's confidantes are Italian. These characters are the receptacle of their friends' secrets and their author's ethnic identity.

If Mrs. Tyler sees "secrecy" as the only means by which to maintain "her two separate realities" (122)--she sees herself as a "double agent" (120)--the narrative of *Split Skirt* self-consciously dramatizes Rossi's own "separate realities," her ethnic "split," by developing into a series of alternating sections in which the two characters take turns telling their stories, playing the parts of both author and audience. Destabilizing authorial power, the dual narrative of *Split Skirt* enables each character to recount her story as an autobiographical oral narrative, a genre characteristic of the early stages of ethnic literature, which typically present the speaker as an authorized witness. [29]

In her study of ethnic writers, Bonnie Tusmith argues that the "specific motivation behind" the use of such strategies as vernacular speech patterns is the "artistic validation of one's ethnic culture and value system against a hegemonic European American standard in literature" (25).[29]   Rossi's narrative, which emphasizes the oral aspect of storytelling, questions the "validation" of the ethnic experience by shifting the focus onto the individual and away from the group experience, and thus connects authenticity with self- instead of group-authorization. Throughout the novel, Rossi struggles to forge a viable relationship between self and other, rejecting notions of community based solely on loyalty to the ethnic group, and thus articulating her position as a writer who draws upon her ethnic experience by rewriting its narratives and rethinking ideas of authenticity and tradition.

While both Mrs. Tyler and Rita commit themselves to speaking the "truth" (23), to going back to origins, they soon realize that they are so enmeshed in roles and plots they did not fabricate for themselves that the "truths" they tell are always provisional and require scrutiny and questioning. Thus these narrators engage in a process of continuous re-authorization, which also includes re-evaluating their positions in old plots and even self-consciously questioning the plots they envision for themselves.   What has distinguished Italian/American women writers from their male counterparts has been a greater willingness to expose the evils of their culture, despite the ostracism that oftentimes follows from such a choice.[30]

Like other multicultural writers, Rossi rejects the notion of an exclusive narratorial power in favor of a decentered narrative that allows an egalitarian narratorial situation. In the last section of *Split Skirt*, Rossi resorts to a third-person narrative: acting as a removed camera-eye that privileges Rita's perspective, the narrative records the two protagonists' re-union outside the county jail. However, the seemingly omniscient narrative gaze does not come across as an all-powerful, all- controlling device, but as a shift towards yet another subject position, one in which the authorial voice brings together different perspectives.

In a multicultural society, John Brenkman argues, it is necessary that everyone become "fluent enough in *one another's* vocabularies and histories to share the forum of political deliberation on an equal footing," and that everyone engage "others' contingent vocabularies" (89) as well as one's own. *Split Skirt* illustrates such an engagement with "others' contingent vocabularies," through its inclusion of the voice of Luz, the Hispanic teenage prostitute who speaks in the first-person in the penultimate section. Luz's connection to Rita and her role as a "sister" (127), another sister, enables her to participate in the narrative space Rita and Mrs. Tyler have been forging together. Appropriately, Rossi dedicates the novel to her own "sisters." Typically, multi-voiced narratives by "ethnic" authors create a space which, in privileging certain voices, also excludes non-members. *Split Skirt* departs from such exclusionary narratives. If Rossi employs the dialogue between her two characters as the means by which to establish a conversation between her own Irish and Italian ethnicities, the inclusion of Luz signals an effort to enlarge the ethnic space and to create a narrative that emphasizes not sameness and consensus, but difference and communication.

Discussing what he calls a "third generation renaissance" of Italian/American writers, Gardaphé explains:

> When we examine later writers, those who are grandchildren of immigrants, we enter a period in which the immigrant past is recreated, not through self-reflection, but through a more distant historical perspective, a perspective gained by removal from the ethnic experience and resulting in the recreation of the immigrant experience in America through more distinctively fictional forms. ("Third Generation" 71)

Mrs. Tyler's recollection of her fear of being mistaken for an "immigrant" (49)--the only reference to the journey that brought her family to America--epitomizes in its uniqueness the status of ethnic memory for writers like Rossi. Her fiction represents an effort not so much to recover that memory, but to reinvent it. If the past, as Salman Rushdie writes, is "a country from which we have all emigrated . . . [and] its loss is part of our common humanity" (12), Rita, Mrs. Tyler, and Luz transcend the specificity of their experiences by sharing their memories and participating in each other's sense of loss and displacement. [31]

Yet clearly defined narrative boundaries prevent the other from being subsumed into the self. Rita and Mrs. Tyler cannot see Luz and Madeline, her cellmate. Separated by the walls of their cells, they can only hear each other's voices. Their words thus act both as self-centered monologue and self-less conversation, directed inward and outward, asserting both uniqueness--difference-- and connection. Rossi's multi-voiced narrative maintains the specificity of Italian/American, Irish/American, and Latina experiences, but it also explores possibilities for a broader dialogue that recognizes the creative potential of intersections and opens the borders of the ethnic/authorial space.

Demonstrating the specificity of the cultural displacement experienced by Italian/American women, Rossi compels the reader to define and question the kind of recognition sought by Italian Americans and members of other unrecognized or unlegitimatized ethnicities. The inadequacy of prevailing stereotypical representations of Italian/American culture in the United States prompts authors like Rossi to narrate different and untold aspects of the ethnic experience--and Rossi is not alone. For example, in her poem "Ethnic Woman," Rose Romano proclaims: "My ethnicity isn't something I drag out/of a closet to celebrate quaint holidays/nobody heard of" (*Wop* 57), thus rejecting the label of "ethnic" that reduces cultural identity to a series of tokens, devoid of referential ties to the variety and richness of Italian/American social reality. In "Mutt Bitch," she claims: "If I have no culture/I can say nothing;/therefore, if I say nothing,/I have no culture" (*Vendetta* 37). Romano, like Rossi, rejects the notion of a quintessential Italian/American identity. These and other Italian/American women writers establish themselves as intellectual voices that move beyond nostalgic and blindly celebratory views of their ethnicity. In doing so, they demonstrate the power of literary texts to explore, interrogate, and offer forceful alternatives to current social and political realities. Their writings negotiate and trouble categories of the personal and the public, exposing how the lives and voices of individuals in the minority are products of dominant discourses of identity, even as they show how such people can become effective agents of resistance and change. These works challenge the mainstream imagination and its stereotyping; they present alternative visions of ethnicity that both include an awareness of the hostile powers working against its expression and dare to imagine a future--and to create a present--in which such forces would cease to have relevance.

Exposing the devastating effects of "good-natured bigotry," Romano claims that she could "write" her "life/story with different shapes in/various sizes in limitless patterns of/pasta laid out to dry on a thick, white/tablecloth," and she asks the implied audience/reader of "Ethnic Woman": "Must I teach you/to read?" The signs of Italian/American culture have become so stultified that for Romano it is imperative to reclaim those signs, and to re-inscribe new significance in them. Like Romano, in her work Agnes Rossi captures the problematic status of Italian/American culture by simultaneously articulating and suppressing the signs of its presence, and similarly requires a reader willing to learn how to read the almost-silent signs, how to hear the voices that speak with an accent that wants to be heard.

Edvige Giunta

Acknowledgments

Portions of this essay have appeared in two earlier essays: "Reinventing the Authorial/Ethnic Space: Communal Narratives in Agnes Rossi's *Split Skirt*," *Literary Studies East and West. Constructions and Confrontations: Changing Representations of Women and Feminism East and West* Vol. 13 (1996); "Narratives of Loss: Voices of Ethnicity in Agnes Rossi and Nancy Savoca," *Canadian Journal of Italian Studies. Special Issue on Italian American Culture* 19 (1996): 55-73.

Excerpts from "Public School No. 18, Paterson, New Jersey," from *Winter Light* (1985) and "Growing Up Italian" from *Taking Back My Name* (1991) by Maria Mazziotti Gillan. Reprinted by permission of the author.

Excerpts from "Mutt Bitch" from *Vendetta* and "Ethnic Woman" by Rose Romano.

Excerpt from "Italian Women" from *Italian Women and Other Tragedies* (Guernica 1994) by Gianna Patriarca. Reprinted by permission of the publisher.

Research for this essay was conducted during an NEH Seminar on "Emergent American Literatures" directed by John Brenkman in 1995.

I am grateful to Joshua Fausty for his meticulous readings and helpful insights.

Notes

1.. In "I'm Here: An Asian American Woman's Response," Amy Ling questions of definitions of "fine literature" and argues for the need to study literature as "the written voice of a specific group of people at a specific time" (742).

2.. Sollors claims that the conflict between "descent" and "consent" "is at the root of the ambiguity surrounding the very terminology of American ethnic interaction" (5).

3.. "The difference is between a malintegration one has learned to cope with or whose hopelessness is fully understood and a more radical malintegration exacerbated by the greenhorn status" (Ostendorf 577).

4.. The same is also true, of course, for those who belong to groups that are marginalized because of their class or sexual orientation. In this essay I will focus specifically on ethnic discrimination.

5.. On the status of Italian Americans in American culture, see Tamburri and Bona eds., Tropea et al. eds. and Gambino.

6.. See Gardaphé, "What's Italian About Italian/American Literature."

7.. See Barolini's discussion of stereotypes of Italian/Americans in "Becoming a Literary Person Out of Context" (272).

8.. Anthony Tamburri has argued that the experience of hyphenation is literally reproduced in the signs used to refer to Americans of Italian descent. In *To Hyphenate or Not To Hyphenate*, he argues that the slash, unlike the hyphen, establishes an egalitarian and dialectical relationship between the terms Italian and American.

9.. On women and ethnicity, see Dearborn. On Italian/American women authors, see Barolini, "Introduction," *The Dream Book*, 3-56; Bona, Introduction, *The Voices We Carry*, 11-29; Gabaccia, Gardaphé, "Autobiography as Piecework"; and Giunta, "'A Song from the Ghetto'."

10.. On Barolini, see Gardaphé, "Autobiography as Piecework" and Giunta, "Blending Literary Discourses." See also Barolini's introduction to *The Dream Book* and her essay, "Becoming a Literary Person Out of Context."

11.. On representations of Italian Americans in film see Giunta, "The Quest for True Love."

12.. See Chambers and Bammer. As Micaela Di Leonardo points out, though "critics and advocates alike implicitly or explicitly assume that contemporary identity politics categories--gender, race or ethnicity, nationality, sexual orientation--are ur-identities, the most fundamental divisions in human experience, but depending on which era of American history we consider, we would want to later alter or expand this list" (109).

13.. Personal letter from Agnes Rossi, 5 January 1994. Early drafts of *Fancy* also contained Italian/American references.

14.. Rossi claims that the omission of the Italian/American reference had to do exclusively with the direction the narrative had taken. Telephone conversation, 28 February 1994.

15.. In her first book of poems, a chapbook entitled *Taking Back My Name*, Gillan turned self-silencing into the subject matter of her poetry.

16.. See Pelton's review of *Your Name Here*   . Examining issues of ethnic visibility and invisibility in Italian/American literature, Fred Gardaphé argues that writers such as Don De Lillo and critics such as Frank Lentricchia either suppress ethnic clues or portray their ethnicity obliquely through other ethnicities. See his article "(In)visibility."

17.. For a discussion of third-generation Italian/American writers, see Gardaphé, "A Third-Generation Renaissance."

18.. On the status of Italian/American literature see the introduction to *From the Margin*, eds. Tamburri, Giordano, and Gardaphé. See also Gardaphé, *Italian Signs, American Streets*.

19.. In his book *Italian Signs, American Streets*, reversing the association between Italian Americans and organized crime, Gardaphé argues for the need "to make sure that the cultural crimes of the past do not increase others' ignorance of Italian American culture" (4).

20.. On the development of a female Italian/American literary tradition, see the introduction to *The Dream Book*, ed. Helen Barolini. See also Barolini's "Becoming a Literary Person Out of Context," Bona's introduction to *The Voices We Carry*, Gardaphé's "Autobiography as Piecework," and Giunta, "'A Song from the Ghetto.'" See Caroli on the history of Italian women immigrants in North America.

21.. For a discussion of "positionality," see Brenkman 99-100.

22.. Rossi claims that she has developed a self-awareness of her ethnicity in the recent past ("On Being Italian American," unpublished notes, 2). Marie then actualizes the author's own relationship to her ethnic experience.

23.. "Perhaps the most revealing cultural difference between southern Italy and America, especially relating to literary representations of selfhood, is the Southern Italian's distrust of words itself [sic]. A firm belief in the value of deeds over words was held sacrosanct by the peasant stock in southern Italy . . . . the southern Italians' traditional distrust of words perpetuated a heritage of silence for both genders" (Bona 89).

24.. "That Italian American women have been underpublished is undeniable; just as exclusionary, however, is that the few who are published are not kept on record and made accessible, even bibliographically, in libraries and in study courses. Not only do Italian American women writing their own stories publish with great difficulty . . . but once in print, they must confront an established cadre of criticism that seems totally devoid of the kind of insight that could relate to their work" (Barolini, *The Dream Book* 44-5).

25.. For a discussion of identity politics and white ethnicity, see di Leonardo.

26.. Yet Mrs. Tyler herself questions her own identity as she slips "in" and "out" (98) of the clothes her mother in law purchases for her.

27.. Sandra Mortola Gilbert, Dorothy Calvetti Bryant, Marianna De Marco Torgovnick, and Linda Bortolotti Hutcheon are just a few Italian/American authors who relinquished their Italian names through marriage. Gilbert wrote to Barolini: "And my mother's name was Caruso, so I always feel oddly falsified with this Waspish-sounding name," which I adopted as a 20-year old bride who had never considered the implications of her actions!" (Barolini, *Dream Book* 22).

28.. Interestingly enough, the recent publication of ethnic memoirs by second- and third-generation Italian/American critics such as Frank Lentricchia, Louise DeSalvo and Marianna De Marco Torgovnick suggests that the cycle has come full circle, recreating the early literary forms of the immigrant experience.

29.. Tusmith's common though somewhat facile distinction neglects to take into account ethnic intersections. Her juxtaposition of two large, broadly defined, groups, European/American and non-European/American, oversimplifies differences among various European/American groups and subgroups, such as the Northern Italians and Southern Italians. In addition, her juxtaposition ignores the way in which immigration policies have shaped the idea of "Americanness" developed by certain ethnic groups, including Italian Americans. To overlook the history of discrimination suffered by certain European American groups, especially Eastern and Southern European, would mean to ignore the history of citizenship in the U.S. In the early twentieth century "preparedness" experts argued that "military service was the only way to 'yank the hyphen out of the Italian Americans' and other 'imperfectly assimilated immigrants'" (Vaughan 450). "The history of citizenship," Brenkman argues, "is also the history of the denial of citizenship" (89). See Brenkman's critique of Sollors's classic distinction between descent and consent (98-9).

30.. Oral histories of immigrant families diverge along gender lines; women "more willingly discussed family problems than men, who more typically presented sanitized or romanticized memories" (Gabaccia 43).

31.. Gardaphé argues that when writers are free from "the chain of the immigrant's memory and reality, and have . . . to rely on imagination . . . their writing reaches into the more mythic quality of the Italian-American experience, thus creating literature that transcends a single ethnic experience" ("Third Generation" 83). Rossi's novel self-consciously transcends the "single ethnic experience" in more ways than one.

Works Cited

Bammer, Angelika ed. *Displacements: Cultural Identities in Question.* Indianapolis: Indiana University Press, 1994.

Barolini, Helen. "Becoming a Literary Person Out of Context." *The Massachusetts Review,* 27.2 (1986): 262-74.

----- ed. *The Dream Book: An Anthology of Writings by Italian American Women.* New York: Shocken, 1987.

Boelhower, William. *Through a Glass Darkly: Ethnic Semiosis in American Literature.* Oxford: Oxford University Press, 1987.

Bona, Mary Jo ed. *The Voices We Carry: Recent Italian/American Women's Fiction.* Montreal: Guernica, 1994.

..... and Anthony Julian Tamburri eds. *Through the Looking Glass: Italian & Italian/American Images in the Media.* Staten Island, NY: American Italian Historical Association, 1996.

Brenkman, John. "Multiculturalism and Criticism." *Inside and Out: The Places of Literary Criticism.* Eds. Susan Gubar and Jonathan Kamboltz. New York and London: Routledge, 1993. 87-101.

Caroli, Betty Boyd, Robert F. Harney, and Lydio F. Tomasi eds. *The Italian Immigrant Woman in North America.* Proceedings of the Tenth Annual Conference of the American Italian Historical Association, 1977. Toronto: The Multicultural History Society of Ontario, 1978.

Chambers, Ian. *Migrancy, Culture, Identity.* London: Routledge, 1994.

Ciresi, Rita. *Mother Rocket. Stories.* Athens: University of Georgia, 1994.

Dearborn, Mary V. *Pocahontas's Daughters: Gender and Ethnicity in American Culture.* New York: Oxford University Press, 1986.

De Rosa, Tina. "An Italian American Woman Speaks Out." *Attenzione* (May 1980): 38-9.

DeSalvo, Louise. *Casting Off.* Brighton, UK: Harvester, 1987.

-----. *Vertigo.* New York: Dutton, 1996.

di Leonardo, Micaela. "White Ethnicities, Identity Politics, and Baby Bear's Chair." *Social Text,*
41 (Winter 1994): 165-91.

Fausty, Joshua S. Review of *Mother Rocket. VIA: Voices in Italian Americana,* 6.2 (Fall 1995):
204-207.

Gabaccia, Donna. "Women and Ethnicity: A Review Essay." *Italian Americana,* 12.1
(Fall/Winter 1993): 38-61.

Gambino, Richard. *Blood of My Blood: The Dilemma of the Italian Americans.* Garden City,
NY: Anchor/Doubleday, 1975.

Garcia, Cristina. *Dreaming in Cuban.* New York: Ballantine, 1992.

Gardaphé, Fred L. "Autobiography as Piecework: The Writings of Helen Barolini." *Italian
Americans Celebrate Life, the Arts and Popular Culture: Selected Essay from the 22nd
Annual Conference of the American Italian Historical Association.* Eds. Paola A. Sensi
Isolani and Anthony Julian Tamburri. American Italiani Historical Association, 1990.

-----. "(In)visibility: Cultural Representation in the Criticism of Frank Lentricchia." *Differentia:
Review of Italian Thought,* 6-7 (Spring/Autumn 1994): 201-18

-----. "Italian-American Fiction: A Third Generation Renaissance." *MELUS,* 4.3-4 (Fall/Winter
1987): 69-85.

-----. *Italian Signs, American Streets: The Evolution of Italian American Narrative.* Durham, NC:
Duke University Press, 1996.

-----. "What's Italian About Italian/American Literature." Paper presented at the Purdue
University Conference on Romance Languages, Literatures and Film. Purdue University.
West Lafayette, IN. October 13-15 1994.

Gattuso Hendin, Josephine. *The Right Thing to Do.* Boston: David R. Godine, 1988.

Gillan, Maria Mazziotti. *Taking Back My Name.* San Francisco: malafemmina press, 1991.

-----. *Where I Come From: Selected and New Poems.* Montreal: Guernica, 1994.

Giunta, Edvige. "Blending 'Literary' Discourses: Helen Barolini's Italian/American Narratives."
Romance Languages Annual 6 (1995):

-----. "'A Song from the Ghetto.'" Afterword. Tina De Rosa. *Paper Fish.* 1980. New York:
The Feminist Press, CUNY, 1996. 123-57.

-----. "The Quest for True Love: Nancy Savoca's Domestic Film Comedy." *MELUS,* (1997). Forthcoming.

Hurston, Zora Neale. *Their Eyes Were Watching God.* 1937. Urbana: University of Illinois Press, 1978.

Lentricchia, Frank. *The Edge of Night.* New York: Random House, 1994.

Ling, Amy. "I'm Here: An Asian American Woman's Response." *Feminisms: An Anthology of Literary Theory and Criticism.* Eds. Robyn R. Warhol and Diane   Price Herndl. New Brunswick, NJ: Rutgers University Press, 1991. 738-45.

Manfredi, Renèe. Excerpt from *Running Away with Frannie. VIA: Voices in Italian Americana.* Special Issue on Italian/American Women. 7.2 (Fall 1996). Forthcoming.

Mangione, Jerre and Ben Morreale. *La Storia: Five Centuries of the Italian American Experience.* New York: Harper, 1992.

Mazza, Cris. *Your Name Here_____.* Minneapolis: Coffee House Press, 1995.

Ostendorf, Berndt. "Literary Acculturation: What Makes Ethnic Literature 'Ethnic'?" *Callaloo,* 8.3 (Fall 1985): 577-86.

Patriarca, Gianna. *Italian Women and Other Tragedies.* Toronto: Guernica, 1994.

Pelton, Ted. Review of *Your Name Here_____. VIA: Voices in Italian Americana.* Special Issue on Italian/American Women. 7.2 (Fall 1996). Forthcoming.

Romano, Rose. *Vendetta.* San Francisco: malafemmina press, 1990.

-----. *The Wop Factor.* San Francisco: malafemmina press, 1994.

Rossi, Agnes. *Athletes and Artists: Stories.* New York: Persea, 1987.

-----. *Fancy.* Unpublished novel.

-----. Letter to Edvige Giunta. 5 January 1994.

-----. *The Quick: A Novella and Stories.* New York: Norton, 1992.

-----. *Split Skirt.* New York: Random House, 1994.

-----. "On Being an Italian American." Unpublished notes.

Rushdie, Salman. *Imaginary Homelands: Essays and Criticism 1981-1991*. New York: Penguin, 1992.

Sollors, Werner. *Beyond Ethnicity: Consent and Descent in American Culture*. New York: Oxford University Press, 1986.

Tamburri, Anthony Julian. *To Hyphenate or Not To Hyphenate. The Italian/American Writer: An "Other" American*. Montreal: Guernica, 1991.

-----, Paolo Giordano and Fred L. Gardaphé, eds. *From the Margin: Writings in Italian Americana*. West Lafayette, IN: Purdue University Press, 1991. 357-   73.

Tan, Amy. *The Joy Luck Club*. New York: Ballantine, 1989.

-----. *The Kitchen God's Wife*. New York: Ballantine, 1991.

Torgovnick, Marianna De Marco. *Crossing Ocean Parkway: Readings by an Italian American Daughter*. Chicago: University of Chicago Press, 1994.

Tropea, Joseph et al. eds. *Support and Struggle: Italians and Italian Americans in a Comparative Perspective*. Staten Island, NY: The American Italian Historical Association, 1986.

Tusmith, Bonnie. *Community in Contemporary Ethnic American Literature*. Ann Arbor: University of Michigan Press, 1994.

Vaughan, Leslie J. "Cosmopolitanism, Ethnicity and American Identity: Randolph Bourne's 'Trans-National America.'" *Journal of American Studies,* 25 (1991): 443-59.

Walker, Alice. *The Color Purple*. New York: Harcourt Brace Jovanovich, 1982.

5.

LOSS AND GROWTH OF IDENTITY
IN SHIMON WINCELBERG'S
RESORT 76

In his play Resort 76, Shimon Wincelberg dramatizes the ethnic
discrimination by Nazis against Jews. He demonstrates how his protagonist
cherishes, loses, and then rejects one identity and then shows how that character
decides to kill himself rather than sacrificing the new identity he has painfully
achieved. The playwright deftly creates an ironic and unique situation in which an
anti-Semite, because of his zealous effort to purify Germany by ridding the country
of Jews, is forced to live among the people he despises. Krause, a Nazi pharmacist
and World War I veteran, decides to re-enlist in the German army because of his
prejudice against Jews. During the routine, mandatory background search, the Nazis
discover that Krause's grandfather was Jewish, rendering the Nazi a Mischling, a
person of mixed birth. To his horror, Krause learns that the Nazis classify him as a
member of the ethnic group that he abhors and order him to live in the Jewish ghetto
in Lodz, Poland. As Wincelberg's play develops, Krause begins to realize that the
Jews he now lives with are indeed human beings--not subhuman animals, as he had
imagined. Krause's feelings of superiority begin to dissolve when he realizes that he
has always been a member of the ethnic group that his Nazi party despises. Because
he has always been partly Jewish and because he discovers that, like other human
beings, Jews possess moral character and that they too experience pain when
persecuted, he must re-evaluate the values that he has maintained throughout his life
since what he learns about Jews leads to self-recognition. Wincelberg demonstrates
that although one may easily harbor prejudices and discriminate against "the other"
when little contact exists between that person and the despised ethnic group, when
one lives and interacts with members of that group, prejudices disappear because one
begins to identify with, and understand, people who previously appeared foreign.

Krause's realization about Jews eventually leads him to commit an act of self-destruction that is, paradoxically, a form of self-affirmation.

As Wincelberg's play begins, Krause searches for the place he dreads--Resort 76. The Nazi government has transported him to the Lodz ghetto and has ordered him to report to the factory. The ironic name of the factory, which implies that the inmates reside in a resort, insults the victims, just as the phrase on the gates of Auschwitz (ARBEIT MACHT FREI) was a cruel joke on those prisoners. Like many members of Wincelberg's audience, the pharmacist knows not what to expect. During the course of the drama, the inhabitants of Resort 76 indoctrinate Krause as well as the audience into the misery and desperation that pervade the ghetto. Manifesting his naiveté upon entering the factory, Krause declares that "Twice I almost got shot by our own soldiers"[1] and that Hauptmann, a Resort 76 inhabitant, should fight for the Nazis: "Doesn't he know, in times like these, his country needs every able-bodied man?"[2] Krause naively overlooks the fact that although the Nazis fight on his side, the soldiers are enemies of the Jews. Germany, therefore, would refuse to accept Jews (such as Hauptmann) in her army, and members of the German armed forces are not, from the Jewish perspective, "our" soldiers. Krause fails to comprehend that Jews would refuse to fight for the German army against the Allies--regardless of Axis propaganda--and that Germany and its occupied territories are not "his [Hauptmann's] countr[ies]." In fact, the Nazis do not consider Jewish people to be either Germans or Poles--merely Jews, an inferior people. Krause's statement that Hauptmann should fight is also ironic because the Nazis would certainly not allow the ghetto dweller in their army when they refuse a Mischling such as the pharmacist. Krause's failure to discern the irony of his statement demonstrates that Nazi propaganda has brainwashed him; he still advocates Nazi ideology even after becoming its victim. At this point in the play, his sense of identity is badly confused.

Like many Aryans in Nazi Germany, Krause becomes influenced by propagandists who effectively employ rhetoric to turn Aryans against Jews. In Resort 76, Wincelberg has deliberately characterized an Aryan who has succumbed to Nazi ideology and has accepted its rhetoric, values, and aspirations. Following the argument of sociologist Ernst Bloch, J. Miller Jones points out that "Nazism in the thirties presented a false utopian face that managed to garner and hold wide support among the German public."[3] Adolf Hitler and Joseph Goebbels created the image of a Judenfrei Germany as a utopia, as the Heimat (the Homeland). In works such as The Protocols of the Elders of Zion, propagandists portrayed Jews as threats to Aryan well-being and contaminators of this potential utopia. While brainwashing German citizens such as Krause to hate and fear Jews, Nazis took extreme measures, even asserting that racial prejudice was divinely sanctioned, that discrimination against Jews was a form of obeying God: in Mein Kampf, for example, Adolf Hitler states that his prejudice is "in accordance with the will of the Almighty Creator: by defending myself against the Jew, I am fighting for the work of the Lord."[4] Blindly accepting Nazi propaganda, Krause believes so strongly that the mistreatment of Jews is morally acceptable that he even expects that those being victimized by Nazis, such as the Lodz factory workers at Resort 76, would also approve and recognize their own inferiority.

Consequently, his discovery that he has Jewish blood in him, when combined with his interaction with Jews in the Lodz ghetto, causes an internal conflict. His confused identity creates a particularly complex predicament. For example, he not only admires, but also fears his government. Although he has served faithfully in the German army during World War I, he expresses no animosity when the Nazis send him to the ghetto during World War II; he shows more confidence in his government than in himself. Furthermore, Krause still accepts Nazi belief in a pure Aryan race even though the Nazis have imprisoned him at Resort 76 upon discovering that his maternal grandfather was Jewish. However, although the pharmacist believes that the Jews deserve their suffering because their blood is impure, he constructs a double standard (and an inherently unstable identity) for himself: he remarks to the ghetto inhabitants, "I wasn't even born then! How can I be held responsible for the kind of man my grandmother married when she was an empty-headed little slut of seventeen? The dirty swine! Polluting an innocent Aryan girl with his bestial Asiatic lusts!"[5] The pharmacist fails to comprehend that his grandmother married a Jew well before the rise of the Nazi regime, before economic problems caused Germans to employ Jews as scapegoats and to consider Semites evil and subhuman. During his diatribe, the pharmacist also neglects to consider that he and other Nazis hold Jews responsible for their ancestors despite his unwillingness to accept his own progenitors. Although he acknowledges that he never knew his grandparents, he assumes that because a Jew married his Aryan grandmother, the man must have been motivated by his animalistic, subhuman lust and that a union between an Aryan and Jew pollutes and contaminates the former. Although Krause cannot deny the identity the Nazis have assigned him, at this point he refuses to embrace it. While attempting to come to terms with the new identity with which the Nazis have branded him, he tries to see himself as its victim rather than as a victim of prejudice.

Krause's confused identity is reflected in his misguided thinking. His reference to bestiality derives, for instance, from Nazi propaganda implying that Jews were subhuman. The Third Reich employed this indoctrination to discourage Aryans from interacting and having children with Jews. The Nazi government realized that it would be easier for Aryans to discriminate against Jews (and more difficult to sympathize with them) if they did not associate with Semites and saw them as inferior. Consequently, the "Law for the Protection of German Blood and German Honor, September 15, 1935" stated, "Marriages between Jews and subjects of German or kindred blood are forbidden."[6] In fact, Aryans involved in romantic relationships with Jews were labeled Rasseschanders and suffered punishments for the offense. The Nazi government clearly stated that Jews were of a different species and thus likened sexual intercourse with a Jew to bestiality. Henry R. Huttenbach claims that the prejudice derived from "the dehumanization of the victim. Those that reasoned toward the annihilation of the Jews predicated their murderous action on an abstraction, 'the Jew' (Der Jude), devoid of all human qualities."[7] Although Krause at first accepted this attitude, he now realizes that he too has become a social outcast and has always possessed something inherent that, according to his beliefs, has rendered him bestial, subhuman. To the extent that he accepts Nazi definitions of Jewish identity, his own identity is threatened.

Mulling over the Nazi theory regarding bestiality and blindly accepting Nazi doctrine, Krause concludes that he, like all Jews, suffers from contamination. He confesses that "We do, after all, have a bureaucracy which is the envy of the civilized world. And if they have decided I am not fit to live among human beings, they probably know what they're talking about."[8] The pharmacist exhibits great faith in bureaucracy--an establishment that, according to German sociologist Max Weber, succeeds the more it is dehumanized, the more it denies individual identity.[9] Richard L. Rubenstein adds that "Bureaucracy can be understood as a structural and organizational expression of the related processes of secularization, disenchantment of the world, and rationalization."[10] Krause's statement regarding bureaucracy manifests the cause of his naiveté: the pharmacist accepts Nazi ideology blindly-- even when it undermines his own sense of self. The resulting confusion is reflected in his language in the above quotation. Thus, by using the first person plural pronoun "We," he reluctantly allies himself with Jews, undesirables whom he detests. His use of the pronoun "they," however, connotes his realization that his heritage is impure, that he is no longer a Nazi; his very existence, therefore, ironically stands in the way of his wife's and daughter's happiness. His wife threatens to leave

him, as does his daughter, Ursula, one of the most devoted members of the Youth
Movement:

> . . . It was all I could do to keep her from putting her head in the oven.
> (Suppressing tears.) Do you call that justice? . . . At least you people know why
> you're here. . . . I mean, at least none of this comes as any   surprise to you. . . .
> But what about me? I never even knew I had a   grandfather.[11]

Krause laments that his daughter wants to place her head in an oven (a desire that
foreshadows his own suicide) because her great-grandfather was Jewish, yet his
words simultaneously remind the Semites of the ovens of destruction in Nazi
concentration camps, rendering it more difficult for the Jews to pity him. Krause
tactlessly informs the inhabitants of Resort 76 that he believes he deserves more
sympathy than they do because Jews have been persecuted for years and should
therefore have accepted and grown accustomed to it, whereas the revelation
concerning his Jewish grandfather has taken him by surprise. In other words, Krause
sees persecution as part of a settled Jewish identity, but such mistreatment seems
alien to his own sense of self.

Although Krause egoistically complains to Jewish victims of the Holocaust
about the unfair treatment he has received, surprisingly, ghetto inhabitants such as
Schnur and Blaustain do actually pity his plight, a problem that pales in comparison
with their own. Part of the alteration in the pharmacist's attitude towards Jews
occurs because he gradually realizes the depth of the factory workers' sufferings and
admires the Jews for empathizing with him despite their own worries. Paradoxically,
their ability to show concern for him testifies to the strength of their own identities.
As Wincelberg's play progresses, Krause comprehends that his dilemma is
inconsequential compared to the tribulations of such ghetto residents as Blaustain
and his wife (Esther), Schnur, Beryl, Madame Hershkovitch, and Anya. Krause
comes to admire them because, in addition to empathizing with him, they maintain
their dignity--their essential selfhood--even when being destroyed. Although the
Jews in the play face desperate situations, they manifest a strong desire to avoid
behaving as cruelly and inhumanely as the Nazis. The playwright contrasts the
virtuous behavior of the Jews with the derogatory manner in which Nazi ideology
portrays them. Persecution ironically confirms, rather than destroys, their moral
identities. Robert Skloot notes that Wincelberg's characters "leave us with the
strongest possible image of humane behavior under abominable circumstances."[12]
As Krause witnesses the humanity of the Jews, especially under horrific conditions,

he finds that he can no longer adhere to the propaganda with which he has been indoctrinated.

The pharmacist comes to admire his new cohabitants as he observes them act morally in desperate times. Krause watches as Blaustain, in addition to supervising the carpet factory, nurses his starving, pregnant wife and guards the cat that Madame Hershkovitch has captured. At one point, Blaustain contemplates aborting the baby his wife carries. Esther's pregnancy renders her a weak invalid who consumes not only her bread but much of her husband's as well. Childbirth, or simply carrying the baby for several months while barely eating, may kill her, and the baby--in the unlikely case that it would live--clearly would have a bleak future. Anya says to Blaustain, "You want to bring a child into this beautiful world? Ask Mme. Hershkovitch what they [Nazis] do. She cleans up around the hospital. Ask her how it feels to throw away a smashed baby along with the rest of the garbage!"[13] Furthermore, ghetto law forbids procreation by Jews. As George Eisen says,

> In line with the Nazi plan of reducing the Jewish population was the forced reduction of the fertility rate through segregation of the sexes, marriage bans, and compulsory abortion. . . . For instance, in ghetto Siaulaui, Lithuania, decrees were posted notifying women that forced abortions would take place within a period of several weeks. When his policy did not produce the expected results, the SS proclaimed the death   penalty for childbirth, for the mother, the infant, and the whole family.[14]

This policy held true for Jews throughout Europe.

Jewish law and human decency, however, finally dictate Blaustain's decision to avoid an abortion. Blaustain realizes that destroying the baby would also be an act of moral self-destruction, partly because it would deny his identity as a Jew. Jewish law, for example, strictly forbids abortion under any circumstances. God informs Jeremiah that "Before I formed thee in the belly I knew thee, and before thou camest forth out of the womb I sanctified thee; I have appointed thee a prophet unto the nations."[15] This Biblical passage implies that because God knows and sanctifies a person's identity even before birth, a fetus is a human being and abortion is murder. Since God orders, "Thou shalt not kill,"[16] abortion, according to Jewish doctrine, represents a violation of one of God's most sacred commandments. Blaustain, touched by Schnur's willingness to sacrifice his life in order to preserve Talmudic study (which Schnur considers essential to his moral identity), emulates his action by risking his own life to save the life of his unborn child. The engineer chooses Jewish law over civil law and decides that aborting the baby would be barbaric and cruel and thus not dissimilar to the acts of the Nazis. It would destroy the baby, but it would also help shatter his sense of self. Blaustain's decision to risk his life in order to obey Jewish law (and thus preserve his identity) impresses Krause, who previously accepted blindly the Nazi propaganda that portrayed Jews as unscrupulous.

Krause also comes to admire Blaustain for making ethical decisions such as to act mercifully towards the stray cat and to remain in the ghetto. Madame Hershkovitch and the other Resort 76 inhabitants consider the cat an effective bargaining tool for acquiring food and a "safe" ghetto job. Anya counters that she can trade the cat for certificates of baptism for Blaustain and herself, which would allow them to escape and join the partisans, even though Esther, because of her pregnancy and ill health, would be unable to join them. Although Blaustain yearns to leave the ghetto, he refuses to desert his wife and workers, who would probably die if he left them, for the carpet factory would then prove unprofitable and the workers, expendable. For instance, the leader of the Lodz ghetto, Mordechai Rumkowski, proclaimed in several speeches that the Jews would survive only if they worked productively and enhanced the Nazi war effort: "I am certain that if the ghetto does its work well and in earnest the authorities will not apply any repressive measures. . . . I will be able to demonstrate, on the basis of irrefutable statistics, that the Jews in the ghetto constitute a productive element, and that they are, perforce, needed."[17] Recognizing that the other workers depend on him, Blaustain chooses social responsibility over self-preservation and decides to continue with his factory work despite his realization that the carpets he manufactures for the Germans derive from Holocaust victims' clothes, such as the blue dress his mother wore when the Nazis murdered her. The ghetto inhabitants free the cat, manifesting that they, unlike the Nazis, choose not to be captors or oppressors. Krause must question his anti-Semitism as he watches the ghetto inhabitants benevolently release the cat.

The starving factory workers could eat the cat for nourishment, as Krause himself suggests, yet they are unwilling to risk their moral identities, despite their great hunger. Holocaust scholar Shmuel Krakowski notes that starvation "was the chief problem the [Lodz] ghetto had to contend with throughout its existence. The average daily food ration per person was less than 1,100 calories." Krakowski adds that 43,500 inhabitants died of starvation, cold , and disease (often brought about by hunger) during the four years (1941-1944) of the Lodz ghetto's existence.[18] In the September 19, 1943 entry in The Chronicle of the Lodz Ghetto, 1941-1944, Lucjan Dobroszycki notes that the lack of food "is rapidly developing into a catastrophe.

The meager reserves are even forcing the soup kitchens to lower the amount of potato in soups to 150 grams. People wander in despair through the streets, trying to find something to eat."[19] Although the Jews in the factory are starving, they realize the evil that the killing of the cat entails. In fact, the Jews treat the cat better than the Nazis treat them, and the Germans comport themselves more benevolently towards animals (who do not threaten their identities) than towards Jews (whom they perceive as threats). Krause, still clinging to the tattered remnants of his former self, declares proudly that the Nazi government has made vivisection illegal, for the Germans shun "Any sort of experimentation that might inflict cruelty on a living animal. . . We may have our faults as a nation, but thank God, we are civilized."[20] Unlike the ghetto inhabitants, the pharmacist fails to discern the irony of a genocidal government that considers vivisection reprehensible. The Nazis deem that vivisection is immoral but consider experimentation on Jews, such as the work of Josef Mengele, morally acceptable. Vivisection would challenge their sense of superiority, but anti-Semitism confirms their self-regard.

The oppressed Jewish workers initially seize the opportunity to exercise power over the vulnerable cat, but eventually they comprehend that by doing so, they mirror, on a microcosmic level, their persecutors. Schnur, for example, insists that despite the desperate situation at Resort 76, Jews who commit acts of violence and evil deny that they have been created in God's image; Schnur says to Beryl that he should never stoop to the level of Nazis "[b]ecause you are a man! A man, and not an animal."[21] For Schnur, being true to one's self means being true to one's creator. When Krause realizes that starving Jews preserve the cat's life and treat it better than he earlier would have treated Semites, he feels shame and recognizes the dignity of those he formerly despised. He realizes that although in one sense they are powerless, their moral integrity gives them a self-respect he does not yet possess. The pharmacist also comprehends the specious nature of Nazi propaganda that has sanctioned the discrimination against Jews.

Ironically, Krause loses his faith in Nazi ideology even as the persecuted Jews maintain their trust in God and their integrity of self. The pharmacist comes to admire his new cohabitants, who have been mercilessly persecuted, for their resistance against despair, for their continuous faith. Previously disdaining Judaism, Krause now expresses amazement when Jews refuse to relinquish hope in God or in one another. For instance, Schnur, the former butcher who risks death by instructing Beryl about Judaism, believes in and teaches the Talmud faithfully. Of course, a question that pervades Holocaust literature concerns how a benevolent and omniscient God can allow such misery and mass destruction. Beryl even declares to Schnur that he is "finished with God! You have lied to me. He is not our father. If this is how a father loves his children. . . then let me be an orphan!"[22] Schnur points out, contrariwise, that in adversity, Jews must maintain their faith--as if to suggest that God has allowed the Holocaust in order to test Jewish faith, mettle, and identity. Surmising that faith is even more essential in times of crisis, he asks Beryl, "Don't you know it is only the breath of children studying the Law that keeps the world from falling apart?"[23] He believes that Jews should love God and should not only thank Him for the pleasures life affords but should also be grateful for every day of life. Even during hardships, he believes, they should exhibit unquestioning faith. These words influence Beryl, who realizes the foolishness of his despair and decides to remain true to his faith (and thereby to himself), just as Blaustain does when he decides that although an abortion could save his life and Esther's, he cannot allow it because it violates God's commandment. Even when the unfortunate Jews express momentary doubts in God, they refuse to violate His laws. Gradually, their conduct begins to alter Krause's self-perception as well as his judgment of others.

As he observes Beryl and Blaustain reaffirm their faith in their religion, Krause finds it necessary to reject his convictions in Nazi ideology. Although he makes no secret of his disdain for Jews while in the ghetto, they show compassion and pity for him, thus making him admire them and feel shame for his past misdeeds. The pharmacist realizes that Jews are indeed human beings, people who live by a code of ethics and who empathize with others. Although critic Robert Skloot says that Krause "kills himself because he cannot face the shame he will encounter when his release is finally obtained,"[24] he fails to consider the learning experience and self-recognition that have taken place in the ghetto that day. The pharmacist's shame derives not from what the Nazis will think of him, but from his own mortification over his earlier prejudice and abuse towards Jews. Because of his political connections, Krause could have legally nullified his Jewish heritage (his pastor declares his mother illegitimate), permitting him to leave the ghetto and the Jewish victims behind. He cannot, however, abandon the new identity he has achieved during his time there. The bribe that provides him with permission to return to Nazi society and erase his Jewish ancestry manifests to Krause the superficiality of the differences between Nazis and Jews; the pharmacist, who had always maintained that actual physical, spiritual, moral, and intellectual differences exist between races, discovers to his dismay that mere money and deceit can transform a Jew into an Aryan. As a result of all these experiences, Krause recognizes that Jews are not inferior to Aryans and do not deserve to be persecuted. This realization, coupled with his shame for harboring prejudice and hatred towards Semites in the past, makes the pharmacist experience misgivings about returning to Germany so that he may oppress more Jews. Because Krause decides that he cannot return home to his Aryan wife and aid a doctrine he now despises, he commits physical suicide to preserve his new moral self. His suicide affirms, rather than negates, the new essential identity he has developed through his ironic exposure to the very prejudices he once espoused. Wincelberg's play, therefore, attests that when people who persecute others for being "different" are forced to identify with members of that group, the oppressors begin to identify with them and question the prejudices they have maintained throughout their lives.

Eric Sterling

Notes

1. Shimon Wincelberg, *Resort 76*, In The Theatre of the Holocaust, ed. Robert Skloot (Madison: The University of Wisconsin Press, 1982), p. 56. All quotations from Wincelberg's play come from this text.

2. Wincelberg, p. 70.

3. J. Miller Jones, "Why the Nazis Are Such Perfect Fiends: The Uncanniness of the Utopia/Dystopia of National Socialism," Paper presented at the European Studies Conference, The University of Nebraska, Omaha, October 8, 1994.

4. Adolf Hitler, Mein Kampf, trans. Ralph Manheim,1943 (Boston: Houghton Mifflin, 1971), p. 65. The italics are Hitler's.

5. Wincelberg, p. 74.

6. "Law for the Protection of German Blood and German Honor, September 15, 1935," In A Holocaust Reader, ed. Lucy S. Dawidowicz (West Orange, NJ: Behrman House, 1976), p.48.

7. Henry R. Huttenbach, "At the Heart of the Holocaust: 'Life Unworthy of Living,'" The Genocide Forum: A Platform for Post-Holocaust Commentary 2.6 (1996): 1.

8. Wincelberg, p. 75. Wincelberg's italics.

9. Max Weber, "Bureaucracy," From *Max Weber: Essays in Sociology*, trans. and ed. H.H. Gerth and C. Wright Mills (New York: Oxford, 1946), pp. 215-216.

10. Richard L. Rubenstein, *The Cunning of History: The Holocaust and the American Future*, 1975 (New York: Harper Colophon, 1978), pp. 27-28, Rubenstein's italics.

11. Wincelberg, p. 74, Wincelberg's ellipses.

12. Robert Skloot, *The Darkness We Carry: The Drama of the Holocaust* (Madison: The University of Wisconsin Press, 1988), p. 34.

13. Wincelberg, pp. 87-88.

14. George Eisen, *Children and Play in the Holocaust: Games Among the Shadows* (Amherst: University of Massachusetts Press, 1988), p. 15.

15. The Holy Bible, *Containing the Old and New Testaments, Translated Out of the Original Tongues: American Standard Version* (New York: Thomas Nelson, 1929), Jeremiah 1:5.

16. *The Holy Bible*, Exodus 20:13.

17. Lucjan Dobroszycki, ed., The Chronicle of the Lodz Ghetto, 1941-1944, trans. Richard Lourie, et al. (New Haven: Yale University Press, 1984), pp. 114-115.

18. Shmuel Krakowski, "Lodz," *In Encyclopedia of the Holocaust*, ed. Israel Gutman, 4 vols. (New York: Macmillan,1990), III, 904.

19. Dobroszycki, pp. 382-383.

20. Wincelberg, p. 101, Wincelberg's ellipsis and italics.

21. Wincelberg, p. 106.

22. Wincelberg, p. 105, Wincelberg's ellipsis and italics.

23. Wincelberg, p. 105.

24. Skloot, p.15.

6

TIME AND PLACE HAVE HAD THEIR SAY :
LITERATURE AND ETHNIC DISCRIMINATION IN
ZORA NEALE HURSTON'S AESTHETICS

From its inception, the African American literary tradition has been characterized by a twofold concern with aesthetics on the one hand, and with the politics of liberation and equality on the other. This double concern was forced upon the Afro-American writer by a history of ethnic discrimination and by the need to claim justice with the weapon at his or her disposal: the written word. For the black author, literature has been a means of influencing and transforming reality.

Not surprisingly, Zora Neale Hurston, the controversial black woman writer who has recently been restored to the position where she belongs in the context of African American Letters, was not alien to racial discrimination. She acknowledged being discriminated against in articles such as "How It Feels to Be Colored Me," (1928), or more explicitly in "My Most Humiliating Jim Crow Experience" (1944), published for an Afro-American audience in *The Negro Digest*. Like her contemporaries, she also suffered the restrictions imposed upon her work by both white patrons of the Arts and by white audiences. However, her literary work, published from the 1920s to the 1950s, seemed to her critics to be devoid of any hint of protest. It was first classified as purely folkloric, exempt from the socio-political content that was so appreciated since the 1930s. In fact, during her lifetime Afro-American literary authorities such as Alain Locke, Richard Wright, and Ralph Ellison, all emphasized the folklore nature of her fiction, dominated by the portrait of Eatonville, her native town. As a result, they considered it was opposed to serious social protest fiction. Nevertheless, it is the characterization of Eatonville as an idyllic black town whose life revolves around the store porch that has become "the backbone of Hurston's legendary status," to quote Deborah McDowell.[1] Yet, Hurston's lack of popularity among black writers until the late 1970s grew as the conditions that made the Harlem Renaissance possible disappeared and as her journalistic writing during the decades of the 1940s and 1950s revealed her as a conservative. So, while she was applauded by the white public for contributing to the improvement of race relations, she became more of an outcast in the Afro-American literary world.

Her rediscovery by Afro-American women has shown the feminist side of her work and has underlined Hurston's preoccupation for gender politics. This aspect has drawn most of the scholarly attention to her second novel, *Their Eyes Were Watching God* (1937), which tells the story of a black woman in search of herself. Conversely, her last published novel, *Seraph on the Suwanee* (1948), shatters the progressive stance on gender transmitted by Janie in *Their Eyes*, and seems to back the interpretation of Hurston's political evolution from a "cultural revolutionary"—as Alice Walker calls her[2]—in the 1920s to a reactionary at the end of her life. Nevertheless, Hurston has come to occupy a prominent position as a foremother and precursor within the canon of black women's writing in particular and within the Afro-American literary canon in general. She owes this position mainly to her use of both Afro-American folklore and the language of the folk as the basis of her fiction[3]. Convinced of the intrinsic value of Afro-American folklore, she tried to demonstrate that it was possible to create *high art* from Afro-American vernacular culture.

Despite the political implications of her position, and disregarding the *feminist* content of her work, the view of Hurston's fiction as politically uninvolved, spread by her contemporaries and perpetuated by the classification of her work within the pastoral tradition by Robert Bone and later by Bernard Bell, is still prominent in the criticism of her work.[4] However, a close study of Hurston's novels shows that her fiction is not as politically aseptic as it has been maintained, and that she wove her views on racism and discrimination in her fiction. Similarly, a review of her life and her journalistic articles will reveal that Hurston was above all a black nationalist, proud of her roots, but also critical of her people, two positions that seemed incompatible to many.

PART I
The Evolution of Hurston's Political Thought

Zora Neale Hurston was raised in Eatonville, Florida, an atypical self-governing all-black town where she grew immersed in the oral Afro-American tradition and its folklore, apparently unaware of the evils of racial discrimination. As a child, she learned to master the rhetorical Afro-American games and absorbed a view of reality which allowed to conceive of Afro-Americans as an assertive, proud people. By then little Zora also observed that Eatonville did not present a homogeneous portrait of the black community. Hurston explains in her autobiography that very often black people's comments and attitudes "tended more to confuse than to clarify" her curiosity about her "race of people," as she put it, since opposite points of view could be defended by the same person at different times. But at any rate, Hurston confesses "[t]he village seemed dull to me most of the time. If the village was singing a chorus, I must have missed the tune"[5]. She did not become fully aware of the importance of her background until she arrived in Harlem and connected with the New Negro ideals about returning to the people for a true picture of the genuine Afro-American values. Her studies in Anthropology also helped her in this direction, providing a scientific context that guaranteed respect toward Afro-American folklore as a discipline, as she acknowledged at the beginning of her folklore anthology *Mules and Men* :

> From the earliest rocking of my cradle, I had known about the capers Brer Rabbit is apt to cut and what the squinch Owl says from the house top. But it was fitting me like a tight chemise. I couldn't see it for wearing it. It was only when I was off in college, away from my native surroundings, that I could see myself like somebody else and stand off and look at my garment. Then I had to have the spy-glass of Anthropology to look through at that.[6]

Consistent with the idea of black self-assertiveness and also imbued by the idea of primitivism and the "noble savage" that permeated Harlem in the 1920s, Hurston, in accordance with the views defended by the New Negroes, found the essence of blackness in the people. But black people were not a homogeneous group any longer. After the migration North of masses of black people, a black proletariat, clearly distinct from the rural peasant of the South, came into existence. Hurston accounts for the Great migration in *Jonah's Gourd Vine,* her first novel (1934). Here, the Afro-American exodus North in search for a job is compared with Moses' biblical exodus, prefiguring thus the kind of allegory that would be the basis of her later novel *Moses, Man of the Mountain* (1939):

> Whereas in Egypt the coming of the locust made desolation, in the farming
> South the departure of the Negro laid waste the agricultural industry—crops
> rotted, houses careened crazily in their utter desertion, and grass grew up in
> streets. On to the North! The land of promise.[7]

Besides, the inseparable relationship between economics and racial politics is
pinpointed. Thus, Hurston notes with irony the disappearance of prejudice—
though not of discrimination—as Afro-Americans are hired in the North when
labor is needed:

> The factories roared and cried, "Hands!" and in the haste and press white
> hands became scarce. Scarce and dear. Hands? Who cares about the color of
> hands? We need hands and muscle. The South—land of muscled hands.[8]

Yet, despite Hurston's awareness of the great change in the lives of many Afro-
Americans after their migration North, she preferred to seek inspiration for her
work in the rural black folk of the pre-industrial South and, although Hurston
testified to the Afro-American exodus to the urban North in some of her short
stories—"Muttsey," "Book of Harlem," "Story in Harlem Slang"—she always
portrayed picturesque characters that responded to the myth of the Bohemian
Harlem rather than to the image of a black proletariat. Her characters, nonetheless,
responded to Thurman's claim that they "retained some individual race qualities
and . . . were not totally white American in every respect save color of skin."[9]
Because Hurston turned her back to the social transformations that were taking
place within Afro-American society, it became easier for her to remain faithful to
the New Negro ideals when the Depression hit Harlem—and the whole country—
and when it became imperative for the black writer to turn to a more committed
position for the social reality of the urban black.

The thrust to Hurston's literary career came when, encouraged by Alain
Locke—who worked by then at Howard University, Washington D.C., where
Hurston got her degree in English—she submitted her story "Spunk" and a play
entitled *Color Struck* to the 1925 *Opportunity* contest and won prizes for both. It
was the right timing, and Harlem was the right place for any new black writer
looking for a chance to be known. The growing interest in black culture on the part
of the white public during the decade of the 1920s had resulted in the willingness
of several white publishers to print black literature while the emergence of black
magazines such as *The Crisis* or *Opportunity* provided a same race outlet for the
work of black authors. This new availability of black literature to the general
public led many black intellectuals to believe that the work of the new generation

of black artists who were arriving in Harlem from all over the country would finally gain the respect and appreciation of a multi-racial audience.

However, not all black intellectuals agreed in how black literature should serve the interests of the race. Whereas the old generation, led by Du Bois, insisted on its socio-political role, the new leaders underlined the importance of the aesthetic aspect in literature. Thus, when in 1925 Dr. Alain Locke helped to configurate the ideas that would characterize the Harlem Renaissance with the publication of the anthology *The New Negro,* he was convinced that black art should represent an aesthetic, rather than a political ideal. This manifesto of black aesthetics responded to a twofold impulse. On the one hand, *The New Negro* became a "testimonial to Negro Beauty, dignity, and creativity,"[10] under the influence of the Black nationalism that followed the First World War. On the other hand, it shared the precepts of modernism: Locke argued that the "newer motive, then, in being racial is to be so purely for the sake of art".[11] By stressing the importance of form over content, Locke pinpointed the New Negroes' adherence to modernism. However, the adoption of a modernist aesthetics, characterized by the dissociation of art and social responsibility, contradicted somehow the political aim of these minority group artists struggling to assert their black identity and to be recognized by the dominant group.

Thus, Du Bois, aware of the socio-political intent of Afro-American literature from its inception, drew Locke's attention to the fact that the modernist literature of *The New Negro* was not beyond politics or propaganda:

> Mr. Locke has newly been seized with the idea that Beauty rather than propaganda should be the object of Negro literature and art. His book proves the falseness of this thesis. This is a book filled and bursting with propaganda, but it is a propaganda for the most part beautiful and painstakingly done.[12]

But by then, Locke had already admitted that the New Negro artists played a socio-political role when he argued: "The especially cultural recognition they win should in turn prove the key to that revaluation of the Negro which must precede or accompany any considerable further betterment of race relationships." [13]

Hurston seemed to epitomize Locke's stance by being consistent throughout her life in her declarations in favor of detaching art from propaganda. As early as 1928 she writes: "I do not belong to the sobbing school of Negrohood who hold that nature has given them a dirty deal and whose feelings are all hurt about it."[14] Ten years later, when the whole economic, political and cultural panorama had changed[15], she reaffirms herself in her opinion against the socio-political role of Afro-American literature in her essay "Art and Such":

> Can the black poet sing a song to the morning? Upsprings the song to his lips but it is fought back. He says to himself, "Ah this is a beautiful song inside me. I feel the morning star in my throat. I will sing of the star and the morning." Then his background thrusts itself between his lips and the star and he mutters, "Ought I not to be singing of our sorrows? That is what is expected of me and I shall be considered forgetful of our past and present. If I do not some will even call me a coward. The one subject for a Negro is the Race and its sufferings and so the song of the morning must be choked back. I will write of a lynching instead." So the same old theme, the same old phrases get
>
> done again *to the detriment of art.* To him no Negro exists as an individual— he exists only as another tragic unit of the Race. (emphasis mine[16])

Hence, Hurston denounced that the pressure on black writers to restrict themselves to the single subject of racial discrimination had a direct effect on diminishing the quality of Afro-American literature. Consistent with her ideas on the role of literature, Hurston immersed herself in the modernist Harlem Renaissance aesthetics, and started experimenting with the form of her fiction. She adapted modernist innovations—such as the focalization in the private narratives of the characters by means of the use of the stream of consciousness—to black vernacular forms. As a result, she invented what Henry Louis Gates, Jr. has called "the speakerly text": a narrative voice informed by "a profoundly lyrical, densely metaphorical, quasi-musical, privileged black oral tradition on the one hand, and a received but not yet fully appropriated standard English literary tradition on the other hand."[17] Thus, in her most acclaimed novel, *Their Eyes Were Watching God,* published in 1937, Hurston transmits the inner mental world of the female protagonist through the language of the black folk conveyed in the form of free indirect speech. By concentrating the narrative of the novel within a single day through the consciousness of its protagonist, Hurston somehow abandons the traditional chronological arrangement. Besides, by devising a narrative within a narrative, the text becomes self-reflexive, drawing the reader's attention towards its own strategies.

The same interest in formal experimentation can be observed in Hurston's short stories. Between 1921 and 1942 Hurston creates successive narrative voices whose differentiating trait is the gradual approach to and eventual identification with the language of the folk. By doing so, Hurston demonstrated that it was viable for the Afro-American writer to acknowledge the folkloric oral tradition as the foundation of a genuine Afro-American written tradition[18]. In this way she contributed to one of the main political objectives set up by the group of New Negroes when they rejected white models of expression and declared the necessity of celebrating black vernacular forms. Langston Hughes formulated this need of ethnic self-assertion in his literary manifesto "The Negro Artist and the Racial Mountain" (1926), where he states:

> To my mind, it is the duty of the younger Negro artists . . . to change through the force of their art that old whispering, 'I want to be white,' hidden in the aspirations of his people, to 'Why should I want to be white? I am Negro and beautiful.'

So, by focusing on the experimentation with black language and speech structures, away from the explicit social protest fiction that Richard Wright would impose in the decades of the 1930s and 1940s, Hurston conjugated the modernist concern about form with the black nationalistic feeling of the Harlem Renaissance.

Hurston's emphasis on the language and culture of the rural black folk was consistent with her idea that the average Afro-American needed to be represented in literature in order to give a "true picture of Negro life in America" instead of the distorted image provided by the portrait of "the fractional 'exceptional' and the 'quaint'" that characterized, in her view, Afro-American fiction from the 1930s on.[19] However, her rural characters did hardly represent the reality of the Afro-American community at the time. Nevertheless, Hurston's novels are not so out of touch with the politics and national and international realities of the time when they were published. All of them deal overtly with the subjects of race and sex, which adds to them a political quality that passed unnoticed by her contemporaries due to the great difference between Wright's dominant style and hers. One of these texts, *Moses, Man of the Mountain,* a tale of race wars, is even deeply embedded in the discourses born from the xenophobic atmosphere that preceded and accompanied World War II.

At the same time Hurston was translating her ideas about art and literature into fiction, Richard Wright started his literary career.[20] In 1938 he published *Uncle Tom's Children,* and from Hurston's review of the book, it becomes clear that her own fiction stands opposite to Wright's. Thus, to the race hatred and pathos she finds in *Uncle Tom's Children,* she would oppose race celebration. In contrast with Wright's violence, "perhaps enough to satisfy all male black readers"[21] , Hurston chooses romance, appealing to female readers. To the "shocking power of a forty-four" of some of his sentences and "the broken speech of his characters", Hurston responds with the lyricism of her prose and the dialect of the Southern Afro-American.[22] Finally, Wright's social determinism, linked to communism—"state responsibility for everything and individual responsibility for nothing," in Hurston's words—clashes with Hurston's acute sense of individuality. It is impossible to understand Hurston's stance on race, or gender, or religion, or politics, or even on literature if her belief in individuals is overlooked. Much of the bewilderment caused by the apparently opposite postures represented by different characters in her successive novels, for instance, disappears if we stop thinking about them as representative of stances defended by the author and understand them just as different stances and attitudes which correspond to different individuals. This is the opinion Hurston defended in her autobiography *Dust Tracks*, and particularly in the chapter "My People! My People," where she states:

> I do not share the gloomy thought that Negroes in America are doomed to be stomped out bodaciously, nor even shackled to the bottom of things . . . It would be against all nature for all the Negroes to be either at the bottom, top, or in between. It has never happened with anybody else, so why with us? No, We will go where the internal drive carries us like everybody else. It is up to the individual. [23]

Similarly, the chapter "Seeing the World as It Is," excised from the final version of the autobiography because of its controversial statements about race and politics, revolved around the idea of individuality condensed in sentences such as "All clumps of people turn out to be individuals on close inspection," or "What seems race achievement is the work of individuals."

So, at the same time that Hurston finds an essence of Afro-Americanness in the vernacular Afro-American language and culture that she will try to apply to literature in order to establish a characteristic Afro-American literary tradition, she preaches the blurring of the distinctions of race.[24] The consideration of the individual as having the ability to rise above race, gender, social class, or religion becomes the basis of her political thought. As soon as 1928 Hurston had begun to write about race and gender as categories that need a context to exist, that is, as subjective categories. In "How It Feels to Be Colored Me" she states "I do not always feel colored. Even now I often achieve the unconscious Zora of Eatonville before the Hegira. I feel most colored when I am thrown against a white background," and she goes on saying "At certain times I have no race, I am *me*." In other circumstances she underlines gender instead of race: "I belong to no race nor time. I am the eternal feminine." And she contradicts Du Bois' theory about Afro-Americans' double-consciousness by stating "I have no separate feeling about being an American citizen and colored." She ends the article with a metaphor about all people being just the same inside.[25]

Since then, Hurston would affirm her work through her conviction that the previous step to fight racism and discrimination is to destroy the concept of difference and establish the common humanity of all Americans. Thus, decades later she wrote in "What White Publishers Won't Print" (1950):

> for the national welfare, it is urgent to realize that the minorities do think, and think about something other than the race problem. That they are very human and internally, according to natural endowment, are just like everybody else. So long as this is not conceived, there must remain that feeling of unsurmountable difference, and difference to the average man means something bad. If people were made right, they would be just like him.[26]

As Barbara Johnson has pointed out, Hurston suggests in this article that it is necessary to represent difference in Afro-American literature in order to erase it[27]. Hurston's fiction, as well as her non-fiction, was directed at showing the humanity of blacks by portraying them as individuals who shared things in common or who stood opposite to each other, regardless of their race or any other factor.

PART II

Tracing Hurston's Idea on
Ethnic Discrimination in Her Novels

I

Hurston's first novel, *Jonah's Gourd Vine* (1934), starts with a discussion between Amy Crittenden and her husband Ned, a discussion that unveils their different understanding of life and of their position in society. The point of the argument is to establish who has the authority in the family. Hurston introduces thus one of the themes that would characterize her prose: power, whether it is the power of the word in connection with religion and politics, like in *Jonah,* in *Moses,* or in *Their Eyes,* or the power relation between the sexes, which is explored in her four novels with each presenting different outcomes. In her first novel Ned has assimilated both the patriarchal mentality that induces him to boss his wife and his children, and the racist mentality that sets up a hierarchy depending on the color of the skin. Amy stands for the opposite views, articulating some of the political stances defended by Hurston in her non-fiction. Against Ned's idea of treating his sons as he was treated by his master during slavery, enforcing authority because of his position as the family's patriarch, Amy proposes love towards her own: "'Twan't no use in treasurin' other folkses property. It was liable to be took uhway any day. But we's free folks now, mebbe hit'll take some generations, but us got tuh 'gin to practice on treasurin' our younguns." As we have seen, the idea of valuing and respecting what one is and has underlies the nationalistic feelings of the Harlem Renaissance. Similarly, the theory that several generations must pass before Afro-Americans assimilate their freedom is also present in the thought of the Harlem Renaissance intellectuals, as we will see below in relation with *Moses, Man of the Mountain.*

As for Ned's attempt to rule his wife, Amy's commonsense and her mastering of folk language disarm her husband again and again. This is the case when Ned orders Amy, in a way reminiscent of Jody's attitude toward Janie in *Their Eyes,* "'Don't you change so many words wid me, 'oman! Ah'll knock yuh dead ez Hector. Shet yo' mouf!'," and she replies "'Ah change jes'ez many words ez Ah durn please! Ahm three times seben and uh button'."[28]

The tug of war between Ned and Amy is soon centered on race relations after Amy's elder son announces that some white folks are passing by. He is immediately reprimanded by his stepfather for looking at them "right in de face": "Yo' brazen ways wid dese white folks is gwinter git you lynched one uh dese days," Ned admonishes. Although this attitude is a protective one in principle, it also enforces the internalization of a social structure where the black man must show his respect for any one with white skin, regardless of his social position or his behavior. Amy, conscious that race does not equal superiority, disallows her husband when she realizes that it is only old Beasley: "He ain't no quality no-how." Amy's words testify to the difference between people, regardless of their color.[29]

As this scene demonstrates, Hurston seems more interested in turning our attention to the attitude towards race within the Afro-American community than in showing us the direct confrontation between blacks and whites. In the conversation between Amy and her husband, Amy acknowledges the common bond of all Afro-

Americans by accepting heterogeneity within the black race when she says "Wese uh mingled people," becoming thus the representative of Hurston's thought about individuality within the Afro-American community—"being just like a flower garden with every color and kind."[30] In contrast, Ned attacks her elder son "washin' his face wid his color and tellin' 'im he's uh bastard" in an attempt to deprive John of his alleged privileged position due to his light color.[31] According to Amy, Ned did actually prefer John to his own sons, until he was convinced by his mother and his sister that his preference was due to John's color. Following Amy's interpretation, he is now reacting against the feeling of having internalized the racist prejudice that a light skin is better than a dark one: "So he tryin' side wid dem [his mother and his sister] and show 'em he don't [discriminate]."[32]

The great difference between Amy and Ned is that Amy analyzes reality based on her own perception while Ned relies on others to form his opinions. In the case just mentioned he relies on his mother and sister's authority. But most often he looks for the whites' judgement. Thus, he defends his claim that "Yaller niggers ain't no good nohow" arguing that "Dese white folks orta know and dey say dese half-white niggers got de worst part uh bofe de white and de black folks." Amy, in her turn, rejects this argument saying that it is the result of poor whites' jealousy for being denied the prominent positions that mulattos had traditionally had in a rich man's house.

II

In *Their Eyes Were Watching God* Hurston studies again the reactions to color difference within the Afro-American community by choosing a light-skinned protagonist with Caucasian features. She also creates occasions when the black community and the white world come into contact. The outcome is a balance of positive and negative encounters. Thus, the beginning of Janie's narrative displays Hurston's integrationist point of view when she tells of the way she was raised by both her grandmother and Mis' Wahsburn, the white woman she worked for, together with four white children. Let us not forget that integration, not separation, was the main thrust of the New Negro[33]. It is in this context that some of Hurston's polemic assertions must be set up. An example of her controversial writing is her apology of slavery in "How It Feels to Be Colored Me," where she writes:

> Someone is always at my elbow reminding me that I am the grand-daughter of slaves. It fails to register depression with me. . . The terrible struggle that made me an American out of a potential slave said "On the line!" The

Reconstruction said "Get set!"; and the generation before said "Go!" I am off
to a flying start and I must not halt in the stretch to look behind and weep.
Slavery is the price I paid for civilization, and the choice was not with me. It is
a bully adventure and worth all that I have paid through my ancestors for it.[34]

It is clear from this excerpt that Hurston has no doubts about her American
identity—in contrast with the emphasis put on the African character of black
Americans by leaders such as Marcus Mosiah Garvey, and his call back to Africa.
To Hurston, black people are Americans in their own right who, besides sharing
western values ("civilization") with the white society, have a culture of their own
which has to be translated for the dominant society so that integration can become
a reality. But despite her belief in integration, she expressed years later her opinion
that integration should not be achieved at the expense of the pride of being Afro-
American. So, in her article "Court Order Can't Make Races Mix" (1955) she
regarded the U.S. Supreme Court decision on ending segregation in the public
schools of the South as insulting for black people. Her argument against it was
based on "the self-respect" of Afro-Americans. Hurston believes that this court
order rests on the assumption that " there is no greater delight to Negroes than
physical association with whites." But, she wonders, " [h]ow much satisfaction can
I get from a court order for somebody to associate with me who does not wish me
near them?"[35]   Instead of enforcing integration, Hurston felt that the Supreme
Court should have enforced "the compulsory education provisions for Negroes in
the South as is done for white children." To Hurston "[i]t is a contradiction in
terms to scream race pride and equality while at the same time spurning Negro
teachers and self-association." [36]

In *Their Eyes* Hurston exemplifies what she understands by real
integration by stressing that all the children under Nanny's and Mis' Washburn's
care received the same treatment, to the point that Janie did not know that she was
black until she saw a photograph of all of the children together. This fact supports
the idea that race is a social construct. In contrast with the behavior of these
"quality white folks," Janie first experiences racial discrimination from her own
ethnic group when she attends school. There she is teased by the rest of black
children for living with whites and for wearing better clothes than they. But their
main and cruelest asset was to discard Janie's fine appearance by reminding her
that she was an illegitimate child, the result of a rape: "Dey made it sound real bad
so as tuh crumple mah feathers." Implicit is a critique to the Afro-American
community for rejecting heterogeneity within it, in an attitude that mirrors the

patterns of behavior of the white society and allies with the oppressor. In view of the situation Nanny, Janie's grandmother, decides to move to a place of their own and then again "Mis' Washburn helped our uh whole heap wid things."[37]

Nanny's account of her experiences during slavery stands in contraposition to the positive image of whites provided by Janie. Her story matches those of so many slaves sexually abused by their masters and hated by their mistresses for it. In her case, the birth of her daughter Leafy, who looked white, unleashed her mistress' fury. The prospect of being whipped, probably to death, and her daughter sold, made her flee. By setting the personalities of two white women in contraposition, Hurston insists on considering individuals rather than on generalizing systematically about race.

But Nanny's view of the world does not only contemplate racial relations but also the complex relation between race and gender. Women, and black women particularly, are exploited by men both physically and sexually. Labor exploitation is addressed when she explains Janie:

> Honey, de white man is de ruler of everything as fur as Ah been able tuh find out . . . So, de white man throw down de load and tell de nigger man tuh pick it up. He pick it up because he have to, but he don't tote it. He hand it to his womenfolks. De nigger woman is de mule uh de world so fur as Ah can see.[38]

Both race and gender are taken into account for her view of social stratification. Later on, she implies that black women are sexually oppressed by men, their race notwithstanding: "Ah can't die easy thinkin' maybe de menfolks white or black is makin' a spit cup outa you."[39] Janie will experience both kinds of oppression throughout her life. Her first husband, Logan Killicks, attempted to use her as labor force in the fields, while Joe Starks, her second husband, used her as a sexual ornament that contributed to his prominent position in town. He enforced her submission to the point that Janie did not recognize herself in the woman married to Jody: "Then one day she sat and watched the shadow of herself going about tending store and prostrating itself before Jody, while all the time she herself sat under a shady tree with the wind blowing through her hair and her clothes."[40] This split self becomes her survival strategy for some time until she finally confronts Jody publicly, robbing him "of his illusion of irresistible maleness."[41]

Consistent with her belief in showing that Afro-Americans are not just a "clump of people," but a variegated community of individuals,—which makes

Afro-Americans the same as any other human group—, Hurston undertakes again a study of the mulatto theme contrasting the figure of Mrs. Turner, a mulatto woman who thinks that her looks "set her aside from Negroes," with Janie. Janie's response to Mrs. Turner's suggestion that mulattos "oughta class off" is identical to that of Amy's in *Jonah's* : "'Us can't *do* it. We's uh mingled people and all of us got black kinfolks as well as yaller kinfolks." Against Janie's approval of difference within the Afro-American ethnic group, Mrs. Turner yearns for assimilation within white society in an attempt to remove herself from her ethnic origins. She repudiates black skinned Afro-Americans as loud-talkers, bad-mannered, gaudily-dressed people. In her opinion, " If it wuznt for so many black folks it would be no race problem. De white folks would take us in wid dem. De black ones is holdin' us back." When Janie observes that there is also an economic factor that separates the black community from white society, Mrs. Turner insists "'Tain't de poorness, it's de color and de features." Like Pecola, in Morrison's *The Bluest Eye,* Mrs. Turner "had built an altar to the unattainable—Caucasian characteristics for all."[42] Her belief in the superiority of white skin makes her worship Janie, who is lighter and with more Caucasian features than herself, and endure Janie's occasional hard words. It was the price to pay for paradise.

III

In *Moses, Man of the Mountain* Hurston illustrates how a people that has been crushed by ethnic discrimination may in turn adopt the same discriminating attitude against others. The clearest example is Miriam, who believes she is Moses' sister. Afraid that her role as the leader of the Hebrew women might be taken by Moses' wife, Zipporah, she tries to get rid of her, basing her argument on Zipporah's dark skin: "We don't want people like that among us mixing up our blood and all," she says. She is punished for hiding her jealousy behind a racist argument and becomes a leper and "a horrible sight in her leprous whiteness."[43]

These characters who intend to build their superiority on the basis of their light skin in detriment of others of their own group respond to Hurston's discovery that "the Negro race was not one band of heavenly love." "I learned," she explains in *Dust Tracks,* "that skins were no measure of what was inside of people. . . I began to laugh at both white and black who claimed special blessings on the basis of race. Therefore I saw no curse in being black, nor extra flavor by being white."[44] Her enumeration of negative attitudes by black people, as well as the creation of positive black characters, serves to demonstrate that Afro-Americans are not a monolithic block, that there is a great diversity within this ethnic group, and that the difference among its members makes Afro-Americans the same as any other group. Hurston expects to destroy the simplistic view of the Afro-American as either "seated on a stump picking away on his banjo and singing and laughing," or the "intellectual" "mumbling against injustice."[45]

The fact that Hurston is profuse in her critique of Afro-Americans does not mean that she does not extend her criticism to the white world, and especially to the American government policies that support the contradiction of preaching democracy abroad while allowing racist discrimination home. One of her more energetic statements against institutionalized racist discrimination appears in the *Negro Digest* of 1945. Once again, she proves to be more overtly critical of the white world when she writes with a black audience in mind. In her article "Crazy for This Democracy" she denounces Franklin D. Roosevelt's words about the United States being "the Arsenal of Democracy" when the country laws and institutions prevented black citizens from participating in the democratic spirit, and when U.S. international politics "has shouldered the load of subjugating the dark world completely."[46] Making use of irony, she argues that she must have misunderstood "Arsenal of Democracy" for "arse-and-all of Democracy." While all mass media talk about Democracy, she says "I don't know for myself, but I have been told that it is really wonderful." Then she adds: "I accept this idea of Democracy. I am for trying it out. It must be a good thing if everybody praises it like that . . . . The only thing that keeps me from pitching headlong into the thing is the presence of numerous Jim Crow laws on the statute books of the nation"[47]. For this reason Hurston urges to change the laws:

> I am all for the repeal of every Jim Crow law in the nation here and now. Not in another generation or so. The Hurstons have already been waiting 80 years for that. I want it here and now.[48]

The same attitude against this state of affairs is evident in her autobiography, especially in the chapter "Seeing the World As It Is," deleted from the first edition because of the editorial censorship. Here she expresses herself freely against the United States' imperialistic policies abroad and the racist domestic policies. But it is also possible to find such criticism in her fiction. In *Jonah's Gourd Vine*, for example, the critique to American politics comes through a communal voice: "De black man ain't got no voice but soon ez war come who de first man dey shove in front? De nigger!"[49]. A more explicitly political novel, however, is *Moses, Man of the Mountain* (1939), as Deborah McDowell has brilliantly defended.[50] It was classified by Blyden Jackson as a protest novel, although "it lacks virtually all of the characteristics endemic to the Negro protest novel".[51] The parallelism between the people of Israel and the United States is implicit in this novel. Both nations are considered by Hurston as aggressor powers that justify their imperialistic behavior by considering themselves interpreters of God's wishes and God's representatives on earth. We find evidence for this in the novel in the way Moses acts as a military leader who leads his troops against different peoples in the name of God. Thus, Israel fights and conquers the Amalekites because Moses "stood with outstretched arms, fighting for Israel with his powers. He was calling on the invisible powers from Mount Sinai to fight and they fought for him."[52] The parallelism between the United States and Israel is also clearly drawn in "Seeing the World as It Is," where Hurston relativizes justice by arguing that a cause is just or not depending on the point of view. As an example she resorts first to the Old Testament and then to several international powers, among them the United States:

> The Old Testament is devoted to what was right and just from the point of view of the Ancient Hebrews. All of their enemies were twenty-two carat evil. They, the Hebrews, were never aggressors. The Lord wanted His children to have a country full of big grapes and tall corn. Incidentally, while they were getting it, they might as well get rid of some trashy tribes that He did not think much of, anyway . . . If the conquest looked like a bloody rape to the Canaanites, that was because their evil ways would not let them see a point that was right upon their nose.[53]

The similarity with the United States is established in the following terms: "We, too, consider machine gun bullets good laxatives for heathens who get constipated with toxic ideas about a country of their own . . . . . there is a geographical boundary to our principles. They are not to leave the United States unless we take them ourselves. Japan's application of our principles to Asia is never to be sufficiently deplored."[54]

The march of the Hebrews from Egypt to the promised land is more explicitly an allegory that tells the story of Afro-Americans in their quest for freedom and equality in the United States. The relation between Hebrews and the people of Egypt is that between Afro-Americans and white America. Their condition as slaves and the lack of control over their labor and over their sons serves as the starting point of the novel.

But Hurston, implicitly draws another parallelism between the people of Israel and the persecution of Jews by Nazi Germany in the years that preceded World War II by opening the novel with the extermination of the Hebrew male babies. As McDowell has observed, "That Hurston was concerned with questions of racial purity in a novel published in 1939 gains significance when we consider that this was the year Hitler ordered the attack on Poland and led Germany into a world war."[55] The same as Hitler, Pharaoh seemed to be worried about the danger of having Egyptian blood mixed with Hebrew blood. The Hebrews themselves comment: "Plenty of Hebrew blood [in Pharaoh's] family already. That is why [he] wants to kill us off. He is scared somebody will come along and tell who his real folks are." Pharaoh must actually face the problem of racial purity in his own house when Prince Moses is identified by Miriam as a Hebrew. The uncertainty about Moses' origins would mark his conflictive relations with those around him throughout his life. From the moment when Miriam announces that Moses is her brother, and therefore a Hebrew, Moses' first wife "had shrunk away from him as if he had been a crocodile."[56] His plea for justice against oppression on behalf of the Hebrews only made matters worse for him, setting the Egyptian court against him and making up Pharaoh's mind to seize him as an enemy of Egypt.

This did not mean that he was accepted by the Hebrews without reservation, either, for when Moses decides to take the Hebrews out of Egypt and of slavery, they suspect him of being an Egyptian and leading them to a certain death. Their lack of trust in Moses even results in their revolting against him twice before their journey starts. By the end of the novel Moses, who feels that his role as a leader has been imposed on him, asks God "Why should I lead people whose ways are strange to me and who neither understand me nor trust me."[57] By leaving the issue of Moses' origins unresolved, Hurston insists once again on the idea that ethnicity is a social construct.

In close connection with the extermination of the Hebrew male babies is female oppression, since the fruit of women's bodies is controlled by the male power of the Pharaoh. Although Jochebed, a Hebrew woman who allegedly gives birth to Moses, fights the Pharaoh's law and her husband in order to keep her son alive, she must finally abandon her baby on the river, afraid that he might be discovered by the "secret police" and murdered after all. In the same way, any attempt on the part of women to get power—remember Miriam and her ambition to be a leader—is frustrated by the patriarchal forces. Hurston shows a world of men and for men.

Hurston's work is a critique to American domestic as well as international politics, but it also condemns Afro-Americans and their leaders. As part of her critical view of Afro-Americans, Hurston repeatedly denounces the little help and encouragement that members of the Afro-American community get from their own when they try to improve their status. The idea is expressed in her first novel by a minor character who reminds the protagonist:

> You know our people is jus' lak uh passle uh crabs in uh basket. De minute dey see one climbin'up too high, de rest of 'em reach up and grab 'em and pull 'im back. Dey ain't gonna let nobody git nowhere if dey kin he'p it."[58]

Similarly, in *Their Eyes* the community joins to criticize Janie in an act of "mass cruelty," to use the narrator's words, when she returns from burying Tea Cake. They envy her looks, her money, her independence and the class position that her former husband left her. So, they use their power of speech in an attempt to dethrone her: "She sits high, but she looks low," Lulu Moss sentenced.

In *Moses*, where the subject of leadership is central to the novel, a Hebrew foreman complains that he is not respected by his people: "being one of them, my people despise me so much that they won't pay me no mind". Then Moses admonishes, "'You must be united among yourselves and you must obey your foreman. You must respect yourselves if you want others to respect you." But Hebrews scorn Moses' words saying "'He ain't no better than I am. I don't mean to take nothing off of him at all." When he himself falls under suspicion of being just anxious for power, he reflects, "So! The will to humble a man more powerful than themselves was stronger than the emotion of gratitude. It was stronger than the wish for the common brotherhood of man." [59]

Moses becomes so disillusioned with the generation of Hebrews he led out of Egypt, represented by Aaron and Miriam who only understand the role of a leader as a way to enrich themselves and accumulate power, that he lays all his hope on a new generation. The narrative voice says about the liberated slaves : "they acted like they knew they were free by ear but they couldn't conceive of it. They couldn't believe they could take on any responsibility for themselves at all. They kept clamoring for somebody to act for them." When on their way to Mount Sinai the Hebrews complain about being hungry and Moses replies that there is no food around, they tell him "we figure it ain't none of our business. You brought us there, didn't you?." They refuse to accept any responsibility on their own destinies—even that of feeding themselves—and demand to be looked after by Moses. Hence, he "turned the hosts of Israel back into the wilderness to serve their forty years and grow men and women in place of slaves ... the generation which he had brought out of Egypt had failed him." Moses fully expects, however, that the third generation "will feel free and noble."[60] This hope in a new generation corresponds with the feeling that the promoters of the Harlem Renaissance had about the New Negroes. Charles Johnson expressed it in Locke's *The New Negro* with the following words:

> the newer spirits are beginning to free themselves from the slough of that servile feeling (now happily classified by the psychologists as the "inferiority complex") inherited from slavery and passed along with virulence for over fifty years. The generation in whom lingered memories of the painful degradation of slavery could not be expected to cherish even those pearls of song and poetry born of suffering. . . The newer voices, at a more comfortable distance, are beginning to find a new beauty in these heritages, and new values in their own lives"[61]

Just as Hurston criticizes greedy and unscrupulous leaders and passive Afro-Americans, she applauds in her article "Negroes without Self-Pity" (1943) some upper-class Afro-Americans who had finally understood that they must involve themselves in civic affairs, that they "merely by being Negroes, are not exempted from the natural laws of existence." Then, in a passage that applies perfectly to the above mentioned Hebrew attitude, she explains her particular view of Afro-American history as follows:

> If you take in the twenty-odd years of intense Abolitionist speaking and writing that preceded the Civil War, the four war years, The Reconstruction period and recent Negro rights agitations, you have at least a hundred years of indoctrination of the Negro that he is an object of pity. Becoming articulate, this was in him and he said it. "We were brought here against our will . . . We are in no way responsible for anything. We are dependents . . . Look upon us with pity and give!"[62]

Finally, in this article Hurston celebrates the fact that Afro-Americans are starting to accept responsibility for their own lives. Indeed, in *Moses* Hurston criticizes the idea of a single leader to represent a whole people, or to make a people free. Moses himself thinks after leading the Hebrews to Canaan that "No man may make another free. . . . All you could do was to give the opportunity for freedom and the man himself must make his own emancipation." However, by the end of the novel, when Moses is old and experienced he warns young Joshua:

"You can't have a state of individuals. Everybody just can't be allowed to do as they please. . . A great state is a well-blended mash of something of all of the people and all of none of the people. . . How can a nation speak with one voice if they are not one?" In addition, Moses tells Joshua "And don't let the people take up too many habits from the nations they come in contact with and throw away what they got from God." At this point Moses seems to favor the adoption of a national identity that homogenizes a group of individuals and sets them in contrast with other groups. His evolution responds to Hurston's belief in the compatibility of a personal identity with a national one.

IV

   Between 1939 and the publication of her next—and last—novel in 1948, Hurston focused her attention on writing articles in journals and magazines addressed to white audiences. Her novel, *Seraph on the Suwanee,* which is about the lives of white characters, is just one more effort on Hurston's part to become a "universal" author whose readership is not restricted to the Afro-American community but extends itself to the white audience. Hurston had two reasons for wishing a white readership. One was ideological, against the segregation of the black artist and black art. The other had to do with earning her living. The white audience was larger than the Afro-American one, and therefore her work stood a better chance to be sold in greater numbers, a reason of no little importance for a writer like Hurston, who knew what it was to make both ends meet. Since her arrival in Harlem in 1924 "with 1.50$, no job, no friends, and a lot of hope,"[68] she, like Langston Hughes, Claude McKay and the painter Aaron Douglas, was supported economically by their common benefactress, Mrs. Rufus Osgood Mason.[64] But unlike these artists, Hurston was accused of representing the naïve, outrageously-funny, primitive black for a white audience in exchange of getting money from them. This is the view supported by Langston Hughes in his autobiography *The Big Sea:*

> Zora Neale Hurston was certainly the most amusing [of the Harlem literati]. Only to reach a wider audience, need she ever write books—because she is a perfect book of entertainment in herself. In her youth she was always getting scholarships and things from wealthy white people, some of whom simply paid her just to sit around and represent the Negro race for them, she did it in such a racy fashion. . . To many of her white friends, no doubt, she was a perfect

"darkie," in the nice meaning they give the term—that is a naïve, childlike, sweet, humorous, and highly colored Negro.[65]

Claude McKay showed a more sympathetic attitude when he declared in his autobiography, *A Long Way from Home* (1937), that Hurston was only one of the many artists of the Harlem Renaissance who needed to attract the benevolence of rich white patrons.

Money—or rather the lack of it—was a preoccupation for Hurston during all her life. Her first-hand experience of poverty led her to write about it in her autobiography in the following terms:

There is something about poverty that smells like death. Dead dreams dropping off the heart like leaves in a dry season and rotting around the feet; impulses smothered too long in the fetid air of underground caves. The soul lives in sickly air. People can be slave-ships in shoes.
This wordless feeling went with me from the time I was ten years old until I achieved a sort of competence around twenty. Naturally, the first five years were the worst. Things and circumstances gave life a most depressing odor.[66]

But while a lack of money was a constant with her until the end of her life, it was not the main reason why Hurston turned to a white audience. The reliance of the black writer on white audiences was not new, since whites had been the primary audience for black writers from Phillis Wheatley to the New Negroes of the Harlem Renaissance, and after.[67] The dilemma that this fact posed for the black writer was voiced by James Weldon Johnson in 1928: "To whom should he address himself, to his own black group or to white America?"[68] During the Harlem Renaissance the interests of both groups were opposed. Whereas the white reader looked for the primitive and comic black character that would confirm his own conception of black people, the black audience had internalized the values of the dominant society and expected black literature to depict the black middle-class as an irreproachable bourgeoisie. The black writer, caught between these two forces, was encouraged by Johnson to forget about the problem of address until the moment when both audiences could merge. It was his hope that, once the black audience saw the positive and true depiction of Afro-Americans in black art, they would support it, and the black artist would no longer depend on the whims of a white audience. The same need of separating art from audience had been anticipated by Langston Hughes in 1926 when he declared:

> We younger Negro artists who create now intend to express our individual
> selves without fear or shame. If white people are pleased we are glad. If they
> are not, it doesn't matter. . . . If colored people are pleased we are glad. If they
> are not, their displeasure doesn't matter either.[69]

Despite Hughes' vindication of artistic autonomy, however, it was very difficult for the black artist of the 1920s to escape the pressure of the white audience, especially when "as the decade progressed, it became increasingly evident that something was missing: the black audience."[70] Therefore, and despite the emergence of black magazines, the black artist relied to a high degree on the response of the white audience to his/her work. Hurston was perfectly aware of her dependence on white publishers and was inclined to yield to their demands in exchange of getting her works published. Thus, when asked in 1944 about the key to her literary success she was very clear: "Rather than get across all of the things which you want to say you must compromise and work within the limitations [of those people] who have the final authority in deciding whether or not a book shall be printed."[71]. And it paid: her autobiography *Dust Tracks on a Road,*, published one year before, was well received by the white public and critics, winning the *Saturday Review*'s $1,000 Anisfield-Wolf Award for her contribution to improving race relations. As Hemenway has pointed out, in this book she "periodically manipulates her experience . . . to present an integrationist position."[72]   But, whereas the white public applauded Hurston, the black community headed by Arna Bontemps and Harold Preece harshly criticized her.[73]

As time went on and Afro-American literature became dominated by social protest, any approach on the part of black writers to the integrationist and reconciliatory position was welcome by the white public. Although the U.S. Supreme Court decision on ending segregation in the public schools of the South in 1954 was the decisive step to integration, forces of integration had influenced society long before that date. The racial climate of the United States started to change in the 1940s, and with it the Afro-American literary atmosphere. Little by little, black writers set aside protest literature cemented on segregation and started adopting different strategies. Some looked for new themes within the racial framework, and instead of focusing on interracial problems, they turned to look into the conflicts within the Afro-American community—which is what Hurston had always done. The black middle-class became their center of attention.[74]

A different solution was to avoid black subjects completely and to write about white characters. Ann Petry, William Gardner Smith, Willard Motley, Frank

Yerby, Richard Wright and Hurston herself were some of the black writers who published postwar novels about whites.[75] This decision was applauded by many white critics who had come to think that black novels about black subjects were synonymous with political pamphlets; that is, they were, in their view, works which sacrificed their artistic value to propaganda. Hurston, who had never agreed with the protest tradition, seemed to embrace the integrationist position—although we have already called the attention to her very particular views on integration in "Court Order Can't Make Races Mix." She even defended what she called "The Pet Negro System" in a controversial article published in 1943. In a humorous and ironic style which imitates the black preacher's oratory, Hurston explains that this system favors the unconditional support of influential whites to particular Afro-Americans. For these white people, their protégés are the exception to the rule: intelligent, honest, hard-working people who can be trusted and who are "as white inside as any one else."[76] Hurston argues that the privileged black person, or "the pet Negro," using her own words, "symbolizes the web of feelings and mutual dependencies spun by generations and generations of living together and natural adjustment."[77] Although she says that she is not defending the system, she writes: "The lowdown fact is that it weaves a kind of basic fabric that tends to stabilize relations and give something to work from in adjustments . . . It may be the proof that this race situation in America is not entirely hopeless and may even be worked out eventually."[78] By the end of the article she reaffirms herself in the observation that the "pet Negro system" works: "The thing doesn't make sense. It just makes beauty."[79]

Hurston's reaction against the dominant atmosphere of protest during the 1930s and well into the 1940s caused her to gradually separate herself from the positions about the distinctiveness of the Afro-American vernacular tradition that she had defended at the beginning of her career. This was especially manifest by the time she started giving shape to *Seraph on the Suwanee* in 1947. Whereas in her article "Characteristics of Negro Expression" written by 1930, she emphasized the uniqueness of Afro-American language and folklore, in the late 1940s she tries hard to blur the distinction between blacks and whites in the South, arguing that blacks and whites have influenced each other to the extent of merging the western and the African traditions into a single American one. As examples of this fusion she took language and music. Whereas in 1930 she considered the extensive use of simile and metaphor by the Afro-American as "the Negro's greatest contribution to the language," in her autobiography (1942) she defended that "an average Southern child, white or black, is raised on simile and invective. And five years later, in

1947, she would radicalize her position claiming that "what is known as Negro dialect in the South is no such thing. Bear in mind that the South is the purest English section of the United States." Consequently, she adds that the blacks have not influenced the speech of the Southern whites but, on the contrary, "the Africans coming to America got [their language] from them." According to Hurston, music too had undergone a similar transformation:

> There is no more Negro music in the U.S. It has been fused and merged and become the national expression. . . In fact, it is now denied , (and with some truth) that it never was pure Negro music, but an adaptation of white music. . . . But the fact remains that what has evolved here is something American.[80]

This evolution of Hurston's thinking has its repercussion on *Seraph on the Suwanee*. Thus, as Hazel Carby has pointed out in her foreword to the novel, Hurston's work revolves around the lives of Southern white characters who speak like the black protagonists of her previous novels. And the fact that black music had become a national expression is represented in the novel by the figure of Kenny Meserve—Arvay's son—who learns to play black music with the help of black Joe Kelsey.

The focus on white characters in *Seraph on the Suwanee*, which has been criticized as a rightist turn on Hurston's part, is explained if we take into account the integration movement which influenced major black writers to abandon both the protest tradition and the black character. But Hurston's decision was also a rebellious act. So, just as she had fought against "the sobbing school of Negrohood"—as she called the protest tradition—, she now rebelled against the traditional literary conventions of her time, which restricted black writers to deal only with black subjects and characters. Thus, in a letter Hurston wrote to Carl Van Vechten in 1942, she had "hopes of breaking that old silly rule about Negroes not writing about white people."[81]

This utterly Hurstonian attitude is not in accordance with the contents of the novel, which cannot be said to transmit a progressive attitude concerning gender relations. Although it concentrates on sexual politics, the tormented inner life of Arvay Meserve is solved at the end with the protagonist's submission to her chauvinistic husband who, from the beginning, let the role that he expected Arvay to play very clear: "'Love and marry me and sleep with me. That is all I need you for. Your brains are not sufficient to help me with my work; you can't think with me" (35). As a photograph negative, the protagonist embodies the opposite values and attitudes defended by Hurston throughout her life with her own behavior. Whereas Hurston could not achieve a long-term stable relationship with her husbands, nor with anyone else, because she felt that both her career and her personality were stifled by them, Arvay devotes herself totally to her husband.

A positive interpretation of the novel is offered by Lillie P. Howard when she considers that "Hurston simply seems to be writing about people, about individuals coming to terms with themselves regardless of their color."[82] In this sense, *Seraph* is as positive as *Their Eyes* since in both novels the female protagonists finally succeed in achieving happiness. The fact that their positions are opposite—whereas Janie rejects the role of servant to her husbands in her search for love and happiness, Arvay finds both when she accepts to serve Jim— does not invalidate Arvay's actions. As Howard points out, "Perhaps Arvay's decision to serve in *Seraph on the Suwanee* illustrates Hurston's belief that people are individuals—that is, what is right for one is not necessarily right for another."[83] This brings us full circle to the beginning of Hurston's thought about individuality as the basis of her understanding of the world.

V

That Hurston's autobiography, her last published novel, and her declarations about the originality of black art and language in the l ate 1940s are in accordance with the integration thought does not mean that this was Hurston's last word on the role and work of the Afro-American writer. In 1951 she had returned to the old idea of writing a "truly indigenous Negro novel." "I have decided,"—she wrote—"that the time has come to write truthfully from the inside. Imagine that no white audience is present to hear what is said."[84] Similarly, her final project was a book about Herod the Great. It had nothing to do with integration but with the personality of a great leader and ally of the Jewish people against the rule of their priests. Hurston thus returned to the theme that had fascinated her while writing *Moses.* Again, the parallelism between the history of oppression of the Jews and that of the Afro-American people was evident in the tentative title *Just like Us* that Hurston offered Scribner with the outline for the book. Since the revisionist biography of Herod was rejected by the publisher and Hurston kept on laboring on it, her fascination for the Jewish struggle for "democracy and the rights of man," in her own words, was to last till the end of her life in 1960.

Hurston's last literary efforts were definitely political, as explicitly political was *Moses, Man of the Mountain,* and many of her essays. It is about time that her problematization of race and her oblique approach to politics, both national and international, is acknowledged as an important constituent of her overall fiction. Only after her image as a folklorist is completed with her views on politics as expressed in her fiction and non-fiction, will her work stand a chance of being justly assessed.

Ana María Fraile-Marcos

Works Cited

Bell, Bernard W. *The Afro-American Novel and Its Tradition.* Amherst: U of Massachusetts P,1987.

Bone, Robert. *Down Home: A History of Afro-American Short Fiction from Its Beginnings to the End of the Harlem Renaissance.* New York: G.P.Putnam's Sons, 1975.

Bruck, Peter, ed. *The Black American Short Story in the 20th Century: A Collection of Critical Essays.* Amsterdam: B. R. Grüner Publishing Co., 1977.

Carby, Hazel V. "Foreword." *Seraph on the Suwanee.* New York: Harper and Row, Publishers, 1991. vii-xviii.

Davis, Arthur Paul. *From the Dark Tower: Afro-American Writers, 1900-1960.* Washington, D.C.: Howard UP, 1974.

Fraile, Ana María. "Zora Neale Hurston's Experimentation with the Narrative Voice in Her Short Stories" *REDEN* (in press).

Gates, Henry Louis, Jr. ed. *The Signifying Monkey: A Theory of African-American Literary Criticism.* New York: Oxford UP, 1988.

Hemenway, Robert E. *Zora Neale Hurston: A Literary Biography.* Chicago: U of Illinois P, 1977.

Holloway, Karla F.C. *The Character of the World: The Texts of Zora Neale Hurston.* New York: Greenwood Press, 1987.

Howard, Lillie. "'Seraph on the Suwanee'." *Zora Neale Hurston: Critical Perspectives Past and Present.* Eds. H. L. Gates and K.A. Appiah. N.Y.: Amistad, 1993. 267-279.

Hughes, Langston. "The Negro Artist and the Racial Mountain," *The Nation,,* CXXII 23 (1926): 694.

—. *The Big Sea* N.Y.: Alfred A. Knopf, 1940.

Hurston, Zora Neale & Langston Hughes. *Jonah's Gourd Vine.* New York: Harper and Row, Publishers, 1990 (1934).

—. *Mules and Men.* New York: Harper and Row, Publishers, 1990 (1935).

—. *Their Eyes Were Watching God.* New York: Harper and Row, Publishers, 1990 (1937).

—. *Moses, Man of the Mountain.* Urbana and Chicago: U of Illinois P, 1984 (1939).

—. *Dust Tracks on a Road.* Ed. Robert E. Hemenway. Urbana: U of Illinois P, 1984 (1942).

—. *Seraph on the Suwanee.* New York: Harper and Row, Publishers, 1991 (1948).

—. *The Sanctified Church: The Folklore Writings of Zora Neale Hurston.* Berkeley, CA: Turtle Island, 1981.

—. "Color Struck: A Play." *Fire!!* 1 (1926): 7-15.

—. "Sweat." *Fire!!* 1 (1926): 40-45.

—. "How It Feels to Be Colored Me." *World Tomorrow* 11 (1928): 215-16. Reprinted in Alice Walker's *I Love Myself When I Am Laughing... And Then Again When I Am Looking Mean and Impressive: a Zora Neale Hurston Reader.* New York: The Feminist Press, 1979. 152-155.

—. "Stories of Conflict" *Zora Neale Hurston: Folklore, Memoinrs, and Other Writings.* Ed Cheryl A. Wall. N.Y.: Literary Classics, The Library of America, 1995. (1938). 912-13.

—. "The Pet Negro System." *American Mercury* , 56 (1943): 593-600. Reprinted in Alice Walker's *I Love Myself When I Am Laughing... And Then Again When I Am Looking Mean and Impressive: a Zora Neale Hurston Reader.* New York: The Feminist Press, 1979. 156-162.

—. "Negroes Without Self-Pity." *American Mercury,* 57 (1943): 601-3. Reprinted in *Zora Neale Hurston: Folklore, Memoinrs, and Other Writings.* Ed Cheryl A. Wall. N.Y.: Literary Classics, The Library of America, 1995. (1938). 932-34.

—. "My Most Humiliating Jim Crow Experience." *Negro Digest* 2 (1944): 25-26. Reprinted in Alice Walker's *I Love Myself When I Am Laughing... And Then Again When I Am Looking Mean and Impressive: a Zora Neale Hurston Reader.* New York: The Feminist Press, 1979. 163-4.

—. "Crazy for this Democracy." *Negro Digest* 4 (1945): 45-48. Reprinted in Alice Walker's *I Love Myself When I Am Laughing... And Then Again When I Am Looking Mean and Impressive: a Zora Neale Hurston Reader.* New York: The Feminist Press, 1979. 165-168.

—. "What White Publishers Won't Print." *Negro Digest,* 8 (1950): 85-89. Reprinted in Alice Walker's *I Love Myself When I Am Laughing... And Then Again When I Am Looking Mean and Impressive: a Zora Neale Hurston Reader.* New York: The Feminist Press, 1979. 169-73.

—. "Court Order Can't Make Races Mix." *Orlando Sentinel,* August 11, 1955. Reprinted in *Zora Neale Hurston: Folklore, Memoinrs, and Other Writings.* Ed Cheryl A. Wall. N.Y.: Literary Classics, The Library of America, 1995. (1938). 956-58.

—. "Art and Such." *Reading Black, Reading Feminist: A Critical Anthology.* Ed. Henry Louis Gates, Jr. New York: Meridian, 1990. 21-26.

Johnson, Barbara. "Metaphor, Metonymy, and Voice in 'Their Eyes Were Watching God'." *Black Literature and Literary Theory.* Ed. Henry Louis Gates, Jr. New York: Methuen, 1984. 205-19.

---. "Thresholds of Difference: Structures of Address in Zora Neale Hurston." *"Race," Writing, and Difference.* Ed. Henry Louis Gates, Jr. Chicago: U of Chicago P,1986. 317-328.

Johnson, James Weldon. "The Dilemma of the Negro Author,"*American Mercury* 15 (1928): 477.

Locke, Alain, ed. *The New Negro.* New York: Atheneum, 1968.

McDowell, "Lines of Descent/Dissenting Lines." *Zora Neale Hurston: Critical Perspectives Past and Present.* Eds. H. L. Gates and K.A. Appiah. N.Y.: Amistad, 1993. 230-240.

Nixon, Will. "Black Male Writers: Endangered Species?" *American Visions* , 5.1 (1990): 24-28.

Scruggs, Charles. "'All Dressed Up but No Place to Go': The Black Writer and His Audience During the Harlem Renaissance." *American Literature,* 48 (1976): 543-563.

Story, Ralph D. "Patronage and the Harlem Renaissance: You Get What You Pay For." *CLA Journal,* 32.3 (1989): 284-295.

Turner, Darwin T. *In a Minor Chord: Three Afro-American Writers and Their Search for Identity.* London: Southern Illinois UP, 1971.

—. "W. E. B. Du Bois and the Theory of a Black Aesthetic." *The Harlem Renaissance Re-examined.* Ed. Victor A. Kramer. New York: Ams Press, 1987. 9-30.

Wald, Priscilla. "Becoming 'Colored': The Self-Authorized Language of Difference in Zora Neale Hurston." *American Literary History* 2.1 (1990): 79-100.

Walker, Alice. *I Love Myself When I Am Laughing... And Then Again When I Am Looking Mean and Impressive: a Zora Neale Hurston Reader.* New York: The Feminist Press, 1979.

—. *In Search of Our Mothers' Gardens: Womanist Prose.* San Diego, New York, London: Harvest / HBJ, 1983.

Wall, Cheryl A., ed. "Zora Neale Hurston: Changing Her Own Words." *American Novelists Revisited: Essays in Feminist Criticism.* Ed. Fritz Fleischmann. Boston, MA: G.K. Hall and Co., 1982.

Notes

[1] McDowell, "Lines of Descent/Dissenting Lines." *Zora Neale Hurston: Critical Perspectives Past and Present.* Eds. H. L. Gates and K.A. Appiah. (N.Y.: Amistad, 1993), 240.

[2] See Alice Walker, *In Search of Our Mothers' Gardens: Womanist Prose.* (San Diego, New York, London: Harvest / HBJ, 1983), 89.

[3] Some outstanding works on Hurston's lyric language and on her narrative strategies are Henry Louis Gates, Jr, "Zora Neale Hurston and the Speakerly Text." *The Signifying Monkey: A Theory of African-American Literary Criticism.* (New York: Oxford UP, 1988), 170-216; Karla F.C. Holloway, *The Character of the World: The Texts of Zora Neale Hurston.* (New York: Greenwood Press, 1987); Barbara Johnson, "Metaphor, Metonymy, and Voice in 'Their Eyes Were Watching God'." *Black Literature and Literary Theory.* Ed. Henry Louis Gates, Jr. (New York: Methuen, 1984), 205-19, and "Thresholds of Difference: Structures of Address in Zora Neale Hurston." *"Race," Writing, and Difference.* Ed. Henry Louis Gates, Jr. (Chicago: U of Chicago P,1986), 317-28; Cheryl A. Wall, "Zora Neale Hurston: Changing Her Own Words." *Zora Neale Hurston: Critical Perspectives Past and Present.* Eds. Henry Louis Gates, Jr. and K.A. Appiah. (N.Y.: Amistad, 1993), 76-97.

[4] Robert Bone, *Down Home: A History of Afro-American Short Fiction from Its Beginnings to the End of the Harlem Renaissance.* (New York: G.P. Putnam's Sons, 1975). Bell, Bernard W. *The Afro-American Novel and Its Tradition.* (Amherst: U of Massachusetts P,1987).

[5] *Op. Cit.,* 46.

[6] *Mules and Men.* (New York: Harper and Row, Publishers, 1990 (1935)), 1.

[7] *Jonah's Gourd Vine.* (New York: Harper and Row, Publishers, 1990), 151.

[8] *Ibid.,* 149.

[9] As quoted by Robert E. Hemenway in *Zora Neale Hurston: A Literary Biography* (Chicago: U of Illinois P, 1977), 45. *Fire!!* is considered the real manifesto of the Harlem Renaissance aesthetics, brought together as an attempt to challenge the guidelines proposed by the older generation of black intellectuals.

[10] Hayden, "Preface to the Atheneum Edition. *New Negro.* ed. Alain Locke. (New York: Atheneum, 1968), xii.

[11] *Op. Cit.,* 51.

[12] In Turner, "W. E. B. Du Bois and the Theory of a Black Aesthetic." *The Harlem Renaissance Re-examined.* Ed. Victor A. Kramer. (New York: Ams Press, 1987), 17.

[13] *Op. Cit.,* 15.

[14] "How It Feels to Be Colored Me." Ed. Alice Walker. *I Love Myself When I Am Laughing... And Then Again When I Am Looking Mean and Impressive: a Zora Neale Hurston Reader.* (New York: The Feminist Press, 1979), 153.

[15] By the time when Hurston started publishing her novels, the Depression had influenced Black writers in more than one way. The economic crisis hit hard the Harlem Renaissance magazines and promoters. The literary prizes organized by *The Crisis* and *Opportunity* disappeared, and many white patrons stopped or reduced their allowances to the New Negroes. The end of the Harlem Renaissance, however, did not come abruptly. In 1930 *The Green Pastures*—dramatization of Roark Bradford's *Ol' Man Adam an' His Chillun,* by Marc Connelly—, was a hit in Broadway. Langston Hughes published his novel *Not without Laughter.* In 1934 Zora Neale Hurston published her first novel, *Jonah's Gourd Vine.* Although the Harlem Renaissance was still giving some of its best literary fruits, a new era of social denunciation had begun, spurred by the different economic and social spirit of the time. The riot that took place in Harlem on March 19, 1935, marked a definitive turn in the black intellectuals' attitude towards race relations and their role as artists. Richard Wright's *Native Son* would be published in 1940. In a world where the aesthetics of the social realism became predominant Hurston remained, nevertheless, faithful to the New Negro ideals.

[16] In *Reading Black, Reading Feminist: A Critical Anthology.* Ed. Henry Louis Gates, Jr. (New York: Meridian, 1990), 23-4.

[17] Gates. *The Signifying Monkey: A Theory of African-American Literary Criticism.* (New York: Oxford UP, 1988), 174.

[18] See Ana María Fraile, "Zora Neale Hurston's Experimentation with the Narrative Voice in Her Short Stories" *REDEN* (In press).

[19] "Hurston, "What White Publishers Won't Print," 173.

[20] The impact of Richard Wright's work was so great that still today Afro-American writers such as Charles Johnson are urging his fellow writers to "search beyond the tradition of great angry novels, such as Richard Wright's *Native Son,* for literary inspiration of other kinds." In Nixon, "Black Male Writers: Endangered Species?" *American Visions,* 5.1 (1990): 24-28. 27.

[21] "Stories of Conflict." *Zora Neale Hurston: Folklore, Memoirs, and Other Writings.* Ed Cheryl A. Wall. (N.Y.: Literary Classics, The Library of America, 1995. (1938)), 912.

[22] In her harsh critique of Wright's rendition of black dialect, she wrote: "Since the author himself is a Negro, his dialect is a puzzling thing. One wonders how he arrived at it. Certainly he does not write by ear unless he is tone-deaf" (913).

[23] *Ibid.,* 237.

[24] We will see in connection with *Seraph on the Suwanee* how Hurston's thought about the distinctiveness of Afro-American language and culture evolves to positions diametrically opposed to the views she defended at the beginning of her career.

[25] See Barbara Johnson's "Thresholds of Difference: Structures of Address in Zora Neale Hurston." *"Race," Writing, and Difference.* Ed. Henry Louis Gates, Jr. (Chicago: U of Chicago P, 1986), 317-28, and Priscilla Wald's "Becoming 'Colored': The Self-Authorized Language of Difference in Zora Neale Hurston." *American Literary History* , 2.1 (1990): 79-100.

[26] "What White Publishers Won't Print." *I Love Myself When I Am Laughing... And Then Again When I Am Looking Mean and Impressive: a Zora Neale Hurston Reader.* Ed. Alice Walker. (New York: The Feminist Press, 1979), 169-73. 171.

[27] Johnson, *Op. Cit.,* 323.

[28] *Op. Cit.,* 5.

[29] *Jonah's,* 2.

[30] *Dust Tracks on a Road.* Ed. Robert E. Hemenway. (Urbana: U of Illinois P, 1984), 220.

[31] *Jonah's,* 3.

[32] *Ibid.,* 11.

[33] Robert Hayden observes in his preface to Locke's anthology: "Stressing the role of the Negro writer as interpreter of his people, Dr. Locke drew upon the work of Countée Cullen, Jean Toomer, Langston Hughes, and Claude McKay, all of whom had won recognition" (xii). This does not exclude that one of the main objectives of the New Negro was to awaken in black people a sense of their own beauty and worth.

[34] *Op. Cit.,* 153.

[35] "Court Order Can't Make Races Mix. "Zora *Neale Hurston: Folklore, Memoirs, and Other Writings.* Ed Cheryl A. Wall. (N.Y.: Literary Classics, The Library of America, 1995. (1938)), 956.

[36] *Ibid.,* 958.

[37] *Their Eyes Were Watching God.* (New York: Harper and Row, Publishers, 1990), 10.

[38] *Ibid.,* 14.

[39] *Ibid.,* 19.

[40] *Ibid.,* 73.

[41] *Ibid.,* 75.

[42] *Ibid.,* 134, 135, 139.

[43] *Op. Cit.,* 297, 301.

[44] *Op. Cit.,* 235.

[45] "What White Publishers," 171.

[46] "Crazy for this Democracy. "I *Love Myself When I Am Laughing... And Then Again When I Am Looking Mean and Impressive: a Zora Neale Hurston Reader. Ed. Alice* Walker. (New York: The Feminist Press, 1979), 166.

[47] *Ibid.,* 165.

[48] *Ibid.,* 167.

[49] *Op. Cit.,* 148.

[50] McDowell, *Op. Cit.*

[51] Blyden Jackson in his Introduction to *Moses, Man of the Mountain.* (Urbana and Chicago: U of Illinois P, 1984), xix.

[52] *Op. Cit.,* 257.

[53] *Dust Tracks,* 333.

[54] *Ibid.,* 339-340.

[55] *Op. Cit.,* 234.

[56] *Op. Cit.,* 86.

[57] *Ibid.,* 246.

[58] *Jonah's,* 169.

[59] *Op. Cit.,* 93, 94, 95.

[60] *Ibid.,* 248, 252, 316.

[61] *Op. Cit.*, 297.

[62] "Negroes Without Self-Pity." *Zora Neale Hurston: Folklore, Memoirs, and Other Writings.* Ed Cheryl A. Wall. (N.Y.: Literary Classics, The Library of America, 1995), 933.

[63] *Dust Tracks,* 168.

[64] Hurston made her acquaintance of Mrs. Mason in September 1927, after coming back to New York from a not very fruitful six-month trip to Florida in search of black folklore. For more information about Harlem's patronage see Story's "Patronage and the Harlem Renaissance: You Get What You Pay For." *CLA Journal* , 32.3 (1989): 284-295.

[65] Langston Hughes, *The Big Sea* (N.Y.: Alfred A. Knopf, 1940). Excerpt reprinted in Harold Bloom's *Zora Neale Hurston.* (N.Y.: Chelsea House Publishers, 1986), 13-14.

[66] *Dust Tracks,* 116.

[67] See Peter Bruck, "Black American Short Fiction in the 20th Century: Problems of Audience, and The Evolution of Artistic Stances and Themes." *The Black American Short Story in the 20th century: A Collection of Critical Essays.* (Amsterdam: B.R. Grüner Publishing Co., 1977), 1-19. See also Charles Scruggs, "'All Dressed Up but No Place to Go': The Black Writer and His Audience During the Harlem Renaissance." *American Literature,* 48 (1976): 543-563.

[68] James Weldon Johnson, "The Dilemma of the Negro Author," *American Mercury,* 15 (1928), 477.

[69] Langston Hughes. "The Negro Artist and the Racial Mountain." *The Nation,* CXXII (June 23, 1926), 694.

[70] Scruggs, *Op. Cit.*, 553.

[71] Quoted in Hemenway, 286-7.

[72] *Op. Cit.*, 284.

[73] See Hemenway, *Op. Cit.*, 289.

[74] See Arthur P. Davis. *From the Dark Tower: Afro-American Writers, 1900-1960.* (Washington, D.C.: Howard UP, 1974), 139-140.

[75] See Carby, "Foreword." *Seraph on the Suwanee.* (New York: Harper and Row, Publishers, 1991), xi-xii.

[76] "The Pet Negro System." *I Love Myself When I Am Laughing... And Then Again When I Am Looking Mean and Impressive: a Zora Neale Hurston Reader.* Ed. Alice Walker. (New York: The Feminist Press, 1979), 156-162. 158.

[77] *Ibid.*, 157.

[78] *Ibid.*, 160.

[79] *Ibid.*, 162.

[80] Zora Neale Hurston to Burroughs Mitchell, October, 1947. Quoted by Hazel Carby, *Op. Cit.*, x.

[81] *Ibid.*

[82] Lillie Howard's "'Seraph on the Suwanee'." *Zora Neale Hurston: Critical Perspectives Past and Present.* Eds. H. L. Gates and K.A. Appiah. (N.Y.: Amistad, 1993), 278.

[83] Lillie Howard. "'Seraph on the Suwanee'." *Zora Neale Hurston: Critical Perspectives Past and Present.* Eds H. L. Gates and K.A. Appiah. (N.Y.: Amistad, 1993), 277.

[84] Quoted by Hemenway, *Op. Cit.*, 338.

7

REDISCOVERING NATION, RESISTING RACIAL OPPRESSION: THE AESTHETICS OF "PUTTING UP" IN U.S. THIRD WORLD WRITING

I.
FIGHTING RACISM, FINDING NATION: THE MATERIAL CONDITIONS FOR NARRATING THE NATION IN U.S. THIRD WORLD LITERATURE

In his famous defense of Bigger Thomas in Richard Wright's 1940 novel *Native Son*, Boris Max articulates an understanding of racial oppression in the U.S. as a form of colonial or national oppression, as he argues to the jury, "Taken collectively, [African Americans] are not simply twelve million people; in reality they constitute a separate nation, stunted, stripped, and held captive *within* this nation, devoid of political, social, economic, and property rights."[1] This conceptualization of racial minorities in the U.S. as colonized nations is one that has appeared with recursive force since Wright's representation of Bigger Thomas's situation in 1940. At the height of the Third World Movements of the 1960s in the U.S., for example, Stokely Carmichael and Charles Hamilton echoed Boris Max's defense in 1967, asserting that while "economists might wish to argue this point endlessly; the objective relationship stands. Black people in the United States have a colonial relationship to the larger society, a relationship characterized by institutional racism."[2]

Similar positions were articulated by Native Americans, Chicanos, Puerto Ricans, and Asian Americans with respect to their own racial group affiliations.[3]

Nonetheless, despite the prevalence in the twentieth century of the "Third World thesis" regarding U.S. racial minorities, these "national questions" and the internal colonial perspective as a whole have always been opposed by some cultural insistence upon the unity of "American" identity and nationhood, whether it be traditional cultural assertions of the U.S. as a melting pot society, the liberal pluralist ideologies of contemporary multiculturalism, or the abstruse academic discourse of postcolonial theory which implies at every turn the pastness of colonialism. Despite the dominance of these latter visions of racial harmony and national unity, however, a prominent element of the U.S. minority or Third World literary discourse has been and continues to be the construction of a national consciousness geared toward the resistance to racial oppression as internally colonized national political subjects. This paper will explore the discovery and development of national identity and consciousness in U.S. Third World literature within the broader context of U.S. racial discourse and theory, exploring the material and enabling conditions of literary nationalism in relation to the ideological and theoretical resistances to the Third World national paradigm as well as the potential within literary nationalism for the development of and bridge to a genuinely international culture.

The U.S. has long been a nation precariously comprised of many nations or national identities which the ideological dreamwork of a harmonizing liberal pluralism has been unable to contain. While the U.S. liberalist conception of a cultural [read "racial"] pluralism preaches tolerance and a "live-and-let-live" attitude among all peoples regardless of race, this position obscures the fact that particular cultural orientations are not compatible with and in fact are mutually exclusive and hostile to one another. Understanding culture as the complex network of social practices which determine and signify relations of subordination, domination, and equality including the relations and organizations of the mode of production and economic life, it must be recognized, for example, that the genocidal practices of U.S. imperialism and colonialism at home and abroad are hardly compatible with the ways of life, the cultures, that U.S. colonialism destroys in the name of such cultural mandates as "Manifest Destiny." James Welch illustrates this point forthrightly in his recent work *Killing Custer*. Discussing the significance of "Custer's Last Stand," he writes,

> The Indians would say they were defending their territory, or exercising their right to be free upon it, to follow the buffalo as they had for centuries; the white authorities would say that they were punishing the Indians for depredations against the white settlers, traders, rivermen, wood gatherers, and

miners, or for leaving the reservation without permission.   In any case,
contrary to some opinion, these actions resulted from a clash of cultures. What
caused this clash is evident.   The Indians lived on territories that the whites
wanted. Most such collisions occur when one culture wants something from
the other. It is always astonishing when the invading culture feels it has the
divine right (call it Manifest Destiny or whatever) to take that something in this
case, land--from the other.[4] (My emphasis)

Welch here clearly exposes the material organizations of everyday life
underpinning cultural orientations and gives an accurate accounting of the material
stakes of cultural struggle. Simply put, questions of cultural difference are not
simply questions of ideas but of ways of life, and if one way of life involves the
destruction of another, then those cultures or ways of life are not compatible,
making a "live-and-let-live" approach hardly effective or viable and exposing the
moral and explanatory bankruptcy of liberal pluralist approaches to race, ethnicity,
and cultural difference.

Moreover, the U.S. contemporary and historical racial policies and social
orders suggest that the ideals of liberal pluralism have hardly realized themselves
in a way that allows all to live and let live on equal terms. Gunnar Myrdal noted in
1944 that the inequality, segregation, and racial discrimination African Americans
faced in U.S. society contradicted the "American creed" of democracy, equality,
and justice. Yet his proposal that immediate assimilation and integration of
African Americans into U.S. culture would solve this "American dilemma" failed
to recognize the racialist norms inherent in "American" culture which made race a
central element of the U.S. capitalist economy and social hierarchy by which
access to and distribution of wealth were regulated. Racialized populations
effectively constituted colonized nations within the U.S. nation.   And it is this
status as internally colonized nations which has served as the context and enabling
condition for many U.S. writers of color in developing in their writing a literary
nationalism that nurtures a consciousness of this national dimension to "race" in
the U.S. and imagines resistance to racial discrimination in the form of national
liberation struggle. Indeed, forty-three years after Wright's *Native Son*, the Chicana
writer Cherrie Moraga asserts and describes the continuation of these colonial and
genocidal conditions, writing in her experimental autobiography *Loving in the War
Years*:

Unlike most white people, with the exception of the Jews, Third World people
have suffered the threat of genocide to our races since the coming of the first
European expansionists . . . for when they keep us in ghettos, reservations, and

> barrios which ensure that our own people will be the recipients of our
> frustrated acts of violence; when they sterilize our women without our consent
> because we are unable to read the document we sign; when they prevent our
> families from getting decent housing, adequate child care, sufficient fuel,
> regular medical care; then we have reason to believe--although they may no
> longer technically be lynching us in Texas or our sisters and brothers in
> Georgia, Alabama, Mississippi—they intend to see us dead.[5]

Moraga here articulates a Third World perspective which sees people of color in
the U.S. as internally colonized minorities, as an internal Third World, who
undergo experiences analogous to those of populations in Third World nations
abroad. Far from being invited to take part in the dominant U.S. culture, Moraga
asserts, racialized populations have been ordered to disappear, consigned to work
the lowest paying jobs and to live in the internal colonies of the barrio, the
reservation, and the ghetto. The Third World colonial experience of people of
color in the U.S., Moraga suggests in this passage, has conditioned the nationalist
context for the production of a U.S. Third World literature.

    In exploring the literary nationalist response to racial discrimination, this
essay will rely heavily on Robert Blauner's theory of internal colonialism in
exploring the objective material conditions of people of color in the U.S. and in
theorizing the cultural/literary response of resistance by U.S. writers of color to
racial oppression in the U.S. Developed in 1972 in his pathbreaking work *Racial
Oppression in America*, Blauner's theory of internal colonialism draws a crucial
distinction between colonized and immigrant minorities and between the
categories of race and ethnicity, arguing that "racial groups in America are, and
have been, colonized peoples; therefore, their social realities cannot be understood
in the framework of immigration and assimilation that is applied to European
ethnic groups."[6] One of the major distinctions that Blauner identifies between the
experiences of immigration and colonization is the mode of entry into the U.S.
economy and society. While white ethnic immigrants of European descent came
by choice to the U.S. and were able to assimilate into a culture predominantly
derived from a Judeo-Christian framework which much more resembled their own,
people of color, the racialized minorities in the U.S., historically entered the U.S.
not by choice or else were native inhabitants of the geopolitical territory now
known as the U.S. These peoples suffered brutal enslavement, special labor
exploitation, initially as unfree labor and later as groups clustered in precapitalist
employment sectors, and, in the case of Native Americans and Chicanos, classic
colonization. A central element of the colonizing and internal colonizing
processes these racial groups endured was the destruction and erosion of their

cultures by the colonizing powers with the intent of replacing those cultures with their own. It is this element of cultural domination that constitutes for Blauner the linchpin in linking the experiences of colonization of people of color in the U.S., the internal Third World, and the Third World abroad:

> Yet the colonial attack on culture is more than a matter of economic factors such as labor recruitment and special exploitation. The colonial situation differs from the class situation of capitalism precisely in the importance of culture as an instrument of domination. Colonialism depends on conquest, control, and the imposition of new institutions and ways of thought. Culture and social organization are important as vessels of a people's autonomy and integrity; when cultures are whole and vigorous, conquest, penetration, and certain modes of control are more readily resisted. Therefore, imperial regimes attempt, consciously or unwittingly, either to destroy the cultures of colonized people or, when it is more convenient, to exploit them for the purposes of more efficient control and economic profit.[7]

As Frantz Fanon describes the process in his essay "On National Culture" in *The Wretched of the Earth* :

> Colonialism is not satisfied merely with holding a people in its grip and emptying the native's head of all form and content. By a kind of perverted logic, it turns to the past of the oppressed people, and distorts, disfigures and destroys it. This work of devaluing pre-colonial history takes on a dialectical significance today.[8]

Because of the centrality of culture in colonial domination, the rehabilitation of those cultural forms and histories has played an equally central role in the resistance of these Third World nations within the U.S. as they challenge the racial hierarchies and cultural norms underwriting the hegemony of the U.S. dominant culture and ratifying racial oppression and discrimination. This strategic cultural nationalism has been central to the national movements in the U.S. from the early twentieth century, to the turbulent 1960s, to the present. In exploring the persistence, necessity, function, and meaning of cultural nationalism as a literary and political mode of resisting racial oppression and discrimination in the U.S., part two of this paper will discuss Rolando Hinojosa's novelistic approach to questions of nationalism and assimilation, exploring his representation of the national dimension and consciousness of the Chicana/o people and the historical rationale his novels supply for a national politics. Looking briefly at moments from the works of Leslie Marmon Silko and Alejandro Morales, part three will explore the possibilities present in Third World literature for developing an international culture and realizing Fanon's precept that "it is at the heart of national consciousness that international consciousness lives and grows."[9]

II. The Pitfalls of Assimilation:
Developing a Literary National Identity

The structuring ideology of U.S. society, perhaps until recently, has long been one of the immigrant's nation, of the melting pot society, where anyone can come and work one's way up the economic ladder and experience the fruits of a society devoted to equal opportunity regardless of race, color, creed, or gender. Yet this ideology obscures the fact that race has long been a central feature of the U.S. capitalist order in targeting people of color for super-exploitation. It this analysis of the "racial labor principle" which centers Blauner's theory of internal colonialism and his distinction between immigrant and colonized minorities. Because "colonial conquest and control has been the cutting edge of Western capitalism in its expansion and penetration throughout the world,"[10] resisting racial oppression for people of color has meant not assimilating into the culture and economy of U.S. capitalism, as white European immigrants were allowed to, but rather challenging the capitalist colonial system itself from the position of oppressed nations. Indeed, not only has assimilation not represented a valid option for minority populations in the U.S., but assimilation into the dominant U.S. culture as equals itself represents a logical impossibility. Assimilating into U.S. culture, which would entail adopting the values and worldview of that culture, would mean embracing and even internalizing the racial and racist norms already informing the dominant U.S. culture and hence would result in the maintenance of that cultural and racial hierarchy rather than the gradual elimination of it.

A nationalist and cultural nationalist response develops as the most effective way of challenging this situation because, in Blauner's words, "the colonial situation differs from the class situation of capitalism precisely in the importance of culture as an instrument of domination," because "colonialism depends on conquest, control, and the imposition of new institutions and ways of thinking."[11] The literary nationalist project of recovering the destroyed culture is not, then, undergone simply so that as a society we might celebrate our diversity, but rather so that people of color, as oppressed nations, can present alternative cultural, social, and economic ways of organizing our life, a vision of themselves to counter the inferior conceptualizations of the dominant culture, and a record of the past to provide an historical materialist analysis of the historical forces and processes that have positioned minorities in the U.S. capitalist order. Such an historical knowledge is necessary as one must understand the forces one is fighting against in order to develop a strategy for resisting racial oppression.

In exploring nationalism as the enabling condition of much U.S. "minority" literature, I want to look at Rolando Hinojosa's novels as paradigmatic of literary nationalism. In writing about the life of Chicanos and Mexicanos on the Texas-Mexican border, Hinojosa's project involves in part rescuing the category of nation and national identity from the merely contingent discursive and imaginary or psychological status which postcolonial theory has consigned it to, a status which evacuates the category of an objective significance and reality by divorcing it from an historical and material context. The work of the vanguard postcolonial theorist Homi Bhabha exemplifies this tendency, as he supports Ernest Gellner's "paradoxical point that the historical necessity of the idea of the nation conflicts with the contingent and arbitrary signs and symbols that signify the affective life of the national culture" and affirms Gellner's assertion that "'the cultural shreds and patches used by nationalism are often arbitrary historical inventions.'" Indeed, Bhabha sees nationalism as necessarily politically regressive, as a "narcissistic neuroses" always premised on a love/hate duality and a process of "othering." He invokes Freud's concept of the "narcissism of minor differences" to explain how deployments of love and hate necessarily inform and define boundaries of national identity, using psychoanalysis to explain national and international relations instead of explaining Third World psychologies through reference to the material international relations in which they are embedded. Premised on the pastness of colonialism, for Bhabha "nation" becomes simply a cultural construction divorced from historical and political necessity and from material economic relations, as he wonders if Fanon's national narratives still "have relevance outside the situation of anti-colonial struggle."[12] Both Bhabha and Gellner lack an understanding of the possible organic relation between culture, history, and the mode of production of any given society. It this relation which is crucial to understanding the necessary relation between national liberation and culture as theorized by Amilcar Cabral. Cabral writes,

> Whatever may be the ideological or idealistic characteristics of cultural expression, culture is an element of the history of a people. Culture is, perhaps, the product of this history just as the flower is the product of a plant. Like history, or because it is history, culture has as its material base the level of the productive forces and the mode of production. Culture plunges its roots

into the physical reality of the environmental humus in which it develops, and it reflects the organic nature of society, which may be more or less influenced by external factors. History allows us to know the nature and extent of the imbalances and conflicts (economic, political and social) which characterize the evolution of a society; culture allows us to know the dynamic syntheses which have been developed and established by social conscience to resolve these conflicts at each stage of its evolution, in search for survival and progress.[13]

As Cabral theorizes culture and as Hinojosa narratively depicts the cultural content of national identity and consciousness, nationalism can hardly be constructed of arbitrary cultural shreds and patches. National identity is not created by fiat but rather is the result of historical circumstances and processes, such that the nation Hinojosa narrates is one grounded in a distinct history and culture that has developed both independently of U.S. society--insofar as it predates the formation of a U.S. nation--and through complex interactions with dominant U.S. culture.

The culture Hinojosa speaks of is not an ideologically motivated mythology such as those we see promulgated on license plates and in such monuments as the Statue of Liberty or Mount Rushmore but rather the result of the processes of everyday life. In an essay titled "The Sense of Place," Hinojosa theorizes this relationship between history and culture that gives birth to a national consciousness and identity. Discussing his sense of the Texas-Mexico border where he grew up and which he writes about, he explains, "I had a sense of it, and by that I mean that I was not learning about the culture of the Valley, but living it, forming part of it, and thus, contributing to it." Culture here is not an artificial construction of patriotic fervor but an organic development forged in the dialectical interaction between a people and its locale and history. He continues, "But a place is merely that until it is populated, and once populated, the histories of the place and its people begin. For me and mine, history began in 1749 when the first colonists began moving into the southern and northern banks of the Rio Grande." It is this common historical and cultural experience--and not the legalistic or geopolitical mapping of borders which are the demarcating signatures of the imperialist histories of the modern nation-state-- that for Hinojosa define the contours and content of a nation:

That river was not yet a jurisdictional barrier and was not to be until almost one hundred years later; but by then the border had its own history and

> culture, its own culture, and its own sense of place: it was Nuevo Santander,
> named for old Santander in the Spanish Peninsula . . .
>
> For me, then, part of a sense of the Border came from sharing: the sharing of
> names, of places, of a common history, and of belonging to a place; one
> attended funerals, was taken to cemeteries, and one saw names that
> corresponded to one's own or to one's friends and neighbors, and relatives. . .
>
> . . . we were borderers with a living and unifying culture born of conflict with
> another culture and this, too, helped to cement further still the knowing exactly
> where one came from and from whom one was descended[14]

Again, the culture informing Hinojosa's literary construction of national
consciousness, as evidenced here, is hardly an arbitrary collection of shreds and
patches.

It is precisely the historical rootedness of the culture that resists absorption or
assimilation into the instrumentality of U.S. capitalist colonialist culture. Indeed,
Hinojosa's task as author is not so much to construct or invent a national identity
but rather to promote a consciousness of the objective national dimensions of the
Texas Mexicans' existence. Realigning history and consciousness and providing
the cultural resources and orientation for comprehending the history of
colonization informing the contemporary predicament of Chicanos in the U.S.,
Hinojosa's writing narrates the conditions for imagining resistance to racial
oppression in the U.S. As the Chicana poet Cherrie Moraga states, "The road to
the future is the road from our past."[15]

Hinojosa's series of novels *Klail City Death Trip* provides fertile ground for
beginning to explore the ways in which U.S. writers of color theorize "race" as
connected to imperialism, conceive of their own literary practice as self-
consciously crafted acts of resistance to U.S. racial capitalism, and attempt to
construct a sense of a Third World national identity in their writing. Hinojosa's
writing in particular must be read as extending and underwriting the cultural
politics of the Chicano Movement of the 1960s and 1970s and challenging liberal
conceptions of race and ethnicity in favor of models that view people of color in
the U.S. as internally colonized. In particular, Hinojosa explores the way in which
the migrant Chicano workers, focal points of his writing, resist this colonization in
the context of their everyday lives and define themselves as a nation in opposition
to the U.S. nation-state. He writes of his characters in the prologue to his novel
Klail City, "Putting up (cf. Resistance) may be genetic; congenital. As Don Quijote

says: 'Anything is possible.' It could, of course, be something else; it could be a legitimate product of living and working and putting up day after day with one's fellow citizens."[16] In Hinojosa's work, this "legitimate product of living and working" gives form to a national, even trans-national, identity that links the U.S. Third World with the Third World abroad through the continual re-enactment in storytelling of moments of Mexican revolutionary uprising from 1848 through the 1930s. The national consciousness Hinojosa's work fosters through historical recovery and cultural memory is one that crosses borders, as he writes in another novel of the series *The Valley*:

> Those old men, and I'll mention but three . . . were all born here, in the United States, but they too fought in the 1910 revolution as did Mexican mexicanos. The parents of these men were also born in this country, as were their grandparents; this goes back to 1765 and earlier, 1749. It may be curious for some, but it's all perfectly understandable and natural for lower Rio Grande borderers, as is the lay of the land on both sides of the border; and if one discounts the Anglo Texans, well, the Texas Mexicans--or mexicanos-- and the Mexico Mexicans--the nacionales--not only think alike more often than not, but they are also blood related as they have and had been for one hundred years before the Americans had that war between themselves in the 1860s; the river is a jurisdictional barrier, but that's about it.[17]

This provocative passage reveals two elements centering Hinojosa's narration of the nation. First, the passage portrays the incommensurability of the jurisdictional or geopolitical boundaries of the nation-state, which demarcate and signify the history of imperialist assault and colonization, with a people's common cultural, historical, and even territorial experience of nationhood. The Texas Mexicans and the Mexico Mexicans, Hinojosa suggests, are bound together as a nation or national identity by the distinct and differential cultural ethos and historical experience which defy geopolitical markers and which inform a national consciousness which does not correspond to that of the U.S. dominant culture. While the U.S. citizens of European descent might identify the "American" revolution against Britain or the Civil War as important moments in the birth and development of the U.S. nation-state, these dates are rather meaningless for the Texas Mexicans, as demonstrated in the passage above in which the U.S. Civil War is referred to as the war the Americans had "between themselves in the 1860s" and in *Klail City* when Hinojosa describes his character Don Marcial de Anda sitting "on a city park bench donated by the Sons and Daughters of Some Revolution or Other."[18] The historical moments that are meaningful are dates such as 1749 and 1848 when "Americans" encroached upon the Mexican people and annexed their lands in the name of Manifest Destiny. For the Texas Mexicans to forget this history is to gloss over their mode of entry into the dominant U.S. socio-economic system as a subordinated and colonized people already viewed as unequal. For Chicanos or Texas Mexicans, to assimilate into the dominant U.S. culture and its attendant national consciousness which celebrates Manifest Destiny and the colonization of the occupied territory now known as the U.S.--indeed the very processes that made the contemporary U.S. nation-state possible--would mean buying into the racializing national telos which justified their own dispossession and their differential and unequal incorporation into U.S. racial capitalism. It would mean forgetting or ignoring that, as E. San Juan, Jr. has noted,

> From its inception, the United States has been distinguished as socio-historical formation with specific racial dynamics. It was contoured by the expulsion of American Indian nations from their homelands and their genocidal suppression, an inaugural and recursive phenomenon followed by the enslavement of millions of Africans, the dispossession of Mexicans, the subjection of Asians, and so on. The historical origin of the United States as a nation-state, traditionally defined by the revolutionary Enlightenment principles enunciated by the "Founding Fathers," cannot be understood without this genocidal foundation. "Race" came to signify the identities of social groups in struggle for resources: land, labor power, and their fruits. Ultimately then, the struggle for command over time/space and the positioning of bodies in the North American habitat politicized the social order and set the course for the future.[19]

Assimilating into the dominant U.S. entails adopting these "Enlightenment principles" which underwrote the genocide of the nation's foundation. Additionally, the problem is that these racial dynamics persist as a "recursive phenomenon," such that forgetting the past with the attitude of letting bygones be bygones, of starting from scratch, does not alter the inequality already historically established and does not abolish the racial values informing U.S. culture which will maintain that racial hierarchy.

In portraying the everyday life of Chicanos in Texas, Hinojosa's fiction explores this "dispossession" that accompanies assimilation. In *Klail City*, for example, he depicts the relation between assimilated and non-assimilated Texas Mexicans in a scene in which his protagonist Rafe Buenrostro changes schools:

> It was quite a surprise. Here we were, going from the 100% Texas Mexican North Ward Elementary to Klail's Memorial Jr. High and then, just like that, we ran across *other* mexicanos; we later found out that these had gone to South

Ward, and they were different from us, somehow. Jehu Malacara, a cousin of mine, called them "The Dispossessed." Now, these mexicanos were one hell of a lot more fluent in English than we were, but they came up short on other things; on the uptake, for one, out on the playground, for another.

Example. When it came to handing out athletic equipment, we pushed and shoved as well as anyone; the American way, right? But these mexicanos hung back. . .

The first week, the assistant coach (no fool) would take note of the scrappiest kids and he'd tap us as prospects: "Say, boy, how'd you like to play seventh grade football for Memorial?"

Some of us'd say yes and some would turn him down, but what we all noticed was that the docile mexicanos from the South Ward usually hung back. Shy, kind-a.[20]

Although Rafe Buenrostro is unable to articulate why those Texas Mexicans from the South Ward are docile and shy and refuse to insist on and fight for the equal distribution of and access to athletic equipment, Hinojosa's narrative makes clear the cultural work assimilation accomplishes in structuring the consciousness of the colonized subject according to the racial norms that maintain the "color line" and structure the racial hierarchy of the U.S. socio-economic formation which provides and limits access to the fruits of social wealth on the basis of race. Indeed, this scene demonstrates and allegorizes the unequal distribution of social resources on the basis of race which takes place on a larger scale in the global colonial system and the role of culture in underwriting that system.

This theme of colonization dominates Hinojosa's writing and is articulated forthrightly earlier in *Klail City* in a conversation between two elder Texas Mexicans don Manuel Guzman and don Aureliano Mora. "We're Greeks, don Manuel," don Aureliano says, "Greeks . . . Greeks whose homes have been taken over by Romans . . . Slaves in the service of the Romans . . . we've got to educate them, these Romans, these Anglos . . . amounts to the same thing."[21] It is the elders in Hinojosa's novelistic community who function as the repositories of historical memory and who remind the younger generations of Texas Mexicans, who continue to experience racial discrimination, of the history of colonization and internal colonization which established and maintains the racial status quo. The knowledge of this history is necessary, Hinojosa suggests, so that the younger generations understand the source of their oppression so that they can challenge racial discrimination at its roots.

In the logic of the novel, historical knowledge provides one with an understanding of who one's friends and enemies are and thus, by extension, of what one's political interests and who one's political allies are. Hinojosa dramatizes this point in an early scene in *Klail City* in which the Klail City veteran Echevarria reminds the community of the past actions of the character Choche Markham so that the community can accurately assess his allegiance to the political interests of the Texas Mexicans. Echevarria says,

> *Our* friend, is he? A champion of the Texas Mexican, you say? Well! When did this come about? What splendid, glorious--miraculous--transformation have we witnessed here? A friend? *Choche* Markham? Ha! Has that word been so devalued that he can fit it and wear it like a glove? Choche Markham a *friend?* My Gawd, people! Is there no such thing as memory?[22]

Echevarria then continues to recount a past incident in which Markham served as witness for an Anglo deputy who had murdered a Texas Mexican in cold blood. Again, this scene suggests that the cultural and historical recovery and revision that predominates in U.S. Third World or minority literatures is not done in the spirit of a liberal pluralist celebration of national diversity, of *e pluribus unum*, but rather in order to expose the material stakes of racism and racial oppression both historically and in contemporary society and to point out, to reiterate James Welch's precept, that culture clashes "occur when one culture wants something from the other."[23]

The development of a national consciousness and nationalist political and cultural orientation should not, however, be understood as necessarily separatist. Indeed, as an attack upon racial capitalism and its cultural ethos, the literary nationalist project is geared toward recovering destroyed cultural and historical resources in order to provide alternative ways and means of organizing, or rather re-organizing, the U.S. socio-economic formation for the interests of all, not just Texas Mexicans. This nationalism is, and historically has been, a form of political internationalism that can provide the basis for the development of a new and just international culture. This impulse of Hinojosa's literary nationalism is clear in don Aureliano's insistence that "we've got to educate them, these Romans, these Anglos." The following section will explore this internationalist dimension to the nationalist project of resisting racial oppression.

III. Towards an Internationalist Cultural Dimension

In an essay in which she discusses conflicts she experiences in teaching Leslie Marmon Silko's novel *Ceremony*, Paula Gunn Allen criticizes Silko for revealing in the novel sacred tribal stories and rituals of the Laguna and Pueblo peoples. She asserts against Silko that "to use the oral tradition directly is to run afoul of native ethics, which is itself a considerable part of the tradition. Using the tradition while contravening it is to do violence to it." The primary "story she lays alongside the novel," Gunn Allen writes, "is a clan story, and is not to be told outside of the clan." Wondering about Silko's motivation to make these traditions public, Gunn Allen speculates, "Certainly, being raised in greater proximity to Laguna village than I, she must have been told what I was, that we don't tell these things outside. Perhaps her desire to demonstrate the importance of breeds led her to this, or perhaps no one ever told her why the Lagunas and Pueblos are so closed about their spiritual activities and the allied oral tradition." In any case, according to Gunn Allen, Silko must have been unaware of "the information that telling old stories, revealing the old ways can only lead to disaster."[24]

In writing her later novel *Almanac of the Dead*, Silko seems quite sensitive to this criticism and in fact seems self-consciously to have dramatized this criticism and her response to it in the plot of the novel itself through her character Sterling. Early in the novel Sterling is exiled from his Laguna reservation because he guides some Hollywood filmmakers to take footage of a sacred monument, the shrine of the giant stone snake. In the final scene of the novel, Sterling returns "home," is allowed to re-enter the reservation amid some lingering suspicions, and reclaims the revolutionary significance of the stone snake, of Native American tribal rituals and traditions. This feature of the plot mirrors Silko's own rejection by Native American critics like Gunn for revealing sacred elements of Native American tribal traditions and her subsequent return to the scene of the crime in *Almanac of the Dead* to realize once again the force and potential for salvation and world transformation in Native American culture.

Indeed, in *Almanac of the Dead*, Silko demonstrates the capacity for Native American culture to offer an alternative to the dominant U.S. culture characterized by exploitation and oppression and to center the development of an international revolutionary culture of world transformation based in genuine concepts of justice, equality, and humanity--a potential that would be lost if these cultural traditions were not publicly thematicized in the novel. For Silko, the purpose of nationalism is not to breed separatism but to develop the alternative cultural possibilities out of which a new culture can be created. Her writing reflects Fanon's sentiment that "the consciousness of self is not the closing of a door to communication. Philosophic thought teaches us, on the contrary, that it is its guarantee. National consciousness . . . is the only thing that will give us an international dimension."[25]

In *Almanac of the Dead*, the central debates between the Mexican Indian tribal leader Angelita La Escapia and the Cuban Marxist Bartolomeo paradigmatically represent Silko's literary and political negotiations between and theorizations of nationalism and internationalism. When La Escapia's tribe puts Bartolomeo on trial "for crimes against the people's history," for example, he responds, "'What history? . . . Jungle monkeys and savages have no history!'", reproducing the very Eurocentric ideologies and principles of the Western philosophic tradition from Hegel onward justifying the European genocidal invasions and colonizations across the globe which have been so central to capitalist development. Bartolomeo's dismissal of Native American history and culture as their "animalistic tribalism" which was "the whore of nationalism and the dupe of capitalism" exposes his own ignorance of the historical experience of Native Americans. It is this very ignorance of and hostility toward the Mexican Indian history and tradition, in fact, which necessitates national struggle as a phase within the larger international class struggle, as Silko demonstrates how certain versions of Marxist practice might themselves be complicit in underwriting Third World oppression. Challenging Bartolomeo's repudiation of nationalism and tribalism as regressive, La Escapia proceeds to inventory the genocidal crimes against American Indians since 1510, her almanac of the dead, citing the figures of each successive holocaust in order to educate her people who "were not in the habit of looking at the 'bigger picture.'" This "bigger picture," Silko's Native American figuration of the Marxist concept of totality (which is also figured in the Hopi's method of "holistic healing"), reveals not only the necessity of nationalism but the validation of nationalism from the perspective of a Marxist historical materialist method.[26]

Certainly the novel constitutes a political epic in the way it features and ties together the various yet related plots of the revolutionary self-organization of the homeless, of the struggles of eco-warriors, AIDS activists, and Vietnam veterans, of national liberation and anti-imperialist movements, and of striking workers. Silko however, privileges and situates firmly in the center as the organizing principle of these struggles the Third World nationalist anti-imperialist movement led by the Hopi leader, a holistic healer whose title signifies his ability to think in terms of totality: "One strategy the Hopi had emphasized had been the 'international coordinated effort.' The Hopi had traveled to Africa and Asia; he had been around the world to meet with indigenous tribal people." Politically, Silko puts into a fuller domestic and global context the significance and necessity of Native American and Third World cultural national struggle in relation to the international class struggle. While she stresses that "a nation is coming! a nation is coming!", this national liberation movement is not separate from the uninterrupted class struggle but simply a necessary and integrated phase. This vision of the uninterrupted class struggle as incorporating anti-imperialist national liberation movements is articulated in the worldview of her character La Escapia who believes "change was on the horizon all over the world. The dispossessed people of the earth would rise up and take back lands that had been their birthright, and these lands would never again be held as private property, but as lands belonging to the people forever to protect." It is a Native American cultural vision, however, that Silko figures as a viable model for the development of new social relations, as she writes that "there would be plenty of space, plenty of pasture and farmland and water for everyone who promised to respect all beings and do no harm."[27]

Gunn Allen is certainly right that Silko takes risks in revealing sacred elements of Native American culture, but Silko's writing suggests that her goal is not the protection of cultural secrets but rather the publication of them precisely because those "secrets" can provide a possible basis for the invention or construction of a new cultural orientation in the U.S. and globally. As is clear in *Almanac of the Dead*, Silko risks the national security of her particular identity group with the hope of restoring that broader Third World solidarity that politically and culturally united the diverse U.S. racial populations in the 1960s.

Indeed, this hope is also mirrored in Alejandro Morales' recent novel *The Brick People*. While this novel provides a fictional rendering of the history of Mexican labor and (im)migration in California, thus tracing the historical process underwriting the development of Chicano identity, it also diagnoses the dangers of constructing that identity too narrowly such that it might become politically entrapping and immobilizing. In an early scene in the novel, for instance, Morales depicts a massacre of Chinese immigrant workers in which Mexican workers participated with Anglos. This historical scene cautions against a restrictive and inflexible sense of racial and national identity which would discourage alignment with other racially oppressed and exploited peoples who might share common interests and which would thus work counter-productively to those very political interests which an historically based national identity formation is meant to anchor, clarify, and direct. One of the predominant thematics of *The Brick People* is the need for a broader Third World and working class coalition to challenge racial oppression and class exploitation on a global basis, as indicated in an early passage in which Joseph Simons worries about the possibility of labor unrest in his brickyard given the emergence of social movements across the globe. Morales writes,

> In different parts of the world social movements threatened to destroy established world powers. Brown men nibbled at portions of the British and Spanish colonies. In the United States, a unionism became stronger and urged labor to fight for pay and improved working conditions. Unions and radical socialists compared the situation of exploited workers in Latin America, Africa, and Asia to laborers in the United States and urged people to guard against unjust treatment.[28]

This passage, as well as the novel as a whole, can be read as a gesture against the splintering of racial identity groups which were once politically united as a Third World liberation front.

As expressed in Morales' worldview, nationalism finally cedes to, transcends itself into, an internationalism that gives birth to a new cultural orientation through the connection and combination of related working-class and national liberation struggles. The process that Silko and Morales describe echoes Fanon's words which validate the nationalist agenda from an internationalist perspective. He writes,

> The struggle itself in its development and in its internal progression sends culture along different paths and traces out entirely new ones for it. The struggle for freedom does not give back to the national culture its former value and shapes; this struggle which aims at a fundamentally different set of relations between men cannot leave intact either the form or the content of the people's culture. After the conflict there is Not only the disappearance of colonialism but also the disappearance of the colonized man.[29]

Indeed, like Dubois's color-line, the borders of the nation, whether imagined in cultural form or mapped in legalistic terms, cannot be leapt over in the class struggle. The colonized author will always stumble--and historically has stumbled--into a recognition of the unevenness of the global economic landscape that produces the Third World. Richard Wright attempted to promote this recognition for other African American writers in his 1937 landmark literary manifesto "Blueprint for Negro Writing," as he observed that "the nationalist character of the Negro people is unmistakable. Psychologically this nationalism is reflected in the whole of Negro culture, and especially in folklore." But while Wright's piece was intended to encourage and direct literary production toward developing, defining, and fomenting this sense of national consciousness, the vision of the manifesto proposed nationalism as only a necessary stage toward achieving the final internationalist solution. "Negro writers must accept the nationalist implications of their lives," Wright continues, "not in order to encourage them, but in order to transcend them. They must accept the concept of nationalism because, in order to transcend it, they must *possess* and *understand* it."[31] For Wright, nationalism is necessary from a cultural perspective because it provides the context, the conditions of possibility, for African Americans to speak and be heard in their own words and forms.

Nationalism, this essay has attempted to demonstrate in following the intellectual tradition of Fanon and Wright, is a way of opening up communication precisely so that the separatism imposed by white racism can be overcome and a genuine internationalism achieved. In its present form, the dominant U.S. culture, riddled as it is with racist norms and class ideologies, does not offer an attractive cultural destiny to justify assimilationist imperatives. The task for readers and critics must be to promote the recuperation of repressed and alternative cultural models for transforming the dominant U.S. culture and national identity, which means, above all, rediscovering the multiple separate nations within the U.S.

                                                                              Tim Libretti

Notes

[1] Richard Wright. *Native Son*. New York: Harper Collins, 1991, p. 463.
[2] Stokely Carmichael and Charles V. Hamilton. *Black Power: The Politics of Liberation in America*. New York: Vintage, 1967, p. 6.
[3] For discussions of these other U.S. Third World Movements, see, for example, Ward Churchill's *Struggle for the Land: Indigenous Resistance to Genocide, Ecocide, and Expropriation in Contemporary North America*, Monroe, Maine: Common Courage Press, 1993; Carlos Munoz's *Youth, Identity, Power: The Chicano Movement*, New York: Verso, 1989; William Wei's *The Asian American Movement*, Philadelphia: Temple UP, 1993.
[4] James Welch. *Killing Custer*. New York: Penguin, 1994, p. 45.

[5] Cherrie Moraga. *Loving in the War Years*. Boston: South End Press, 1983, p. 110.

[6] Robert Blauner. "Colonized and Immigrant Minorities" in *From Different Shores: Perspectives on Race and Ethnicity in America*. New York: Oxford UP, 1994, p. 149.

[7] *Ibid.*, p. 156-7.

[8] Frantz Fanon. *The Wretched of the Earth*. New York: Grove Press, 1963, p. 210.

[9] *Ibid.*, pp. 247-8.

[10] Blauner, p. 152.

[11] *Ibid.*, p. 157.

[12] Homi Bhabha. "DissemiNation: time, narrative, and the margins of the modern nation" in *Nation and Narration*, ed. by Homi Bhabha. New York: Routledge, 1990, pp. 292-3, 303.

[13] Amilcar Cabral. "National Liberation and Culture" in *Return to the Source*. New York: Monthly Review Press, 1973, p. 42.

[14] Rolando Hinojosa. "The Sense of Place" in *The Rolando Hinojosa Reader*, ed. By Jose Saldivar. Houston: Arte Publico Press, 1985, pp. 19-21.

[15] Cherrie Moraga. *The Last Generation*. Boston: South End Press, 1993, p. 171.

[16] Rolando Hinojosa. *Klail City*. Houston: Arte Publico Press, 1987, p.10.

[17] Rolando Hinojosa. *The Valley*. Houston: Arte Publico Press, 1983, p. 78.

[18] Hinojosa, 1987, p. 30.

[19] E. San Juan, Jr. *Racial Formations/Critical Transformations: Articulations of Power in Ethnic and Racial Studies in the United States*. New Jersey: Humanities Press, 1992, p. 5.

[20] Hinojosa, 1987, pp. 70-71.

[21] *Ibid.*, pp. 38-9.

[22] *Ibid.*, p. 16.

[23] Welch, p. 45.

[24] Paula Gunn Allen. "Special Problems in Teaching Leslie Marmon Silko's *Ceremony*" in *American Indian Quarterly*, Fall 1990, XIV: 4, pp. 379, 383-4.

[25] Fanon, p. 247.

[26] Leslie Marmon Silko. *Almanac of the Dead*. New York: Penguin, 1991, pp. 525-526, 530.

[27] *Ibid.*, pp. 731, 724, 532, 518.

[28] Alejandro Morales. *The Brick People*. Houston: Arte Publico Press, 1992, pp. 16-17.

[29] Fanon, pp. 245-246.

[30] Richard Wright. "Blueprint for Negro Writing" in *The Richard Wright Reader*, ed. by Michel Fabre. New York: Harper and Row, 1978, pp. 41-2.

8

WHAT GOD HAS PUT ASUNDER:
THE POLITICS OF ETHNIC BARRIERS IN
CHUKWUEMEKA IKE'S *TOADS FOR SUPPER* AND
ISIDORE OKPEWHO'S *THE LAST DUTY.*

I

One of the controversial figures in Nigeria's turbulent politics, Emeka Odumegwu-Ojukwu[1], once observed in an interview that "the beginning of wisdom in Nigeria is ... the handshake across the Niger" (*The News* 36). This assertion aptly foregrounds the reality of a deep divide in the polity. The "Niger" is more than just a "river" and a natural physical barrier in the context of ethno-political relationship Ojukwu speaks in, and about. The Niger territorializes. For to some Nigerians who are convinced about ethnic purity, difference and territoriality, the River Niger seems to suggest God's own immutable declaration of boundaries - not only physical boundaries but also cultural and socio-psychological boundaries. For them, this declaration needs only to be hallowed and not transgressed by any form of crossing or mixing. In other (transgressive) words, no man should join together what God has put asunder!.

The metaphor of "handshake" (interaction, co-operation, co-existence) therefore is transgressive to a conservative view of ethnic (id)entities. The "handshake" is an attempt to demolish the Berlin wall (another metaphor of territorialization and difference) of ethnic (dis)(crimi)nations - the dissonance it engenders (ideologically speaking), the *criminality* of oppositionality (ethically speaking) and the chauvinism of ethnic nationalism within the modern pluri-ethnic nation. To expand the last point made above, ethnic territorialization could itself be seen as a form of transgression against the mega-nation that has emerged as a product of (Western) colonialism, just as the mega-nation transgresses against the micro-nations by forcing them back into membership, identifying their "self-determi/nations" as rebellions. Indeed, as Peter

Hitchcock has argued, "there is no identity that is not always already transgressed, if not transgressive" (1).

Nigeria emerged as a colonial "bastard" - indeed the name was suggested by a British woman, referred to by Chinua Achebe as Lord Lugard's "girl-friend" (Achebe 6) - it was conceived by the unholy spirit of colonialism, and was born of a colonial virgin! The British merely brought together about 250 ethnic groups, which hitherto existed as separate and independent nations, for their own administrative convenience. They also encouraged ethnicity, as Okwudiba Nnoli has argued in *Ethnic Politics in Nigeria*, as a divide-and-rule strategy (112-113). As long as the different ethnic groups were made to take greater pride in their separate (id)entities and also to discriminate along ethnic lines, British colonial presence was thought to be safe.

The point then is that ethnic discrimination in Nigeria is deeply rooted in Nigeria's colonial history. In the post-colonial period, Nigeria has not been able to achieve political stability primarily due to ethnicity and ethnocentrism which were greatly nurtured in the colonial cradle. Rulership of the country has been greatly ethnicized, and military interventions have also helped in consolidating inter-ethnic prejudices and conflicts. The country fought a thirty-month civil war in which "ethnic security", "ethnic domination", "ethnic rebellion", etc, were among the key words. To the Nigerian (Federal) side of the war, "To keep Nigeria one is a task that must be done", while on the Biafran side, Biafrans were fighting for "self-determination" and "survival".

Even in the current annulment of the June 12, 1993 presidential election in which Chief, M.K.O. Abiola, a Yoruba man, was believed to have won, the major issue has been ethnicity. Many supporters of Chief Abiola, particularly in the Western and Eastern part of Nigeria, have alleged that the annulment was not necessarily an attempt by the Nigerian military to hold on to power, but to protect Hausa-Fulani hegemony in the rulership of the country, or to prevent ethnic groups other than the Hausa-Fulani from producing the President of the country. They have claimed that Chief Abiola took General Babangida by surprise, for the latter had thought that Alhaji Tofa, Abiola's opponent in the presidential race and a candidate of the Hausa-Fulani, would win. The ethnic dimension in the "June 12 Crisis" in Nigeria seems to be further indicated by the fact that three years after the annulment, the agitation for de-annulment has died down in the Middle Belt and in the Eastern part of the country, but is still strong in the Yoruba states in the Western part.

At the socio-cultural level too, inter-ethnic co-operation has been low. Interethnic marriages in Nigeria are still very low. Each ethnic group tries to preserve its own purity and separateness, in spite of the subversive pressures from Christianity, formal (Western) education, and urban exposures.

Also at elitist circles, one can still find ethnically-oriented discriminatory practices, verbal stereotyping and abuse of other ethnic groups, etc. Nigeria's ethno-plurality has therefore not been exploited towards producing the kind of pluri-cultural strengths one would ideally expect from the post-colonial context.

Thus, to link up with the semiotic of the Niger, we note that Ojukwu actually has in mind a co-operation between Yoruba and Igbo ethnic groups that have been maintaining regional dominance on both sides of the Niger, and whose interests have been clashing at the federal level. Indeed, their inter-ethnic conflicts and prejudices were intensified, following the collaboration of the Yoruba with the Hausa-Fulani (of the North) in fighting against the Igbo-led Biafran secession. Thus the River Niger appears to be a signifier of ethno-territoriality for the Yorubas and the Igbos.

There are, indeed, not only physical River Nigers in Nigerian interethnic relations, but also *psychological* River Nigers which ethnic persons have to deal with in their inevitable cross-ethnic interactions. In the same vein, some Nigerian creative writers have also had to deal with the subject of interethnic relations in Nigeria in their works. But, generally, ethnic discrimination appears to be a zone where angels fear to tread; it is not a favorite theme for many Nigerian writers, even though it is an evident social problem in the polity. The avoidance of the theme, which is probably due to security reasons mainly, is itself eloquent; it speaks of the handicap of written literature as an important medium of social discourse and narration of an ethnically divided nation. Individual writers may fear for their security and would not want to be seen as threatening the "face" wants (Goffman) of any ethnic group, either directly or indirectly, since creative writing is part of the construction of social relationships and positionings.

On the other hand, writers in pluri-ethnic societies face the same type of problem that politicians face, namely: their acceptance as *authentic* voices. A writer could lose audience (or part of the audience) by positioning herself or himself as being ethnically conscious. Already, they, as writers in the Nigerian context may, as a result, not have their works recommended for class-room study by some ethnically-minded professors, or may even be given critical acclaim simply because they are perceived as being voices or representatives of their (different) ethnic groups. For some of these writers, therefore, ethnic discrimination is a very sensitive theme especially in a deeply divided country like Nigeria. For them, whether the theme is "a sleeping dog" or one that is awake, a better response is to let it lie.

Some Nigerian writers have, however, handled the subject of ethnic discrimination, its processes and repercussions on the individual and on interpersonal/ intergroup relationships, in their works. For example, Chukwuemeka Ike and Isidore Okpewho have presented ethnic discrimination in their respective novels, *Toads for Supper* and *The Last Duty*. The literary postures and strategies these writers have adopted in interrogating ethnic discrimination (as an aberrant social behavior) deserve critical attention. There is also the need to examine the implications of such postures and strategies for "face" and also discuss the problem of the avoidance of "face-threatening."

Furthermore, both novelists juxtapose the theme of ethnicity with other sensitive themes, for instance, racism. Questions raised by such juxtapositioning for instance include: How does ethnic discrimination relate to, or explain, racial discrimination in *Toads for Supper?* Also, how does ethnicity as a theme modify the writers' thematization of sexual politics (since the novels also deal with male-female relationships)?

Generally, too, what are the relevance of the novels as narrations of a (deeply) divided post-colonial nation? Is ethnic discrimination reducible to ethnic dis/crimi/nation in the two novels, and how successful is the project of deterritorialization in both novels?

II

Ellis Cashmore, writing in *Dictionary of Race and Ethnic Relations*, rightly points out that ethnicity or ethnic awareness, in some cases "can be actively promoted to serve immediate purposes", as in the case of the Chicano Movement which was used in fighting exploitation, while in some other cases, "ethnicity may be, as Sandra Wallman put it, an utter irrelevance or a crippling liability". For Cashmore, therefore, "Emphasizing or exaggerating cultural differences may not only distinguish a group from the rest of a population, but also incur the wrath of the wider society" (99). The foci of Ike and Okpewho in their novels under study are on the negative complications created by ethnicity and ethnocentrism. Ethnicity, which correlates with group interest, is presented in the novels as undermining personal interests and/or needs for existence. It crushes the desire for fulfillment and self-assertion, especially when such desire subverts the "inward-looking" nature of ethnocentrism, (Nnoli 6).

In *Toads for Supper*, ethnicity and ethnocentrism orchestrate a tragic end to desire for a cross-ethnic marriage between Amadi Chukwuka (an Igbo man) and Aduke Olowu (a Yoruba lady), while in *The Last Duty*, they play a significant role in destroying Oshevire's cross-ethnic marriage, and even Oshevire himself, in a time of an ethno-based civil war. Thus, readers are flung back to the age-old socio-philosophical problem of conflict between society and the individual which Ralph Waldo Emerson wittily addresses when he says, in his essay, "Self-Reliance", the "society everywhere is in conspiracy against the manhood of every one of its members" (34). Amadi, a young undergraduate, finds himself wrestling against the voice of ethnocentricity which demands that he marry Nwakaego, the lady imposed on him by his parents. Ethnocentrism, as a cultural voice, abrogates Amadi's (individual) desire not to be imposed upon, or what Lim and Bowers refer to as "autonomy face" (420). To be sure, this voice is heard in the verbal interactions involving some Igbo characters, for instance Chima, another undergraduate, as could be seen in the sample below:

> Come on, Amadi, don't sound so mysterious. Who is she, if you know her? She's Miss Aduke Olowu. What? Miss Olowu? If it's juju, may it not infect me!'. The sudden change baffled Amadi. `Why?' he asked.
>
> Is that the girl who, I hear, is giving you sleepless nights?'. As Amadi tried to answer Chima went on: `My friend this is the University of Southern Nigeria and you are a Freshman. Like a chicken transported to a strange environment, you should stand on one leg till you are sure of your ground'. But I still don't understand'. Chima looked towards Macaulay Has as to make certain that Miss Olowu was not eavesdropping. `Let me act the matter neatly like a scarf. *That girl is Yoruba, you are Ibo* (sic). *The Twain cannot meet*'. Do you mean a Yoruba girl and an Igbo boy cannot be friends?'. I am not speculating. No such thing has happened on the campus of this university since I arrived, and that's about two years now. On the contrary, there have been many woeful failures...'
> (*Toads* 9 - 10, emphasis added).

The-twain-cannot-meet ideology is an assertion of primordial sentiment, an expression of the psychology of the *homo hostilis* (Sam Keen) which operates on the paranoid binarity of "Us" versus "Them". Ojukwu has located this ethno-paranoia in Nigerian interethnic relations:

> Tribalism, as a social philosophy, is based on the construction of a series of imaginary boundaries which establish the `us' and the `them' dichotomy. Based on this dichotomy, ethnic group assumes then an appreciate aggressive posture towards `them' beyond the so-called boundary. It is the persistence of this boundary in our actions and in our reflexes that fosters tribalism in Nigeria.
> (*Because I am Involved* 19).

Chima, though an undergraduate, has acquired ethnic prejudice as a form of culture, and so speaks from the ethno-cultural abundance of his heart. Prejudice is a psychological problem, as Keen has argued in *Faces of the Enemy*.

Note also that this ethnic prejudice may invoke other forms of culture to legitimize itself; for instance Chima in the quote from *Toads* above postures as a cultural sage by using an Igbo proverb, "Like a chicken transported to a strange environment ..." ("*Okuko* e wetara *ohuru* na-eji otu *o*kpa akw*uru*") or (A domestic fowl brought (to a place) newly stands on one leg"). Chima suggests himself as one schooled (properly) in the cultural/folk wisdom of the Igbos, as somebody whose advice is reliable. In other words, the use of Igbo proverb is a credibility or testimonial tactic in the discourse, and it makes Chima a speaker of the culture and its discriminations. As Edward Said, in fact, says, "culture is a system of discriminations and evaluations... it also means that culture is a system of exclusions" (II). The Igbo ethno-culture is presented by Chima's voicing as a distancing of the Yoruba, not just physically, but mentally (excluding Aduke, a Yoruba, from Amadi's affection). In other words, forestalling the "handshake" across the Niger.

Indeed, the ethnocentric voice is not only heard from Chima, it is also presented by the novelist as a psychological presence which Amadi must deal with:

> Amadi!' called his mother. `Write that thing you are writing quickly and get ready. You know it is today that Nwakaego's people are coming to say welcome to you'.

> Oh!' grunted Amadi. He flung the unaddressed envelope on the ground and fell like an understuffed pillow on his bed. You have been caught red-handed', a voice inside him told him sympathetically. `I have always warned you that no man aware of the hazards of blindness rushes into things with his eyes wide open. I have warned you that no sensible man carrying a whole elephant on his head joins in hunting crickets. You have now been caught. But it's not too late to mend. That is, if you are prepared to mend your ways. That letter to Aduke does not show that you are'.

> his head joins in hunting crickets. You have now been caught. But it's not too
> late to mend. That is, if you are prepared to mend your ways. That letter to
> Aduke does not show that you are'.
>
> He shut his eyes tight, but he could not think. He picked up the
> unaddressed letter, looked at it for some seconds and tore it to shreds (*Toads*
> 49).

The voice, which again uses Igbo proverbs ("*no* man aware of .... no *sensible* man
carrying a whole elephant...) aligns with enthnofolk wisdom: It seems to suggest the
stiff opposition of ethnic voice to Amadi's independent thought and action. He still
finds it difficult to suppress this voice or to act against its dictates, i.e. to subvert
ethnocentric psyche.

The voice intimidates him with the negation device used in the proverbs - "*no*
man", *no* sensible man" - showing how unreasonable and deviant he (Amadi) is
becoming. The addition of the word "sensible" suggests that Amadi is acting
unreasonably or senselessly, hence Amadi's embarrassment and repentance (tearing
of the letter he has written to Aduke).

The dominance of this voice over Amadi's own voice is seen in the control the
former wishes to exercise ("I have always *warned* you ...", "I have *warned* you ...").
Warning is a power-oriented act, and is normally appropriated by the High over the
Low, by the Law over the Subject. Amadi's subjectivity and subjection to ethnic
prejudice is therefore being secured.

The washing of the semen-stained pajamas at the Ike Kute stream by Amadi
acquires a symbolic status:

> Amadi was the only person that morning in the stream. As he washed
> the pyjamas, his mind wandered back to Aduke. *He decided to wash her too out
> of his thoughts.* Before removing his covering cloth to have a bath, he held the
> pyjamas at eye level to make sure there was *no trace left of Aduke* (***Toads* 51**).

In his dream, he had made love to Aduke, hence the semen stain on the pyjamas.
The love for Aduke thus remains a dream, a dream which transgresses on ethno-
cultural dream. Aduke is now symbolized as a "parch", a phallic stain on Amadi's
mind, and he tries to wash "her" off. This (negative) image also shows ethnic
prejudice at one level as causing a frustration of desire. The stream water now
washes off "Aduke" and Amadi also takes a bath in it, as if to wash off his "leprosy"

just like Naaman did in the Bible (2 Kings 5:14). Ironically, the stream (the stream of ethno-culture) has been nicknamed "Ike Kute" ("{only} the strong is able to fetch") - "The stream had been given the name *Ike Kute*, as only the strong could return from it with water" (51) - for the path leading to the stream was very slippery. It is therefore suggestively a stream of difficulty, of cross-ethnic difficulty in the Amadi-Aduke case.

The voice of ethnic discrimination eventually triumphs, or rather succeeds, in destroying the Amadi-Aduke relationship, and consequently, in destroying Amadi and Aduke psychologically. This destruction suggests the loss suffered by two ethnic groups as a result of their mutual conflict and prejudice.

The novel also highlights another dimension of ethnic discrimination that is indeed very crucial to a fuller understanding of the social problem particularly in its presence in Nigeria. This dimension is the linguistic/ cultural. Attention has already been called to the coalescence of folk wisdom and the voice of ethnocentricity above. Apart from this, however, we have a significant underscoring of the perception of ethnic barriers as operating at the level of language (and cultural) difference. One of the difficulties encountered by Amadi at Ilesha when he goes to disclose his intention to marry Aduke is his being a non-speaker of Yoruba. This, in addition to his lack of knowledge of other Yoruba cultural behavior (for instance prostrating to elders) rouses hostility against him as an "outsider". Language is one of the instruments often used in consolidating perceptions of ethnic difference (Cashmore 98 - 99) and it has been especially so in the African context (Nnoli 5).

Also, we have some other forms of linguistic ethnic distancing and estrangement in *Toads*. The Yoruba characters, for instance, refer to Igbo characters as "kobokobo" (inferior person) (186). This a form of negative stereotyping or labeling (or verbal devaluation) which are sometimes used by ethnic persons in Nigeria in alienating and expressing disgust for people from other ethnic groups. For further examples, we can sometimes hear the Igbos refer to the Yorubas as "Ndi Ofe Mman*u*" (Those who cook oily soup), or to the Efik - Ibibio as "Ndi imi nk*i*ta (Dog-nose people) or "Mmono" (a mimicry that suggests the vulgarity of the language, or the language as the language of the uncivilized); or the Efik - Ibibio refer to the Igbos as "Unene" (people who are dominance-oriented), etc. These aspects of verbal hostility show the depth of ethnic divide in the Nigerian polity. Labeling enhances territorialization and exclusivization (St. Clair 55), which are important subject matters Okpewho, like Ike, also addresses.

In *The Last Duty*, Okpewho fictionalizes the Nigerian civil war which was partly a war of interethnic conflict, with the Igbo-led Biafra fighting the federal side (led by the Hausa-Fulani and the Yoruba). In *The Last Duty*, Okpewho presents one of the consequences of such a war - the vent given to ethnocentricity, and the plight of families resulting from cross-ethnic marriages. Oshevire is married to a Simba woman, Aku, and the couple live in a border town between the rebel Simba and Igabo. As Ali informs us:

> This is a tribal border town between the Igabo and the rebel Simba. It was quite clear to me that we had to be very careful how we conducted our military duty here. When the federal army liberated this town from the rebels just over three years ago, many Simba people had to flee the town for fear of losing their lives. Time had long ago forged a tie between the two tribes, but I was sure that tempers here would be delicate. (4)

(Civil) war in a multi-ethnic society often intensifies ethnic insecurity. It is not only that ethnic persons naturally develop fear for their security, but also ethnic discriminations and victimizations tend to occur. Indeed, these are what we find in the case of Aku who has had to stay back with her husband among the Kweke (her husband's ethnic group), when members of her own ethnic group who are regarded as "rebels" have withdrawn from the town due to fear of ethnic insecurity. Even though she is married to a Kweke man, she is still seen as an outsider, a "rebel". That negative label "rebel" generates hostile attitudes towards her in the town. As long as the Kweke persons are concerned, she is one of the "enemies", principally because her ethnic group, Simba, is at war with the federal Igabo. This could be gleaned from her report:

> I can hardly walk on the streets, can hardly even venture to the market to buy food for my child and me, because *hostile eyes assail me* from all sides and all but tear the heart out of me.
>
> Where can I run, what can I do? If it weren't for the goodness of the federal army commander here, who has warned that nobody should take the law into his hands, where would I be today? If I can no longer go to the market to buy foodstuffs for my child and myself, then how can we survive? *And one day someone asked me if I was buying up food to send to my people! My people? My people?* Very few people in this town ever want to visit my stall and buy things from me. (*The Last Duty* 11; first emphasis is mine).

Okpewho indeed foregrounds this ethnic hostility against Aku by italicizing part of her report that succinctly presents evidence of this ethnic hostility ("*And one day someone.... My people*?"). He wants to show that Aku is particularly disturbed by this awareness of her insecurity. Also her question, "*My people*? *My people*?", draws attention to the reality of the discrimination she faces, for her being identified as being a Simba person even after marriage.

The novelist shows that he is well-informed about the processes of ethnic hostility in Nigeria, particularly as such hostility manifests in crisis moments like the Nigerian Civil War (1967 - 70). Such crisis situations easily turn "friends" to fiends. People easily fall back to ethnic chauvinism. So, even though, as Ali says in sample text four, "Time had long ago forged a tie between the two tribes...." such that they could intermarry, civil war undermines the ties and returns the two tribes to their primordial perceptions of differences and prejudices.

Toje, a rubber merchant, thus uses the opportunity offered by ethnic hostility in the war to state his envy against Oshevire, framing up the charge against him that he is aiding Simba rebels. As a result of this false charge (which resembles the truth, since Oshevire is married to a Simba woman), Oshevire is arrested, and Toje again uses the opportunity offered by his absence to test his potency on Aku, Oshevier's wife. So, a chain of complex relationships emerges from Okpewho's text: civil war in pluri-ethnic society stimulates and intensifies ethnic hostility and discrimination which in turn facilitate opportunism in interpersonal conflicts and sexual violation. In other words, ethnic hostility may need some other (avoidable?) political problems to rouse and intensify it, otherwise time and interaction could minimize it. Also, ethnic hostility and discrimination are reproductive in relation to other socio-political problems (just as war does). This as a model also holds true for the situation in Ike's *Toads* where ethnic discrimination leads or facilitates other problems at the individual and social levels. The only difference in *Toads* is that Ike does not hold ethnic discrimination as a dependent variable as Okpewho does. For Okpewho in *The Last Duty*, ethnic discrimination is not self-existing; it could be linked to other socio-political problems such as war.

III

In what ways is the subject of ethnic discrimination related to other subject matters in the novels such as war, racial discrimination, and sexual politics?

War destroys relationships, apart from the fact that it has to do with relationships, for, as Balandier has observed, war could result when relationships break down in a polity (500 - 501). Ethnic discrimination and hostility are therefore already a kind of "war", metaphorically speaking. In *The Last Duty*, the civil war rouses the spirit of ethnicity. Thus Okpewho may be calling our attention to the thin line separating the actual war from the cold war of ethnic discrimination, and that since both are so related, social engineering in a deeply divided pluri-ethnic society may require that we avoid one problem so as to avoid another, or to subdue another.

In the same vein, women often become the major victims of social problems like ethnic discrimination, especially as they, by virtue of social expectations on marriage, are subjected to men's situations generally. Thus in *Toads*, Aduke suffers psychiatric trauma in the hands of Amadi who also finds himself in the hands of ethnocentricity, while in *The Last Duty*, Aku suffers psychologically from her husband's absence and sexual starvation, as well as from Toje's impotent sexual experiments with her. Aku is not only alienated but also violated as a woman. In both novels, the agency of man in both ethnic discrimination and sexual abuse is very clearly suggested. Indeed, man is also a sufferer, but a sufferer of what he has caused or has failed to subdue, and as well a sufferer who makes the woman (as the Other) a co-sufferer (in other words, man is paradoxically a patient-agent).

In terms of the connection with racial discrimination, it is only in *Toads* that both discriminations (ethnic and racial) are juxtaposed, and for strategic reasons. The Nigerian characters in the novel express their dissatisfaction and disgust with colonial presence and domination. Again, Chima, who postures as an agent of ethnic discrimination, also attacks white racism (*Toads* 17). A paradox is therefore suggested by Ike - that one who is guilty of discrimination attacks another form of discrimination! In other words, Chima does not (attempt to) remove the "log" in his own eyes before attempting to remove the speck in the white colonialist's eyes. Ethnocentrism and racism are closely related as social vices. Just as the European colonialists derogate and discriminate against Nigerians in the university, so do Nigerian ethnocentric persons relate with their fellow Nigerians from other ethnic groups. So, although racism and ethnicity may be conceptually different, they have similar negative effects on society.

IV

Apart from this relationship of ethnic discrimination to other related subject matters in the novels, what are the literary postures and strategies adopted by Ike and Okpewho in their handling of this very delicate subject, and what are the implications of such postures and strategies for face?.

Both Ike and Okpewho use forms of indirectness in presenting ethnic discrimination since the subject matter is a very sensitive one and they have to deal with historical and cultural settings. In the first place, the narratives are presented as fictions. Okpewho in the opening page of *The Last Duty* marks the fictionality of the narrative by warning, "This story is *all* fiction" (his own emphasis). Thus he invokes security as a text producer, *disarming* readings of the text that may prejudice people against himself (i.e. seeking immunity against censorship). The security of creative writers who dwell on social problems, as we have seen in the Salman Rushdie case, is indeed very crucial.

There are in both novels subtle exploitations of certain elements that surface particularly in discourse on ethnic relations in Nigeria. We have already noted the use of stereotypes and/or negative labels by the characters, which we also find in ethnic conflict in Nigeria. In addition to this, Okpewho refers to slogans, like "To keep Zonda one is a task that must be done" (19), which helps in locating the theme of ethnicity in Nigeria's history of conflict. Clearly, this is an allusion to the common slogan on the federal side of the Nigerian civil war - "To keep *Nigeria* one is a task that must be done". But the substitution of "Nigeria" with "Zonda" makes the fictional difference clear (The-difference-is-clear!). Thus, we can guess the historical context Okpewho is writing about, but if we choose to re-substitute "Zonda" with "Nigeria", that is our own transgression, not Okpewho's! The point then is that "the resemblance between historical and fictional experiences is an aspect of the meaning-making process which an audience is invited to participate in" (Oha 5).

Ike does a similar thing with his substitution of "University of Ibadan" with "University of Southern Nigeria" (*Toads* 9). There is no University of Southern

Nigeria, and there has never been one. Ike is just using the alternative name to keep within the ambience of fictionality. The fictionalization tactic has implications for the face wants of the novelists and the ethnic groups brought into the narratives. It saves face (at the surface level) for both novelists, while at the deep level the ethnic groups criticized would feel that their "fellowship face" wants (Lim and Bowers 420) have been threatened. But certainly no obvious charge could be brought against the novelists as threatening ethnic face.

In the case of Ike, the portraiture of ethnic discrimination from an Igbo angle (i.e. with Igbo characters as major authors of ethnic barrier) again appears to suggest the novelist, who is also an Igbo man, as being fair and self-critical. It is as if he is saying that (un)charity begins at home! It would have made a great difference for readership, particularly the non-Igbo readership, than if Ike had made the Yoruba characters more *culpable* (!) in the practice of ethnic discrimination. Thus, the slanting of the narrative justifies its authenticity and saves face for Ike, though not quite for his ethnic group.

Okpewho, on the other hand, pluralizes the narrative in the postmodern tradition, making it possible for a heteroglossic discourse to ensue. All the characters *talk* to the readers in a very confessional way. Thus the authorship is further fictionalized and pluralized. This enables Okpewho to maintain a greater distance from *his* text, almost tempting us to believe Roland Barthes' notion of the "death" of the author.

V

The two novels, as narrations of an ethnically divided nation, have a lot of relevance, not only to our better understanding of the processes and consequences of ethnicity and ethnocentrism, but also in signifying the measure of success that could be registered in the engineering of the pluri-ethnic society through literary techniques of indirectness. The persistence of the perceptions of boundaries among ethnic groups in Nigeria requires more than political and military solutions. These "solutions", which occur in such forms as crushing of ethnic rebellions (the de-biafranizations), placating of ethnic gods, etc, do not exorcise the ethnic demons. But literary narratives on ethnocentricity are capable of confronting readers in their closets with the evils, the criminality, of ethnic discrimination. Such narratives with their rhetorical postures could produce knowledge, even from transgressive inclinations, that would subvert ethnocentric narrations of the pluri-ethnic nation. Okpewho and Ike, have indeed shown in their novels that, whereas African nations have addressed the issue of racism that colonization played with, there is now a more urgent need to address the issue of ethnic discrimination which has greatly undermined the search for post-colonial peace, stability and security. Victories of decolonization amount to failure in the long run if Western colonialism is outlived by interethnic hostility. For what colonization is greater than that which puts a barrier between one group and another, or which makes one group enslaved to ideas of its own purity and difference?

Obododimma Oha

Notes

[1] Emeka Odumegwu Ojukwu was the leader of the Biafran secession from 1967 to 1970. He is now back into politics in Nigeria.

Works Cited

Achebe, Chinua. *The Trouble With Nigeria.* Enugu: Fourth Dimension Publishers, 1990.

Balandier, G. "An Anthropology of Violence and War". *International Social Science Journal,* XXXVIII. 4 (1986): 499-511.

Barthes, Roland. "The Death of the Author". *Image-Music-Text.* Trans. Stephen Heath. Glasgow: Fontana/Collins, 1979.

Cashmore, Ellis E. *et al., Dictionary of Race and Ethnic Relations* (2nd Edition). London: Routledge, 1992.

Emerson, Ralph Waldo. "Self-Reliance". *Selected Essays.* United States of America: Best Loved Classics, n.d.

Goffman, Erving. *Interaction Ritual: Essays in Face-to-Face Behaviour.* Chicago: Aldine Publishing Co., 1967.

Hitchcock, Peter. "Passing: Henry Green and Working Class Identity". *Modern Fiction Studies,* 40.1 (Spring 1994): 1 - 31.

Ike, Chukwuemeka Vincent. *Toads for Supper* (13th Impression). Glasgow: Fontana/Collins, 1980.

Keen, Sam. *Faces of the Enemy: Reflections of the Hostile Imagination.* San Francisco & New York: Harper & Row, 1986.

Lim, Tae-Seop and John Waite Bowers. "Facework: Solidarity, Approbation and Tact". *Human Communication Research,* 17.3 (1991) 415 - 450.

Nnoli, Okwudiba. *Ethnic Politics in Nigeria.* Enugu: Fourth Dimension Publishers, 1978.

Odumegwu-Ojukwu, Emeka. *Because I Am Involved.* Ibadan: Spectrum Books Limited, 1989.

_____. Interview with Susan Bassey and Seye Kehinde. *The News,* 22 February (1993): 32 - 36.

Oha, Obododimma. "Discourse Strategies in Isidore Okpewho's *The Last Duty*". A Paper Presented at a Symposium in Honour of Professor Isidore Okpewho, Draper's Hall, University of Ibadan, November 9, 1991.

Okpewho, Isidore. *The Last Duty.* Essex: Longman, 1983.

Said, Edward. *The World, The Text,* and *The Critic.* London: Faber, 1984.

St. Clair, Robert N. "The Politics of Language". *Word,* 29.1 (April 1978): 44 - 62.

9

EAST/WEST PARADIGMS OF HISTORY AND FICTION: JOY KOGAWA'S *OBASAN* AND SKY LEE'S *DISAPPEARING MOON CAFE*

The ongoing problematization of historical knowledge in contemporary fiction has unveiled historiographic practice as an ideological strategy to maintain Western (and male) positions of centrality and domination over other temporal, spatial, cultural, and sexual entities. In the new spectrum designed by these texts, history becomes by definition a hybrid discursive formation, susceptible thus, like any other such formation, to de/re/construction, and specially, to (meta)fictional incorporations. On the one hand, the narrativization of the process of historical reconstruction addresses the question of historical and literary representation, drawing the reader's attention to the fictional (constructed) character of what we call 'reference' in both. On the other hand, historical intertextuality also underlines the function of context, as the material--geographical, historical, linguistic--text within which novels are written and read, often revealing a "complex knot of shifting subjectivities that haunt narratives of dislocation in time and space" (Bartkowski 1993, 171).

This essay offers a discussion of the ways in which Joy Kogawa's *Obasan* and Sky Lee's *Disappearing Moon Cafe* inscribe the silenced history of the Japanese Canadians and the Chinese Canadians, respectively, in archeological/genelogical modes that disrupt the continuist narrative of Canadian multicultural history. In doing so, these texts also destabilize the opposition between East/West traditional paradigms of identity/location by denouncing the exclusionary bias of historical and cultural definitions of space, and positioning the writing subjects on the margins of Canadian *and* Japanese/Chinese historical narratives. Although marketed for the general public, without specific allusion to their contribution in the making of an Asian Canadian tradition, *Obasan* and *Disappearing Moon Cafe* represent the first two novels ever written in Canada by and about Japanese Canadian and Chinese Canadian authorship, narratorship and story.[i] Bearing in mind the fact that the first immigrants arrived at the Canadian West Coast in the late 19th century, the almost absence of Asian Canadian texts up to the 1970s seems to prove how well these communities interiorized the historical silence imposed upon them.

All the Asian immigrants who began to come to Canada around the second half of the 19th century encountered a wall of silence and white xenophobia (see Ward 1990b). Whereas the Japanese were classified under the more aggressive "stereotype B," criticized for "aping their betters," the Chinese were considered rather harmless, and thus fell into "steretype A," characterized as "knowing their place" (qtd. in Kim 1982, 123). As we will see, the fictions of Kogawa and Lee replicate exactly these two discursively constructed Others; yet they do so by setting the stereotypes against themselves. Whereas *Obasan* describes a cultural community trying to be assimilated into the "mainstream" of Canadian life, *Disappearing Moon Cafe*'s Chinatown is a separatist enclave, surrounded by the world of "white ghosts," with which the relation is one of mutual hostility (see Brandt 1993). Neither assimilation nor self-ghettoization appears represented as *essential* cultural traits but as counterdiscursive poles to the dominant ethos of white Canada. Ironically, neither option provides these communities with access to the discourses of power.[ii] As a result, they are dispersed (*Obasan*) and ostracized (*Disappearing Moon Cafe*). Thus, although the two novels are rather different from each other in narrative tone, structure, plot, and characterization, they also seem at the same time to join the common project of setting the official discourse of multiculturalism against the impossibility of cultural fluidity.

In order to do so, both *Obasan* and *Disappearing Moon Cafe* interweave personal and communal histories in an interactive mode. Both texts also point to the need to draw on historical data in order to rescue the erased histories of the Japanese Canadians and Chinese Canadians respectively, two interconnected narratives often obliterated by the official history of (white) Canada (see Adachi 1991; Chan 1983). *Obasan*'s stress is set on the dislocation effected by the forced removal, internment and dispersal of all Canadians of Japanese origin after the events of Pearl Harbour.[iii] The novel stages its first-person narrator, Naomi, reading the documents of her own history. The text's processual structure is archeological in that it opens up the site of the official document, with its belief in continuous historical narrative, and identifies the operations of dominant ideology inherent in the discursive manufacturing of events into historical facts. Although Lee's narrator, Kae Woo, is less explicit about her historiographic work, she also seems more self-conscious than Naomi about her role as ethnographer of a non-official culture. Despite the literal search for bones of the Epilogue, *Disappearing Moon Cafe* draws on--as it undermines--a genealogical method, which, set against the history of the Chinese Canadians, traces instead the history of the narrator's descent from the first Chinese who came to Canada. The genealogical structure also underlines the text's emphasis on beginnings, multiple beginnings that configure the story around interruptions of, and departures from, the notion of origin, be this historical or otherwise (see Said 1975). But let us begin with *Obasan*.

The "evacuation," internment and dispersal of the Japanese Canadians, as related in *Obasan* and in historical accounts alike, undermines the logics of the assimilation/unassimilation argument. In times of growing general hysteria (Pearl Harbour), B.C. press and public opinion have recourse indistinctly to one or other guarantee of exclusion of the undesirable Other. Writing in her diary about the pre-evacuation circumstances of the Japanese Canadians, *Obasan*'s Aunt Emily significantly aims at the contradictions and the covert animosity implied in the discourse of racial stereotypes:

> One letter in the papers says that in order to preserve the "British way of life", they should send us all away. We're a "lower order of people". In one breath we are damned for being "inassimilable" and the next there's fear that we'll assimilate. One reporter points to those among us who are living in poverty and says "No British subject would live in such conditions." Then if we improve our lot, another says "There is danger that they will enter our better neighbourhoods." If we are educated the complaint is that we will cease being the "ideal servant". It makes me choke. The diseases, the crippling, the twisting of our souls is still to come. (Kogawa 1983, 87)[iv]

In contrast to official appellations denoting manifest perceptibility (such as "visible minorities"), Kogawa's text is very much about invisibility. The narrative appears as fragmented as the lives of the people that it tells about; its history is not only a history of humiliation and deprivation, but also, and very much so, a history of absences and invisibility: "We grow where we are not seen, we flourish where we are not heard, the thick undergrowth of an unlikely planting" (Kogawa 1983, 226). The victory of the Allies in the Pacific ironically anihilates the possibility of figuring the Japanese Canadian subject. Furthermore, the death of Naomi's mother in the bombing of Nagasaki, a mystery that haunts Naomi's mind throughout the story, links the political implications of historical amnesia, invisibility, and exile across cultures and nations: "The lost mother is thus a trope for the lost racial memory: her exile in Japan during the war, her disfiguration in the Nagasaki holocaust, and the attempt to extinguish her memory through a corresponding conspiracy between Japanese cultural suppression of unacceptable fact and white Canadian oppression of the unacceptable alien" (Lim 1991, 244).

The Nagasaki connection defies thus the binary structure of East/West through the thread of the absent mother, a Kibbei, born in Canada and educated in Japan, and, because of that, crossing over the metaphorical boundaries of culture and nationality. Failing to understand the use of the word "Jap" in the Vancouver papers, Emily writes to her sister: "But over here, they say 'Once a Jap always a Jap', and that means us.[v] We're the enemy. And what about you over there? Have they arrested you because you are Canadian?" (Kogawa 1983, 83). Significantly, the mother is *unrepresented* in the text, thus leaving the task of cultural and ideological negotiation to the daughter, Naomi, a Canadian-born of Japanese origin, for whom the victory of the West brings the stoppage of her process of subject formation: "Time solidifies, ossifies the waiting into molecules of stone, dark microscopic planets that swirl through the universe of my body waiting for light and the morning" (66).

Historical reference constitutes the most powerful intertext in *Obasan*. The fictionalization of archival documents in this novel provides the structure of Naomi's confrontation between written an unwritten versions of the past: "There is one telling. It's not how it was" (Kogawa 1983, 197). The questioning not only of the official version of the evacuation, but also of the Nikkei's (generally stated by Nisei, like Aunt Emily, intent on *representing* history) determines Naomi's difficult engagement with the notions of historical/fictional (re)construction: "Although this novel is based on historical events, and many persons named are real," we read in the preliminary pages of *Obasan* "most of the characters are fictional"; and, in keeping with the ambiguity of such assertion, the text that follows does not seem to subscribe to the opposition between fact and fiction, but rather reminds the reader of the doings of a post-structuralist deconstruction of such binary thought. In this way, the documents presented, recounting the different government and community actions, are centripetal to the text's (counter)memory (Naomi's text), centrifugally pointing to the impossibility of historical representation. What the novel constructs, then, is not the unifying national referent, on which the hegemonies of History and Nation depend (see Bhabha 1991). It rather points to the clashing constructs of nation and territory, historical reference and historical experience (see Zwicker 1993). For the Japanese Canadians there is neither nation nor territory that they can legitimately inhabit.

Obasan's focus is therefore on unveiling the document as a major tool of legitimization, categorization and demarcation of historical authority. Official history is to be understood here in Foucauldian terms as "one way in which a society recognizes and develops a mass documentation with which it is inextricably linked" (Foucault 1977, 7). Against the unifying force of this history, *Obasan* interposes an archeological reading method which requires a constant redistribution of the documents presented, with the consequent continuous transformation of the general structure of historical narrative. Special importance deserves one such document in *Obasan*, a novel divided into 39 chapters, patterned by the alternation of what we could call political and personal plots, plus an excerpt from the 1946 Memoradum sent to Ottawa by the Co-operative Committee of Japanese Canadians protesting the policy of deportation, with which the book actually closes (Kogawa 1983, 248-250). Dissociated from the narration by being (strategically) placed after the last chapter, the Memorandum unsettles the discontinuous, yet identifiable, narrative thread by subverting the circular (and potentially happy) end of the story, fighting the idea of closure (the illusion of resolution), and interrupting narrative chronology, by going back to the repatriation policy in 1946. Additionally, this document ultimately foregrounds the ongoing play between fact and fiction, leaving the reader with a degree of indecision which destabilizes once more any previous loci of authority, and alerts us, in so doing, to the complexities and paradoxes implicit in the present exercise of revision.

However cathartic the narrator's engagement with language may be, then, the problem of historical reconstruction remains largely unsolved. The words 'exile,' 'violation,' 'discrimination,' 'injustice,' 'hostility,' in the excerpt, unsettle the reader. The force of these signs is diminished by the more powerful discourse of political expediency, but also, ironically, by the document's own belief in representational history: the belief that language can objectively reflect historical facts. Visually confronted with Naomi's story, the reading of the Memorandum reinforces the deconstruction of the notion of mimesis the very novel has enacted, laying bare the fact that the relation between signifier and signified, historical reference and experience, is maintained at the cost of the erasure of other (historical) signs. The

Memorandum, in other words, "omits," Heather Zwicker argues, "the consideration of speech and silence that makes *Obasan* the powerful novel it is" (1993, 91-92).

The function of dominant discourses in disguising historical crimes deserves therefore special attention in *Obasan*. Physical and cultural displacement is effected through the government discursive practices, hiding the ideology of racism behind the impersonal rationality of legal print: "'You know those prisons they sent us?'" Aunt Emily asks Naomi. "'The government called them 'Interior Housing Projects'! With language like that you can disguise any crime'" (Kogawa 1983, 34). The text does not reject history as such, but the discursive practices that make history the logos of a national referent, constructed by opposition to, and thus excluding, a national Other. The authority of such national referent relies on the fictionalization of, and eventual victory over, the Enemy/Other. In *Obasan*, language colonizes and invades the Japanese Canadian "enemy" by means of legitimizing the orders for "evacuation," the forced removal of Japanese Canadians east of the "protected area."

The task of unveiling the rampant contradictions of the government discourse falls partly upon Emily, who singles out Ian Mackenzie's "Volunteer or Else" statement: "All Nisei are liable to imprisonment if we refuse *to volunteer* to leave" (Kogawa 1983, 87; emphasis mine). More radically, it is Naomi's readings of Emily's documents that effects a deconstruction of the official document: Sick Bay, Naomi discovers, is not a beach, and the place called "the Pool" is not a swimming pool, but a prison in Hasting Park's exhibition grounds where Grandma and Grandpa Nakane, along with many other 2000 "Japs pending removal," are treated like the cattle previously there (77-88). The "Repatriation Policy" *depatriates* the Japanese Canadians by stripping them from their Canadian birthrights.[vi]

While language's covert ideology imprints its violence on the text, the deconstruction of institutional discourse, as engaged by Naomi, is nonetheless a salutary action: language succeeds in silencing the Japanese Canadian subject, but also serves to unveil the abuse of discursive power. Take, for instance, the scene in which Naomi reads a passage from a short form letter to Uncle: "... While it is not necessary that this title be available in order to complete the sale it is preferred that it be surrendered to the Registrar of Land Titles. Will you be good enough therefore...." (Kogawa 1983, 36). As the reading is interrupted here, the decontextualized words trace the line of dispossession and dislocation, succesfully concluded by the government with the selling of Japanese Canadian property.

Under the misleading name of "Custodian of Alien Property," the government first confiscates ships, cars, businesses, houses and lands, and then sells them to war veterans, an ultimate *order* which effectively secures *order*, by postponing indefinitely the return of the Japanese Canadians to the West Coast.[vii] Considering the possibility of buying the house back, Naomi writes to the people who live now there, but she gets only silence as reply (50).

Naomi, wary of the traps of representation, and unlike her articulate aunt, locates herself at a distance from the discourse of history. This becomes evident as she bitterly puns on the name of a Custodian, B. Good, who has written a letter to Emily in response to her enquiry about the seizure of the family property: "The Custodian's reply to Aunt Emily must have been the same to anyone else who dared to write. 'Be good, my undesirable, my illegitimate children, be obedient, be servile, above all don't send me any letters of enquiry about your homes, while I stand on guard (over your property) in the true north strong, though you are not free. B. Good'" (Kogawa 1983, 37). The ironic deconstruction of the letter's text subverts national ideology by parodying the patriarchal/patriotic national anthem. Instead, it draws our attention to the erasure of difference by the ethnocentric and unifying tendency of national history (see Jones 1990). A Sansei or third-generation Japanese Canadian, Naomi is often exposed to questions such as: "Do you like our country? You speak such a good English. Do you run a café? My daughter has a darling Japanese friend. Have you ever been back to Japan?" (225).

In contrast to the mimetic function of the government discourse, the broken English of Obasan also defies the notion of correspondence between signifier and signified and subverts the narrative of the nation by identifying its gaps and its sites of powerlessness: "'Here,'" she explains to Naomi the circumstances of Uncle Isamu's death, "'medicine was put in, but--oso katta--it was too late'" (14). The language is indeed "broken as those who speak it have been broken" (Matheson 1984, 6). Naomi herself shows a tendency to broken English when addressing her aunt Obasan or her Uncle Isamu, as if she automatically entered their reality: "Slow can go," she says to Obasan as they climb the stairs to the attic (23), unconsciously reproducing the phrase that, as a child, she received from a native old man.[viii] In this context, Emily's occasional attempt at translating a haiku that Uncle has just recited produces an ironic effect, not only because the haiku words of union are set against the literal separation and dispersal of the Japanese Canadians, but also because the translation is found wanting of syllables: "'As the storm rages ... our drawing closer ... keeps us warm'" (217).

As the translation exercise seems to imply, although Naomi succeeds in articulating her critique of white Canada, the presence of narrative and historical *holes* in the text also obstaculizes the reader's unproblematic arrival at a reassuring *whole* at the end. Despite the evidence of the writing, Naomi, in the 1970s, has not improved in communication skills and sits helplessly wondering "what is it [Mrs Barker] smells?". Mrs. and Mr. Barker are the owners of the beet farm where the family is sent after the end of the war. Twenty-five years later, in the narrative present, Mr. Barker's use of broken English when addressing Obasan sounds grotesque and insulting, as does his condemnation of what Canada did to "our Japanese": "Ah, here we go again. 'Our Indians'. 'Our Japanese'. 'A terrible business'. It's like being offered a pair of crutches while I'm striding down the street. The comments are so incessant and always so well-intentioned" (Kogawa 1983, 225). The use of the possessive pronoun reveals the patronizing drive behind the official policy of multiculturalism as well as the ossification of cultures which such a policy might actually entail (see Iwama 1994). Whether the text effectively imprints the complicities between the discourses of nation and racism, the fundamental question of the Japanese Canadians remains:

> Where do any of us come from in this cold country? Oh Canada, whether it is admitted or not, we come from you we come from you. From the same soil, the slugs and slime and bogs and twigs and roots. We come from the country that plucks its people out like weeds and flings them on the roadside. We grow in the ditches and sloughs, untended and spindly. We erupt in the valleys and mountainsides, in small towns and back alleys, sprouting upside-down on the prairies, our hair wild as spiders' legs, our feet rooted nowhere.... We come from our untold tales that wait for their telling. We come from Canada, this land that is like every land, filled with the wise, the fearful, the compassionate, the corrupt. (Kogawa 1983, 226)

A reworking of the Parable of the Sower (Mark 4: 1-20) with ironic allusions to the national anthem, this passage, nearly at the end of the book, underlines the continuation of gaps in the historical questions *Obasan* asks--gaps embodied by Obasan's dry mouth, open in a "small accepting 'o'" (Kogawa 1983, 245), by the dead mother in Nagasaki, by Uncle's only post-mortem mark of his existence: a yellow I.D. card, #00556, signed by a RCMP inspector (24). The articulation of pain accords the narrative with a narrow, although potentially rich, path towards forgiveness, but does not seem to imply wholeness or reconciliation with historical experience. The text rather remains an elegy for the lost community (see Howells 1990, 94; also Kogawa, 1994, 464).[ix]

If *Obasan* portrays a community vainly trying to be assimilated into Canada's dominant ethos, *Disappearing Moon Cafe* seems particularly interesting in terms of its inverse constructions of the racial Other, in ironic replica of "sterotype A" above. This text locates the self-ghettoizing tendency of her Chinese Canadian family in the succession of head taxes imposed on Chinese immigrants since 1886 and leading to the Exclusion Act of 1923, it also clearly draws the reader's attention to the presence of a reverse racism within.[x] The imprints of this attitude can be found early in the parodic description of Gwei Chang's encounter with the Native Indian woman Kelora: "'But you're a wild injun.' He spilled out the insults in front of her, but they were meaningless to her. In chinese, the words mocked, slanglike, 'yin-chin'" (Lee 1990, 3). Later, Gwei Chang advises Ting An not to marry a "blonde demoness" (232), and promises to get him a "real wife from China": "'Like your real wife from China?' [Ting An] asked. "'Not a dirty half-breed, buried somewhere in the bush?'" (233). Elsewhere, the text exhibits the mark of reverse hostility and spite towards "white ghosts." Mui Lan tells her surprised daughter-in-law about the need to stick together, despite Choy Fuk's life of concubinage, in order to survive in a wilderness inhabited by barbarians (61). Years later, Fong Mei reproduces this kind of discourse when she tells Suzie not to make friends with her white schoolmates: "'The less you see of those white girls, the better off you'll be'" (151).

The line of hostile interracial relations reaches its climax with the murder of Janet Smith, the only white woman, except for brief mentions to Ting An's French Canadian wife, who appears, albeit dead, in *Disappearing Moon Cafe*. In 1924, a white woman is killed under strange circumstances, and the prime suspect is a Chinese houseboy called Wong Foon Sing[xi]: "The first instincts of the chinese told them to board up their businesses and barricade Pender Street, with enough rice and salted fish stockpiled to outlast a siege" (Lee 1990, 70). The Janet Smith episode, apparently disconnected from the other narrative plots, marks the text's (hi)story as it locates the novel within the wider narrative of B.C. animosity against Asian Canadians: "'Yeurr stunkee, yelleer, slimee snake! Marrk me werrds, yee willna' gitawa witit!'" a white woman, jumping out of her car, is reported to have yelled to a Japanese pedlar whose trunk had broken down in the middle of a bridge (71). Hearing reports like this, the community men, gathered around the patriarch in order to discuss the implications of the Janet Smith's murder, recall with fear the incidents of the 1907 riots[xii]: "No more could they say, 'I've seen too much of their white hate,' pack up, sell out and move back like so many others before them. More and more, memories of the old villages had faded into a vague distance, too far to retrace now" (70-71).

Furthermore, the account of the murder episode provides the grounds for tracing internal hostility back to this outside animosity. Menaced by the possibility of retribution to the whole Chinese community, the men of the Chinese Benevolent Association anticipate white aggressivity by indicting their victim, the potential Chinese murderer of a white woman, on all possible charges.[xiii] Torturing Foon Sing's weakening body, the Chinese patriarchs reproduce, from within, the verbal and physical violence which they themselves have been subjected to in the hands of the white Fathers. In doing so, they unwittingly confirm the sinister stereotype, which made white people so uncomfortable in their presence: "These overseas chinese were like derelicts, neither here nor there, not tolerated anywhere; an outlaw band of men united by common bonds of helpless rage. Fuming and foaming, talking just as malevolently, wanting to inflame as if that could appease their own pain!" (Lee 1990, 77).

We have previously seen how *Obasan* contradicts the "visibility" allotted to the Japanese Canadians by official discourse. Rescuing the unofficial history of the losers, *Disappearing Moon Cafe* also thematizes the issue of invisibility in a highly effective way. Gwei Chang difficulty in finding the bones of the Chinese rail workers meaningfully opens *Disappearing Moon Cafe*, his mission being to find and send home the human remains of those "strewn along the Canadian Pacific Railway, their ghosts sitting on the ties, some standing with one foot on the gleaming metal ribbon, waiting, grumbling. They were still waiting as much as half a century after the ribbon-cutting ceremony by the whites at the end of the line, forgotten as chinamen generally are" (Lee 1990, 6).[xiv]

As in *Obasan*, too, the East/West coordinates of history touch directly upon *Disappearing Moon Cafe*, by means of displacing the Chinese Canadian subject onto a permanent position on the margins of both Chinese and Canadian historical narratives. This time, the *original* displacement is enacted by the myth of the golden Western land. Gwei Chang, as many other of his compatriots, leaves his homeland in the belief of making money in this foreign land of plenty, only to find himself strolling down Victoria streets, his mind suffling between a job as a servant and a search-for-bones expedition: "In order to make himself feel better, he began to search the ground, hoping to spot a glimmer of gold in the dirt, convinced that the Gold Mountains weren't a myth at all" (Lee 1990, 6). Later, a letter from Gwei Chang's mother in China interrupts the ephemeral plenty of Gwei Chang's Eden-like life with Kelora, his trip to China and back to Canada again setting a historical pattern of displacement in both countries. As for Mui Lan, waiting with her son to be sent for, she becomes as dis-located as her husband by the line of East/West (dis)connections: "All of them desperately weaving tenuous, invisible threads over the ocean, to cling cobweblike to their men and sons in the Gold Mountains" (26).

Once in Canada, the difficult relations between China and Canada--the events of World War II in both the East and the West of the globe, the developments of the communist regime in China, and the beginning of the Cold War era (see McEvoy 1982)--postpone indefinitely the possibility of undoing the Chinese Canadian historical dislocation. Fong Mei knows that there is no future for her children in Vancouver Tang People's Street. Yet, her plans to transplant her children back into China in 1939 are thwarted by Japan's great advances in the Pacific area, which had began long before that date: "'But who would have thought they'd get so far south?' exclaimed my mother's mother, whose singular pursuit of happiness for her three children had left her perception of history in the making somewhat distorted" (Lee 1990, 140). Fong Mei herself keeps her heart in China, where her beloved sister remains, but her wishes for an eventual return are definitely shattered by the proclamation of the People's Republic in 1949: "I like to imagine Fong Mei as this cold war cartoon character I once saw in a magazine, with no other option than to stand in front of those bamboo curtains, banging her fists on them, with what she didn't realize was an empty suitcase at her side" (167).

The novel negotiates the connections between reconstruction and deconstruction: the enmeshment of historical/literary (re)construction questions the official narrative by denying the assumption of independence between fact and fiction, and implicitly deconstructs any given absolute truth inside or outside the text. Against the rootedness of historical signification, *Disappearing Moon Cafe* inscribes thus a process of self-conscious invention: "I should re-examine my own motives," Kae reflects after having given us an unfavourable portrait of Mui lan. "Why do I need to make this ancestress the tip of the funnelling storm, the pinnacle that anchored chaos and destruction close to earth?" (Lee 1990, 31). Later, in a more challenging tone, Kae cuts her narration with a sudden metafictional discourse that unsettles our relation to the story: "In front of me, there is nothing to speak of except torpid text and a throbbing cursor on a black-and-white computer screen ..." (179). The clues to this (meta)fictionality are found earlier in the text, with Gwei Chang's dream-like account of the expedition: "To believe," the men from the Benevolent Associations tell him, "is to make live! You must make your mission live, or else you will not succeed" (2).

It is the performative function of language and discourses to construct both history and fiction that *Disappearing Moon Cafe* as well as *Obasan* then explore. But, if *Obasan*'s stress rather falls on the unveiling of the historical crimes behind the power of performance, *Disappearing Moon Cafe*, instead, recognizes the principle of performativity from within, exploiting to the limit the possibilities of historical and fictional discourses. This is done by setting the process of historiography against and through a genealogical romance with a partly unsolved whodunit structure. As a result, the questions of fact or fiction, truth or falsity, become in this text largely redundant: "Was his story the same as my story?" Kae wonders, profoundly wary of Morgan's version of family history. "Or should I have said, is history the same as mystery?" (Lee 1990, 66). Morgan's theatrical approach to historical data provides a crucial example of the workings of performance in *Disappearing Moon Cafe*: "'O.K. Now Listen!' Morgan cut in. 'You want to know what I found out? It's 1924 ... in the heat of summer, the news rips through Chinatown like wild fire! A white woman is murdered! The prime suspect is a chinese houseboy named Wong Foon Sing! Chopsticks drop and clatter in surprise! Clumps of rice stick in throats...'" (Lee 1990, 66).

Similarly, as in *Obasan* too, Lee's text aims directly at the strategies of legitimization of historical authority. But whereas *Obasan* contests official history by opening an archeological site of documents which contradict the latter's apparent unity and seemingly uncontestable hegemony, *Disappearing Moon Cafe* rejects the transformation of the (public) document into the monument (of history) and rather relies on non-official historical sources: personal letters, storytelling, memory and countermemory. Its genealogical structure is actually constructed, not anthropologically through the search for origins, but, quite to the contrary, through the line of mutations, of discursive (historical, cultural, political, etc.) interruptions that have (de)formed the family tree. The first public document to appear in Lee's novel is a censored rice-papery pamphlet dating well back to pre-communist China. Although visually impressed by Hermia's histrionic access to such an enigmatic cultural heritage, Kae also ironizes about the fetish nature of this document/monument--literally enveloped by the 1971 China's official ideology, the

People's Daily: "It had survived the Great Cultural Revolution to be smuggled out of China, and would probably end up in the hands of an elitist New York connoisseur who would continue to hide it away and cherished like an illicit mistress for over two hundred years" (Lee 1990, 40). Despite the fuss, the document itself is never read. Instead, it is the reading of the first two letters exchanged between Fong Mei and her sister in China around 1919 that provides the historical intertext to both the Canada and the China of the time (41-48).

Kae's own relation to the material discursive practices of historiography is defined by her choice of a genealogy instead of a documentary. Despite the printed words on the page, the making of history in this text does not rely so much in written as in oral discourse. In the process, the narrator's use of pidgin and Chinese transliterations draws the reader's attention to the gaps inscribed in the construction of another, non-official, history. Control of the English language is believed to imply access to the discourses of power: "'You and me ... we'll figure out a way to bypass that 'no candoo' and get more four our money even,'" Mui Lan advises her son, fed up of being cheated by the white iceman. "'There's that little italian iceman. You go talk english to him!'" (Lee 1990, 34). Yet mastery of English does not seem to provide even the third-generation Chinese Canadian subject with the promised entrance into Canadian social and political life: "'So, does Keeman still think that the government anticommunist witch hunt is really an excuse to take away the chinese vote?'" asks Suzie in 1950. However learned in the master language, Chinese Canadians, the text suggests, continue to be stripped from their right to education by the continuing presence of a subtle, but nonetheless operative, racial prejudice. Suzie's acute memory reveals how her sister Beatrice, ostensibly bilingual, is denied a scholarship and entrance altogether into music at the University of British Columbia:

> They said that her english marks were not good enough, but I was sitting out in the hall, waiting for her. Nine years old, and I could see that stinking old man who was supposed to be the head of the department couldn't even look at Bea without hate oozing from every pore. Pure envy and jealousy that a mere girl, and chinese to boot, should be so gifted. (Lee 1990, 201-202)

A generation later, Kae finds herself well within a broader national society by means of capitalizing on her own ethinicity; working as an investment research analyst, she enjoys a life of vanities such as "Hong Kong business luncheons (known to last three days and three nights) and leather limousine seats (cushioning against harsher realities)" (Lee 1990, 124). A nice Chinese face, Kae reflects, has suddenly become of high value in the world of the international market: "Naturally, my bosses figured out that it would be comely if a nice-looking chinese junior sat beside one of the senior partners at the meeting" (124). The narrator's ironic remarks conceal a sharp critique of the processes of ethnic tokenization.

Disappearing Moon Cafe joins efforts with *Obasan* in its powerful critique of Canadian ethnocentrism. In Lee's text, the argument is as simple as follows: "Chinamen didn't make the law of the land, so they would always live outside of it. In fact, it was a crime for them just to be here" (221). In this context, the paradisiacal description of Gwei Chang's life in the mountains at the beginning of the book is significantly jeopardized by the failure of maps, "with sections of the railroad numbered," to locate the spots where the Chinese bones lie, the invisible sites marking the black spots of national history and cartography: "He'd been told that there would be markers, or cairns, or something. How hard could it be ..." (11). Unlike *Obasan*, rather bent on the clashing presentation of the inside and the outside of historical experience, *Disappearing Moon Cafe* juggles the implications of cultural self-erasure from within, in the portrait of a claustrophobic community, a ghetto enveloped upon itself by both white prejudice and Chinese Canadian way of mirroring their own stereotypes: "The cackle-talk of their trap spirits; grim laughter rolling off like distant thunder" (Lee 1990, 106).

Lacking the precise negotiation of a global historical event, such as World War II in *Obasan*, *Disappearing Moon Cafe*, however, also inscribes the traces of the unsolved in such a way as to prevent the arrival at the happy resolution inherent in genealogical romance. Haunting the text to its very end, the narrative of Kelora, one about abandonment and death, is left basically unrepresented. Literally unrepresented also is the hypothetical suicide of Suzie, Kae's aunt, in 1951. The death of Suzie's baby in the hands of a white doctor, however, marks the text with the deadly delusions of a colonizing history: "And then, to be transported down the tiled halls and gleaming corridors of a great institution to be saved! A whirlwind of white faces. White social worker face. White nurse face. White cleaner face. All of them gave me the illusion of hope" (Lee 1990, 204).

Differences notwithstanding, then, the two novels underline the workings of the vertical mosaic behind the seemingly equalizing national icon; certainly, Slocan has very little to do with the promised land of plenty, the "garden story" of North America's New Eden image (see Palmer, T. 1990; also Kroetsch 1985);

neither is the claustrophobic portrait of Chinatown's "violence, with the same, sour odour of trapped bodies under duress" any closer to the promised golden land (Lee 1990, 221). Invisibility, (self)ghettoization, and alienness result in both novels from the characters' forced exclusion from the discourses of power. Still, they have a way of reaching their audience, for as Kathryn Kilgore argues (in relation to *Obasan*, but indeed striking a point of connection between the two texts I have been discussing):

> Some family histories contain a double-edged vision in which the personal, specific events combine and reach into the mythic and the cosmic: a story comes to tell not only the experience of an individual, and through that the experience of a minority culture, but also the delusions of a dominant culture. This kind of fiction is a subtle translation: historical facts are internalized and expressed through scenes that create a sense of place and a sense of out-of-place, a sense of relationship between individuals and community, and a sense of alien. It seems to depend on the repetition of accurately selected, pointed details that work the pattern of the story right through your skin. (Kilgore 1982, 45)

It is, then, through the working of history and fiction *right through one's skin* that *Obasan* and *Disappearing Moon Cafe* contest the discursive officiality of dominant history and culture. They do so, as we have seen, by means of complex patterns of confrontation between the supposed objectivity of historical data and the subjectivity of memory and experience, between the multicultural/assimilative arguments and the covert pressure for cultural and racial invisibility inherent in both. The texts' deconstructions of the discursive practices configuring the historical document/monument, and their articulations of the global coordinates of racism and dislocation succeed in drawing the reader's attention to the ideology of Western epistemology and the arbitrariness of temporal and spatial paradigms of historical knowledge and interpretation. With their different histories, then, *Obasan* and *Disappearing Moon Cafe* rewrite the maps of Canadian history and fiction by choosing a mode of representation which unveils the notions of literature, history, geography, nationality, and culture, not only as discursively constructed but also, and in a very important way, as implicated in the continuing processes of ethnocentrism and social discrimination.

Eva Darias-Beautell

Notes

[1.] Obasan is, however, often included in studies of Asian American writing (see for instance, Lim 1991; also Wong 1993).

2. British Columbia Chinese and Japanese immigrants were disenfranchised in 1875 and 1895, respectively.

[3.] The Japanese Canadians were, by Order-in-Council, first imprisoned, then removed from the West Coast and interned in the ghost towns of the interior of B.C. After the end of World War II, they were forcibly dispersed throughout the country, although most were sent to the sugar beet farms in the Canadian prairies. Not a single evidence was ever found of a supposed Japanese Canadian disloyalty. The removal of all restrictions came on April 1949 (for a general history of the Japanese Canadians, see Adachi, 1991; for critical analyses of the events of World War II, see Sunahara 1981 and Ward 1990a).

[4.] Emily's diary is a rewriting of Muriel Kitagawa's "Letters to Wes," edited, along with other Kitagawa's manuscripts, by Roy Miki (Kitagawa 1985). See also "This Is My Own, My Native Land" (186-197) and "I Know the Nisei Well" (286-290) in this collection, both of which are rewritten in Obasan as part of Emily's manuscripts (Kogawa 1983, 39-40 and 197-198, respectively).

[5.] The phrase is actually A.W. Neil's reply to Prime Minister King's comment, during a session in the House of Commons in February 1941, that the Japanese Canadians had proved their loyalty to Canada (see Adachi 1991, 279).

[6.] This was the "repatriation or relocation" scheme, launched by the government in 1945, and forcing the Japanese Canadians either to leave for Japan or to move east of the Rockies. Three quarters of those who signed up for "repatriation" were Canadian citizens. The Canadian government did everything in hand to encourage the "back-to-Japan" option. The plan become highly controversial and was eventually suspended in 1947, after some 4,000 allegedly volunteers had already been sent to Japan (see Adachi 1991, 270-279).

[7.] The selling of the internees' property was done without the owners' knowledge. Apart from obstaculizing a potential return and accelerating dispersal, the operation alleviated the high cost of the Japanese Canadian internment; that is, the Japanese Canadians were made to pay for their own incarceration (see Sunahara 1981, 163).

[8.] Identifications with the Native Peoples are many in both Kogawa's and Lee's texts. As we will see, Kelora is in Disappearing Moon Cafe the surprising matriarch of a Chinese Canadian family. The making of common cause with the Natives seems particularly problematic in the case of Obasan: the Indian Rough Lock saves Naomi from drowning in the lake (149); Uncle is also pictured as an "'Indian Chief from Canadian Prairie'"--souvenir of Alberta, made in Japan" (2). Yet the complexities of history have it that the B.C. Native Brotherhood and Sisterhood supported compulsory deportation of the Japanese Canadians in 1942 (see Iwama 1994). This endnote perhaps alerts us further, if nothing else, to the complicities and the reversibility of positions between victimized and victimizer with which the texts play.

[9.] After long and continuing pressure from the National Association of Japanese Canadians and other organizations for redress, the Mulroney government somehow managed, in 1988, to close a shameful chapter in Canadian history by offering an official apology as well as an economic compensation to the Japanese Canadian survivors. The effectivity of this (late) official gesture to undo the historical crime has, obviously, been doubted (see Miki and Kobayashi 1991; also Kogawa 1992).

[10.] This Act, euphemistically called "Chinese Immigration Act," virtually ended Chinese immigration, since it excluded all except diplomats, Canadian-born children, students and wives of Chinese Canadian merchants. The act was repelled only in 1947, although the last immigration barriers took twenty more years to be overturned.

[11.] The details of this incident can be found in B.C. historical archives. The murder was never solved.

[12.] This was the September 1907 "Stand-for-a-White-Canada" demonstration, which ended up in violent mobs against Chinese and Japanese businesses and houses in Vancouver Chinatown and "Little Tokyo" (Powell Street). Police reinforcements had to be summoned up to cordon the area and avoid further confrontations (see Adachi 1991 for a Japanese Canadian point of view; Chan 1983 for a Chinese Canadian focus; Ward 1990b for an overall discussion of British Columbia animosity against all Asians).

[13.] These associations, the first of which was founded in Canada in 1884, helped the Chinese newcomers against the wall of racism built by their white neighbors. Taking after similar organizations in China, the Benevolent Associations offered jobs and protected the community in a traditionally hierarchical sense. They constituted a de facto Chinese Canadian government until well into mid-century (see Chan 1983).

[14.] More than 600 Chinese laborers died in the railway construction. Most of these deaths were caused by the lack of security measures, but some are reported to have resulted from premeditated negligence on the part of white laborers. The high number of Chinese casualties led to the spread of a saying, repeated all over Canadian Chinatowns: "for every foot of railroad through the Fraser Canyon, a Chinese worker died" (see Chan 1983, 66-67).

Words Cited

Adachi, Ken. 1991. *The Enemy That Never Was: A History of the Japanese Canadians*. Toronto: McClelland & Stewart.

Bartkowski, Fran. 1993. "Travelers v. Ethnics: Discourses of Displacement." *Discourse: Journal for Theoretical Studies in Media and Culture,* 15.3: 158-176.

Bhabha, Homi K. 1991. "DissemiNation: Time, Narrative, and the Margins of the Modern Nation." *Nation and Narration*. Ed. H. Bhabha. London: Routledge. 291-322.

Brandt, Di. 1993. *Wild Mother Dancing: Maternal Narrative in Canadian Literature*. Winnipeg: University of Manitoba Press.

Brydon, Diana. 1987. "Discovering 'Ethnicity': Joy Kogawa's *Obasan* and Mena Abdullah's *Time of the Peacock*." *Australian/Canadian Literatures in English: Comparative Perspectives*. Eds. Russell McDougall and Gillian Whitlock. Melbourne: Methuen. 94-110.

Chan, Anthony B. 1983. *Gold Mountain: The Chinese in the New World.* Vancouver: New
      Star Books.

Foucault, Michel. 1977 (1969). *The Archeology of Knowledge.* Trans. A. M. Sheridan Smith.
      London: Tavistock.

Howells, Coral Ann. 1990. "Storm Glass: The Presentation and Transformation of   History in
      *The Diviners, Obasan, My Lovely Enemy." Crisis and Creativity in the New Literatures in
      English Canada.* Cross/Cultures. Readings in Post/Colonial Literatures in English 2.
      Atlanta (GA): Rodopi. 87-98.

Iwama, Marilyn. 1994. "If You Say So: Articulating Cultural Symbols of Tradition in the
      Japanese Canadian Community." *Canadian Literature* 140 (Spring): 13-29.

Jones, Manina. 1990. "The Avenues of Speech and Silence: Telling Difference in Joy
      Kogawa's *Obasan." Theory Between Disciplines: Authority/ Vision/ Politics.* Eds. Martin
      Kreiswirth and Mark A. Cheetham. Ann Arbor: University of Michigan Press. 213-229.

Kilgore, Kathryn. 1982. "A Long Way from Home." Review of *Obasan. Village Voice.* 22
      June: 45.

Kim, Elaine H. 1982. *Asian American Literature: An Introduction to the Writings and Their
      Social Context.* Philadelphia: Temple U.P.

Kitagawa, Muriel. 1985. *This Is My Own: Letters to Wes & Other Writings on the
      Japanese Canadians 1941-1948.* Ed. and Intro. Roy Miki. Vancouver: Talonbooks.

Kogawa, Joy. 1983. *Obasan.* Markham (Ont.): Penguin.

Kogawa, Joy. 1992. *Itsuka.* Toronto: Viking.

Kogawa, Joy. 1994. Interview. By Jeanne Delbaere. *Kunapipi* 16.1: 461-464.

Kroetsch, Robert. 1985. "The Grammar of Silence: Narrative Patterns in Ethnic Writing."
      Canadian Literature 106 (Fall): 65-74.

Lee, Sky. 1990. *Disappearing Moon Cafe.* Vancouver: Douglas and McIntyre.

Lim, Shirley Geok-Lin. 1991. "Asian American Daughters Rewriting Asian Maternal Texts."
      Asian Americans: Comparative and Global Perspectives. Eds. Shirley Hune et al.
      Pullman: Washington State U.P. 239-248.

McEvoy. F. J. 1982. "'A Symbol of Racial Discrimination': The Chinese Immigration Act and
Canada's Relations with China 1942-1947." *Canadian Ethnic Studies* 14.3: 24-42.

Matheson, William. 1984. "Obasan." Unpublished essay. St. Louis: Washington University.

Miki, Roy and Kobayashi, Cassandra. 1991. *Justice in Our Time: The Japanese Canadian Redress Settlement.* Vancouver: Talon Books.

Palmer, Tamara. 1990. "The Fictionalization of the Vertical Mosaic: The Immigrant, Success and National Mythology." *Literatures of Lesser Diffusion.* Ed. Joseph Pivato. Edmonton: Research Institute for Comparative Studies/University of Alberta. 65-101.

Said, Edward W. 1975. *Beginnings: Intention and Method.* Baltimore: Johns Hopkins U.P.

Sunahara, Ann Gomer. 1981. *The Politics of Racism: The Uprooting of Japanese Canadians During the Second World War.* Toronto: James Lorimer.

Ward, W. Peter. 1990a. "British Columbia and the Japanese Evacuation." *Readings in Canadian History: Post-Confederation.* Eds. Douglas R. Francis and Donald B. Smith. Toronto: Holt, Rinehart & Winston. 462-480.

Ward, W. Peter. 1990b. *White Canada Forever: Popular Attitudes and Public Policy Toward Orientals in British Columbia.* Montreal: McGill-Queen's University and Kingston Press.

Wong, Sau-Ling Cynthia. 1993. *Reading Asian American Literature: From Necessity to Stravaganza.* Princeton: Princeton U.P.

Zwicker, Heather. 1993. "New National Narratives for a New World Order: Contemporary Postcolonial Fiction From Canada and the North of Ireland." Unpublished PhD Thesis. Standford (CA): Stanford University.

10.

WOMEN BEFORE HELL'S GATE:
SURVIVORS OF THE HOLOCAUST AND THEIR MEMOIRS

The horrors of Nazism were best described in 1986 by the German historian Eberhard Jäckel:

> The Nazi extermination of the Jews was unique because never before had a state, under the responsible authority of its leader, decided and announced that a specific group of human beings, including the old, the women, the children and the infants would be killed to the very last one, and implemented this decision with every means at its disposal.[1]

Jäckel's statement eloquently explains why the Holocaust continues to horrify us 50 years after the end of World War II. The Holocaust has become emblematic as a symbol of the cruelty of inter-ethnic hatred and the means and motives of the Nazi tyrants continue to terrify and are the subject of continuing attention. The killing of German Jews in such Nazi concentration camps as Auschwitz, Theresienstadt (Terezin), Ravensbrück, and Oederan occurred not only through exposing the victims to physical privations, because that alone was not the quickest way to guarantee their destruction. Although the indomitibility of the human spirit did not flourish in the camps, it did continue to survive, and in many cases, it prolonged the inmates' tenuous hold on life. It therefore became necessary to assault the detainees psychologically by divorcing them from any sense of their identity as human beings. The techniques of this dehumanization process are vividly described in various survivor memoirs. The goals of this essay are threefold: to examine the philosophy behind the dehumanization of Holocaust victims, to examine specific techniques of dehumanization as reflected in Holocaust literature, and to examine the ways in which some Holocaust survivors were able to resist these processes of dehumanization as reflected in Holocaust literature, and to examine the ways in which some Holocaust survivors were able to resist these processes of dehumanization by rehumanizing themselves and maintaining their will to live.

In examining the philosophy behind these practices of dehumanization it is profitable to turn to the analyses of fascism offered by Theodor W. Adorno, a major 20th-century philosopher. In his 1966 essay, "Erziehung nach Auschwitz," he declares the following: the most important task of education is the prevention of future Auschwitzes.[2] Adorno then proceeds to indict the barbarism that constituted Auschwitz as the very antithesis of education and holds that Auschwitz was the result of powerful societal tendencies that continue to exist. The genocide had its roots in the resurrection of an aggressive nationalism that had its origins in the late 19th century.[3] Indeed, the notion of a state based on religious, ethnic, and cultural homogeneity was a reactionary product of that time whose influence continues today.

Adorno rightly viewed the Nazi genocide as a major ethical issue of the twentieth century. On the other hand, the road that led to Auschwitz was mired in pseudo-ethical *a prioris*. The postulate that German National Socialism could be based upon any concept of ethics, no matter how far-flung, may seem incongruous at first glance. However, the French historian Léon Poliakov points out that Nazism possessed a perverse religiosity. He states that religion has three basic elements: "the perception of a higher power, the submission to that power, and the establishment of relations with it . . ."[4] Hitler was the higher power and in order to mythologize that power he had to create a pseudo-dichotomy between good and evil by portraying the Jewish people as devils incarnate.

The ethical assumptions of Nazism have also been examined by the theologian Peter J. Haas in his 1988 book, *Morality after Auschwitz*. Haas maintains that there was a Nazi ethic, i.e., a codified system for differentiating between good and evil. The Nazi apparatus was the "governing norm" of the entire German "civilization."[5] The Nazi ethic was, according to Haas, based upon the concept of a "just war."[6] This Nazi pseudo-ethic demonized the Jews and delegated them to being viewed as a sub-species of humanity. The Nazi ethic stressed the importance of religious, ethnic, and cultural homogeneity, concepts borrowed from the racist philosophies which flourished during the 19th century.

The historian Dominick LaCapra similarly speaks of the goals of fascism in terms of an "undifferentiated unity or even identity of the German people or nation in a common will."[7] He elaborates:

> One has a narcissistic fusion of a Führer and *Volk* in a spectacular
> relationship. . . . One's very identity as a German was to be generated through
> identification with this leader and this identity was solidified by a racial
> ideology that represented Germans as members of a superior people.[8]

Eliminationist anti-Semitism must therefore be seen as a sine qua non of Nazi
ideology. Despite the fact that the Holocaust imposed great costs on the Nazi war
program and severely compromised the functioning of the Nazi war-making
apparatus, the Nazis continued the persecution due to their belief in the validity of
Jewish inferiority. All this because of a belief that "a whole people, branded by
genetic origin, and not by organized or unorganized political interest, had no right
to live--not anywhere in Europe nor anywhere on the planet."[9]

This genocidal concept is elaborated on by Lawrence Langer in his 1995 book
Admitting the Holocaust, where he described the Holocaust as a "rupture in human
values."[10] The barbaric Nazi system that led to the "Final Solution" was touted as
a positive alternative to the perceived evils of a parliamentary democracy and a
society that worked toward tolerance of a variety of viewpoints during the Weimar
Republic. The system of values espoused by Weimar culture was turned upside
down by a system that promised to replace the putative evils of a heterogeneous
Weimar democracy with the unitary consciousness of a Nazi police state. This
drive for unitary consciousness demanded the effacement of not only political, but
also ethnic diversity and therefore led to the destruction of European Jewry.

In reflecting on the destructiveness of the Nazi system, Adorno remarks that
Auschwitz has provided humankind with a new categorical imperative: For us to
so conduct ourselves that the events of Auschwitz are never repeated.[11] Survivors'
memories of unbridled suffering may indeed take on not only a historical
dimension but also an ethical significance: to the extent that the moving
remembrances of Holocaust survivors can serve to make us more vigilant, more
involved, and more humane world citizens. Considerable moral authority is
possessed by those who have borne witness to the torment which constitutes the
Holocaust, and who, at the same time, continue to win our admiration through their
unabated humanity. In fact, survivors' memoirs have a strong advantage over
objective accounts, because of the ability of eyewitnesses to engage the reader's
sympathy and admiration.[12]

The detainees of Auschwitz were victims of a totally contorted ethical system. The Nazi ethic defined Jews as being subhuman, creating a dilemma for those Nazi potentates who dealt with the Jewish population. Their creed taught them that Jews were subhuman, but when they came into contact with Jewish people they found themselves confronted with human beings: ordinary men, women, and children. They dealt with this dilemma by trying to recreate the Jews according to their pseudo-credal image of them: debasing and dehumanizing their race in an attempt to transform it into the subhuman creatures that the Nazi creed dictated that they were. What emerged was a brutal suppression of the inherent humanity of the Jewish people in order to support an incoherent ethical system that was not in harmony with reality because it tried to impose false divisions upon our species. While denying that Jews had any humanity in the first place, the Nazis tried to systematically strip that humanity away from them. That is proof that the Nazi ethic suffered from a severe internal contradiction and was based on irrational underpinnings.

The perpetrators of the Holocaust knew that for their victims to survive it was necessary for those victims to hold on to their identity as integral human beings. The Nazis therefore attempted to dehumanize the inmates in every way possible. The inmates on the other hand, did everything they could to preserve a sense of human dignity. When reading these memoirs a dialectic between dehumanization and human dignity is clearly observable: a dialectic of the techniques of dehumanization of concentration camp detainees and the methods used by the concentration camp survivors to rehumanize themselves and thereby make themselves more resistant to the fate intended for them.

This dialectic will be examined in four books of Holocaust memoirs: Grete Salus's *Niemand, nichts--ein Jude: Theresienstadt, Auschwitz, Oederan* ("Nobody, Nothing--a Jew: Theresienstadt, Auschwitz, Oederan," 1958), Lucie Begov's *Mit meinen Augen: Botschaft einer Auschwitz-Überlebenden* ("With my own Eyes: The Message of an Auschwitz Survivor," 1983), Anja Lundholm's *Das Höllentor: Bericht einer Überlebenden* ("Hell's Gate: A Survivor's Report," 1988), and Ruth Klüger's *weiter leben: Eine Jugend* ("Life continues: My Youth," 1992). Women writers will be the focus of this study, because such prominent male Holocaust survivors as Elie Wiesel, Bruno Bettelheim, Viktor Frankl, Primo Levi, Jean Améry, and many others have already been the subject of extensive critical attention. Women's Holocaust memoirs have as of yet not gotten the scholarly attention they deserve, and by bridging this gap, a better understanding of the

Holocaust may emerge. This study also aims to concentrate on chroniclers of the Holocaust who are relatively unknown to an English-speaking readership.[13]

All of these female chroniclers describe the use of torture as a means of dehumanization. Six forms of physical and psychological torture are described: Random terror, sadistic roll calls, excremental assault, meaningless hard labor, and--of course--the ever-present threat of the gas chambers. Random terror is best described in the following passage from Grete Salus:

> Plötzlich hörte ich eine Frauenstimme in einer fremden Sprache aufschreien wie in höchster Not--einige Male--. Dann ein Laufen, ein dumpfer Laut--Stille. Von irgendwo Schüsse. Ich hatte das Gefühl, so jetzt bin ich verrückt geworden. Das war ja gar nicht wahr, das war eine Halluzination. Produkt meiner gemarterten Nerven. [Suddenly I heard a woman's voice screaming in a foreign language that resonated with great fear--a number of times. Then there was a running, a muted sound, and then--silence. From somewhere there was the sound of shooting. I had the feeling as if I had gone crazy. That could not be true, I thought, that was a hallucination. The product of my agonized nerves.][14]

Random acts of cruelty on the part of the Nazis were intended to afflict not only the immediate victims but were a technique to terrorize everybody in the vicinity and to create a tortuous effect on the bystanders who felt that they could be next. The innocent bystanders were confronted with a mesmerizingly harsh reality that they did not want to accept because it threatened their psychological well-being and their ability to maintain the will to live.

Yet another way that the Nazis terrorized the inmates was through excruciatingly long roll calls, during which the detainees were forced to stand in formation. Both Grete Salus and Lucie Begov describe the roll call at Auschwitz as a brutal ritual whose memory continues to traumatize survivors. During the roll calls, the prisoners had to stand outside, exposed in their light clothing to the weather and to the random brutalities of their tormentors, for hours on end. According to Salus:

> Antreten zum Zählappell. Wir stürmten alle heraus, mußten uns nun sechs Mann hintereinander aufstellen und stehen, 4 Stunden, 6 Stunden und auch noch mehr. Wir sahen vor den anderen Blocks dieselben Gruppen warten. Endlich nach sechs Stunden kam eine deutsche Aufseherin, ließ sich die Zahl melden, wenn sie stimmte, konnten wir abtreten, wenn nicht, mußten wir stundenlang weiterstehen. . . . Appelle--eine der gefürchtesten und schlimmsten Institutionen

im KZ. Hier im Auschwitz sahen wir ganze Gruppen zur Strafe niederknien.
Manchmal wurde auch während des Appells selektiert, da mußten sich die
Menschen nackt ausziehen--egal in welcher Jahreszeit--.[We were called to roll
call. We stormed out, had to stand in rows of six, four hours, six hours, and
even longer. In front of the other barracks we also saw the same groups
waiting. Six hours later, a German guard finally came and announced the count.
If it was correct, we were dismissed, if it was not correct, we had to continue
standing for several hours more. . . . Roll call was one of the worst and most
feared institutions in the concentration camp. In Auschwitz we saw entire
groups forced to kneel for hours on end as a special punishment. Sometimes
there were "selections" during the roll call, the people were forced to strip
themselves naked regardless of which season it was.][15]

During "selections," those prisoners who were unwell were singled out for
immediate extermination in the gas chambers. Even for those who survived the
selections, there was the spectacle of standing for hours on end in an exhausted and
famished state. Roll calls were exacerbated by the fact that those who complained
about the toll these pointless tortures were taking on them brought further
brutalities upon themselves:

Eine Bekannte, eine ältere Dame, welche bis zur Befreiung durch die Russen
in Auschwitz verblieb, erzählte mir folgendes: Sie hatte Ruhr, mußte Appell
stehen, bat die Blockälteste, ob sie austreten könne, die Antwort--eine Ohrfeige.
Eine deutsche Aufseherin hatte es gesehen, trat auf sie zu und schlug so auf sie
ein, daß sie ohnmächtig zusammenbrach, und für lange Zeit schwer erkrankte.
[An acquaintance, an elderly lady, who remained in Auschwitz until her
liberation by the Russians, told me the following: she had dysentery while she
had to stand for roll call, and asked the barracks leader if she could leave and
received a slap as an answer. A German guard saw it, went over to her and hit
her so hard that she fell into unconsciousness and was dangerously ill for a long
time.][16]

Begov describes the roll call in the following terms:

Wir aber standen und wußten immer noch nicht, worauf wir warteten,
während die Vernichtungsqualen Glied um Glied, Organ um Organ erfaßten,
die besinnungslose Erschöpfung tiefer und schwerer wurde. . . . Dann kam der
Moment, wo die Grenze des Unerträglichen erreicht war. Wir alle erlebten ihn
immer und immer wieder, diesen Moment, wo es nicht mehr weiterging, die
körperlichen Schmerzen den Geist verwirrten, abgebrochene Laute, ein irres
Stammeln über die Lippen kam. [We stood without knowing what we were
waiting for as the destructive pains spread from limb to limb and organ to organ
and the excruciating exhaustion became deeper and weightier. We all
experienced it time and time again, this moment, where it became unbearable,

> where the bodily pain confused the mind, interrupted syllables of a crazy
> stuttering came over the lips.][17]

Begov's remembrance effectively describes not only the physical but also the
psychological privations to which detainees were subjected during roll call. The
agony of the roll calls became so intense that the detainees would start
hallucinating and would begin talking to themselves. All of the survivors are
extremely vivid in describing the hellish impact these painful roll calls had on
them.

Another of the most common types of torture described by all of these writers
is that of excremental assault. According to Harold Kaplan, the purpose of
excremental assault was to produce a sense of self-disgust in the victims and
thereby diminish their will to survive.[18] Lucie Begov vividly describes the
"Scheißkommando" as an example of this excremental assault. While imprisoned
at Auschwitz, she was forced to empty large wagons filled with human excrement
from latrines all over camp. The purpose of this exercise was to humiliate and
degrade her and thereby weaken her resistance to the deathly forces around her.

Anja Lundhölm provides the following graphic description of excremental
assault in the infirmary at the concentration camp, Ravensbrück. She was forced to
empty: " . . . eine solche Konzentration von allem, was nur stinken kann, . . . bis
zum Rande gefüllt mit ekelerrengenden Excrementen: Urin, Kot, Eiter, Gedarm,
schleimigen Auswurf und Leichenteilen, Restbestände der Sezierkunst der
Lagerärzte." ["Such a concentration of everything that can only stink: filled to the
brim with disgusting excrements: urine, feces, pus, entrails, slimy scum, and body
parts: the remains of the dissections of the camp doctors."][19] She describes her
difficulties and her humiliation in trying to empty the awful mixture: "Der
schätzungsweise ein Meter hohe Kannister ist schwergewichtig wie eine kleine
Bombe. Beim Anheben schwappt etwas von der widerwärtigen Brühe über meine
Hände, macht sie glitschig." ["The canister, which was approximately one meter
high, was as heavy as a small bomb. While lifting it, some of the disgusting
mixture slid over my hands, making them slippery."][20]

Ruth Klüger also remembers forms of excremental assault in the Czech
concentration camp of Theresienstadt, where there were not enough sanitary
facilities for all the inmates:

Immer war eine Schlange vor dem Klo. Es lohnte sich, sich an die Zeiten zu gewöhnen, in denen man auf weniger Andrang hoffen durfte. Es gab auf jedem Stockwerk nur zwei Klosette, wenn ich mich recht erinnere. Im Gebäude waren Hunderte von Kindern, unter ihnen immer eine Menge, die an Durchfall, der Dauerkrankheit des Lagers, litten. [There was always a line in front of the bathroom. It was worthwhile to get used to using the bathroom at times when there was likely to be less traffic. There were only two bathrooms on every floor, if I remember correctly. Inside the building were hundreds of children among whom were many suffering from diarrhea, the eternal plague of the camp.][21]

When Ruth Klüger and her mother were transported from Theresienstadt to Auschwitz, they were bombarded with another form of excremental assault. They were transported in crowded cattle cars without food, water, or any form of sanitation: "Bald stank der Wagen nach Urin und Kot, man mußte dafür Gefäße von Mitgebrachten finden, und es gab nur die eine Luke um diese zu leeren." ["The wagon soon stank from urine and excrement; one had to find bottles for it from the things that one had brought with, and empty them through a small hole in the door."][22] Klüger has this comment about cattle cars: "Noch jetzt, wenn ich Güterwagen sehe, überläuft es mich. Es ist üblich Viehwaggons zu sagen, aber auch Tiere werden ja normaleweise nicht so befördert, und wenn, so sollte es nicht sein." ["Even now, when I see goods wagons, I am overcome. It is common to call them livestock wagons, but even animals do not have to endure such suffering, and if they do, it should not be allowed."][23] Many people died while being transported to the east under these unbearable conditions.

The Nazis, feeling it was a moral imperative to dehumanize their victims, also subjected the detainees to hard labor, imposing tasks which were totally lacking in any economic or utilitarian function. Anja Lundholm describes one such sort of dehumanization. Detainees were forced to fill huge crates with sand, drench them to increase their heaviness, carry them for long distances, and then carry them back to their original places and dump them out. This procedure killed some inmates and those who stumbled or fell were often beaten to death by the camp guards. Another form of dehumanization that the Nazis practiced was making malnourished women go through fruit and vegetables intended for the SS and throw away those which were spoiled. On penalty of death, they could not eat any of them. Those who succumbed to the temptation of eating the forbidden foodstuffs were beaten into a state of unconsciousness. The impact on the starving women was one of psychological torture. This incident is reported in Lundholm's book. She comments, "Im Erfinden immer neue Quälereien sind unsere

Bewacherinnen groß. Mich setzen sie mit Vorlieb auf Arbeiten an, die weniger körperliche als seelische Folter bedeuten." ["Our guards are mighty in the invention of ever-new tortures. They prefer to assign me to tasks that are more in the realm of psychological torture than physical torture."][24]

As is well known, the cruelest and most uninhibited machination of the Nazis was that of the gas chambers. The incredibility of these gas chambers cannot be overstressed. When the first word of the gas chambers came out, the inmates themselves did not want to believe it. Ruth Klüger recalls the first time she heard of the gas chambers:

> Nach Theresienstadt kam im August 1943 eine Gruppe Kinder, die ich nicht gesehen habe, und fast niemand dort hat sie gesehen. Sie sollten in einen Spezialtransport ins Ausland, in die Schweiz, wurde behauptet. Sie wurden streng gesondert halten, und nur wenige Betreuer durften während der kurzen Zeit, die sie bei uns waren, an sie heran. Trotzdem hörte man: Diese Kinder wehrten sich verweifelt, als sie sich duschen sollte. Und auch der Grund für diese Weigerung sprach sich herum. Die Erwachsenen hielten die Geschichte von den Duschen, aus aus den statt Wasser Giftgas strömte für ein Phantasieprodukt der Kinder, während Kinder wie ich, sie zumindest in Erwägung zogen. [A group of children came to Theresienstadt in 1943 whom I never saw and almost nobody there saw them. They were to be sent away in a special transport abroad, to Switzerland it was said. They were separated from the rest of us by all necessary means, and only a few advisors [from the Jewish community] could visit them. Nonetheless, we heard that these children desperately refused to shower. And everybody was talking about the reason for this refusal. The adults held the stories of showers out of which poison gas streamed instead of water, for a fantasy product of the children. In the meantime, children such as myself, pondered this issue seriously.][25]

In addition to pointing out how difficult it was for the concentration camp inmates to believe the reality of the gas chambers, this passage points out that children in the concentration camps had to grow up fast. Between Ruth and her mother, who were imprisoned together, there was almost a reversal of the parent/child relationship. Ruth took a more realistic and more accurate view of the dangers confronting them.

After the horrible truth of the gas chambers became known to the inmates, most, like Ruth Klüger's mother, did not want to believe it. They reacted to it with a kind of defensive amnesia, which according to Lucie Begov, amounted to a defense of their murderers and an unwarranted belief that their captors were acting according to some conventional standard of morality. Begov describes her own inability to believe reports of the gas chambers:

> Wie es dann herauskamm, weiß ich nicht, doch plötzlich hatte es alle gehört: So wie es denen ergangen war, die wir im Familienlager glaubten, erging es auch allen, die ins Revier kamen. Sie wurden getötet und zwar "vergast" und im "Kamin" verbrannt. Auch in den Quarantäne--und Arbeitsblocks--war man vor dem "Kamin" nicht sicher und auch wir würden nach und nach "selektiert" und "vergast" werden. Am gefährlichsten war der Aufenthalt im Revier. . . . Ich . . . glaubte das vermeintliche Gerücht mit einem "logischen" Argument widerlegen zu können: Wenn sie uns töten wollen, wozu bringen sie uns vorher in ein Lager, fragte ich. So weit waren war noch davon entfernt, die durchgesickerte Wahrheit zu glauben, die Wirklichkeit, in der wir lebten, zu erkennen, zu erfassen. [I do not know how the word got out, but suddenly everybody had heard it: what happened to those whom we believed to be in the family camp happened as well to everyone who came into the infirmary. They were killed and indeed "gassed" and then burned in the "chimney." Even we would be "selected" and then "gassed." The most dangerous place for such a "selection" was the infirmary . . . I . . . believed I could refute the seeming rumor with a "logical" argument: if they wanted to kill us, why would they bring us to a camp first? We were indeed so far from believing the proven truth and recognizing and understanding the reality in which we lived.][26]

Unfortunately Lucie Begov's defensive amnesia had fatal consequences which went quite contrary to her expectations and intentions. She encouraged her ailing sister to visit the infirmary, and the sister was sent straight to the gas chambers.

The ultimate act of dehumanization was the transformation of inmates into "Muselmänner," which is reflected on in one of Ruth Klüger's poems entitled "Kamin" ("Chimney"):

> Mancher lebte einst vor Grauen/Von der drohenden Gefahr./Heute kann er gelassen schauen,/Bietet ruhig sein Leben dar./Jetzt ist er zermürbt von Leiden,/Keine Schönheit, keine Freuden/Leben, Sonne, sie sind hin./Und es lodert der Kamin./Auschwitz liegt in seiner Hand,/Alles, alles wird verbrannt. [After living full of horror/Of the danger threatening him/Today he can calmly look at it/He peacefully offers his own life/Everyone is worn out from sufferings/No beauty, no joy/Life, sunshine are over/The chimney blazes/Auschwitz lies in its hand/Everything, everything will be burned.][27]

The "Muselmänner" were those inmates who had lost the will to survive and who withdrew from the surrounding world in a manner resembling autism. This poem is Klüger's tribute to those who were unable to survive, who were forced to succumb to the inevitable because the depravity that surrounded them became unbearable. After their withdrawal from reality made them nonfunctional as workers, the Muselmänner were consigned to death in the gas chambers during the "selections." Ruth reflects that she never gave up hope--out of a combination of childhood blindness and fear of death. Yet surviving was as improbable as winning the lottery. She empathizes with the "Muselmänner" who gave up their will to live, because she recognizes the tribulations confronting them. She thereby validates their experience and their perspective--a withdrawal from real life, which made their deaths in the chimneys of Auschwitz more inevitable, but which also ended their suffering. The last line "Everything will be burned" is a reflection of the near inevitability of death in the concentration camps, a situation that the inmates were never allowed to forget.

Despite these cruel yet efficacious methods of dehumanization, many inmates attempted to rehumanize themselves in order to maintain their will to live. It is necessary to examine the ways in which concentration camp inmates tried to maintain their humanity in order to hold on to that quintessential recognition of their dignity without which survival was impossible. Such means included religion, literature, semi-organized instruction, and acts of defiance.

Ruth Klüger recalls seeing the famous rabbi Leo Baeck preaching from the roofs of Theresienstadt, trying to console the inmates. He gave theological sermons on the fact that God's time is not man's time and that humankind must have patience with God's calendar, implying, in a subtle way, that the Nazis would not last forever. Ruth felt personally inspired by the sermon, and she also remembers being inspired by Zionist discussions among her Jewish co-religionists in Theresienstadt. Her conscious thoughts were saturated with Zionism, because it was the philosophy that made the most sense to her. She recalls singing Zionist songs with companions her own age.

Semi-organized instruction was also a vehicle for rehumanization. Although organized instruction for the children of Theresienstadt was forbidden, there were clandestine attempts to calm the children's fears by imparting knowledge of art and literature to them. This was forbidden because the Jewish intellect was viewed by the Nazis as being a danger even in a concentration camp situation due to its power to revitalize the victims they wanted to destroy. The ban on learning made the children value learning all the more. Theresienstadt contained people of a variety of intellectual endeavors and ideological leanings who were capable of providing instruction.   Teachers and professors would lead discussion groups of eager children, groups which learned to break up quickly when a German inspection was imminent.

Klüger also writes about the consoling effect which her knowledge of the German classics had on her. Knowing the best of what German Classicism had produced helped give her the strength to survive the worst of what humankind had produced. She poignantly describes the importance poetry had for the inmates' survival:

> Ich erzählte nichts Ungewöhnliches, wenn ich sage, ich hätte überall, wo ich war, Gedichte aufgesagt und verfaßt. Viele KZ-Insassen haben Trost in den Versen gefunden, die sie auswendig wußten. . . . Meistens werden Gedichte von religiösem oder weltanschaulichem Inhalt erwähnt oder solche die einen besonderen emotionellen Stellenwert in der Kindheit des Gefangenen hatten. Mir scheint es indessen, daß der Inhalt der Verse erst in zweiter Linie von Bedeutung war und daß der uns in erster Linie die Form selbst, die gebundene Sprache, eine Stütze gab. [I am not telling anything unusual when I say I would have recited and composed poems anywhere where I would have been. Many concentration camp inmates found consolation in the verses that they knew by heart. . . . Most of them mention poems with religious or philosophical themes or such poems that had a special emotional value during their childhood. Incidentally, it appears to me that the theme of the poem was of secondary importance: that the most important thing in giving us support was the form of the verse, the rhyme itself.][28]

She writes about using verse and rhyme to convince herself that continued life was a worthwhile goal. Those people facing the worst scourges of humanity could increase their chances of survival by recalling the best that humanity had accomplished, because it had a consoling and benevolently animating effect. Literary scholar Andrea Reiter writes that withdrawal into art offered the detainees a welcome opportunity to temporarily forget the brutal reality of the concentration camps and thereby conquer their fears.[29] It should be mentioned that literary activity seldom took the form of reading or writing, but took the form of reminiscing about favorite books, reciting memorized poems, or trying to create original poems within one's head, and then committing them to memory.

Another factor which had a rehumanizing effect on the victims and increased their chances of survival were small acts of defiance. Such an act is described by Lundholm. After the death of the privileged inmate Wanda, who served as a brothel madam for the SS, an organized group of inmates decided to confiscate her goods and distribute them to other inmates. A Kapo had custody of Wanda's goods, but during an air raid the inmates were able to break into the kapo's apartment and confiscate fruit preserves, bread, butter, salami, and chocolate. The women ate their fill and after realizing that they could not keep their stolen goods in secrecy, they decided to distribute them to women and children in different barracks where the presence of the stolen goods was less likely to arouse suspicion. This in turn had a rehumanizing impact on the women and led them to put forth a greater moral resistance to the forces threatening their survival.

The dialectic between dehumanization and preservation of human dignity is portrayed most vividly by Klüger in her account of the Nazi evacuation of the last concentration camp at which she was detained, Christianstadt. The Nazis, fearing an impending liberation by the allies, wished to erase all traces of the brutal concentration camp. They drove the barefoot inmates on a desperate death march from the Czech concentration camp toward Germany. Human dignity, not to mention courage, is exemplified in the decision of Ruth, her mother, and four Czech companions to escape from the Nazi tyrants. The Klügers made their own way toward Germany and hid there until the Allied Liberation.

One more point remains to be made about the significance of these Holocaust memoirs. The writing of these memoirs is itself an act of courage as well as an act of engagement against the conditions which produced fascism, conditions which continue to exist. In a personal conversation, Holocaust survivor Jack Mandelbaum, the President of the Midwest Holocaust Education Center in Overland Park, Kansas told me that he was psychologically unable to talk about his concentration camp experiences until 20 years after his liberation. Lucie Begov describes the similar difficulty she had in writing her memoirs:

> Daß mir eine derart exakte Schilderung Jahrzehnte nach Auschwitz möglich war, verdanke ich einem umfangreichen Rohmanuskript, das ich gleich nach Kriegsende 1945/46 . . . niederschrieb . . . Ich dachte oft in den seither vergangenen Jahrzehnten oft daran, dieses Rohmaterial zu einem Buch zu verarbeiten, konnte aber die dazu erforderliche seelische Kraft nicht aufbringen. [That it was possible for me to write such an exact description decades after Auschwitz was due to a detailed rough draft that I wrote directly after the end of the war in 1945/46. I often thought of working this rough draft into a book during the past decades, but I could not gather up the necessary psychological power.][30]

The courageous act of memoir-writing is examined by Andrea Reiter in her study of Holocaust literature, *Auf daß entsteigen der Dunkelheit: Die literarische Bewältigung von KZ-Erfahrung* (1995). According to Reiter, the unique thing about these texts is the attempt to portray a life-threatening personal experience and attribute some meaning to this traumatic experience in such a way that the requisites for a satisfactory continuation of life can be guaranteed.[31] In their reports, the survivors emphasize the meaning their telling of the story has for them after the liberation. Although the fact that they are witnesses means they have something important to say to us, the writing also serves a therapeutic function for them. The psychological overcoming of their experiences constitutes a sort of catharsis.[32] Survivors attempting to chronicle the Holocaust must experience a conflict between the internal pressure to express themselves and the psychological barriers of reliving traumatic experiences.[33]

These memoirs have a lesson for us, a lesson that is expressed by Harold Kaplan:

> Be careful what doctrine you believe for it is certain that you will try to bring it to reality. Declare that you have an enemy, and he will become that enemy. Declare a person to be of inferior race, and you will soon write the scenarios that will fulfill your theory.[34]

According to Theodor Adorno, education has a meaningful role to play in the prevention of future Auschwitzes in that it leads to critical self-reflection. The true power against the principle of Auschwitz is the principle of autonomy: the power of reflection, of self-determination, the ability to refuse participation.[35] This gives individuals a defense against blind identification with the collective. Renewed nationalisms in our postmodern age where such social devices are outmoded creates fresh ground for sadistic practices.[36] Finally, these memoirs of dehumanization and subsequent rehumanization under impossible circumstances can have a rehumanizing impact upon us, their readership. The reading of the memoirs has the potential of instilling in its readership the power of reflection, of self-determination, and of non-cooperation with evil which is the only true antidote to the principle of Auschwitz.[37] As we continue to be advocates of an ethically principled social order based on multi-ethnicity, multi-religiosity, multi-ableism, multiculturalsim, and tolerance of social diversity, these memoirs may be of use to us in engendering strong resistance to those who oppose such principles and advocate--subtly or overtly--a return to the politically bereft philosophies advocated by Hitler and other Nazi leaders.

Peter R. Erspamer

Endnotes:

1. Eberhard Jäckel, quoted in Dominick LaCapra, *Representing the Holocaust: History, Theory, Trauma* (Ithaca and London: Cornell University Press, 1994) 49.
2. Theodor W. Adorno, "Erziehung nach Auschwitz" in *Erziehung zur Mündigkeit* (Frankfurt: Suhrkamp, 1975) 88.
3. Adorno, "Erziehung nach Auschwitz," 89.
4. Léon Poliakov, *Harvest of Hate: The Nazi Program for the Destruction of the Jews of Europe,* (New York: Holocaust Library, 1979) 5.
5. Peter J. Haas, *Morality after Auschwitz: The Radical Challenge of the Nazi Ethic* (Philadelphia: Fortress, 1988) 4. As Haas points out:

> Once the Jews could be symbolized as posing, by their very nature, a mortal threat to German culture, there were certain ethical ramifications. These ramifications based on formal notions of self-defense are perfectly understandable in light of our style of ethical discourse, a discourse that has operated in unbroken continuity from the past . . .

6. Haas, *Morality after Auschwitz,* 14.
7. Dominick LaCapra, *Representing the Holocaust: History, Theory, Trauma* (Ithaca and London: Cornell University Press, 1994) 108.
8. LaCapra, *Representing the Holocaust,* 102.
9. Harold Kaplan, *Conscience and Memory: Meditations in a Museum of the Holocaust* (Chicago and London: University of Chicago Press, 1994) 13. Pointing to a crucial component of the Nazi pseudo-ethic, Kaplan states: "There is no question that Hitler fought hard to liberate his people from all moral inhibitions against the use of violence. But he could only do so by making them swear allegiance to himself."
10. Lawrence L. Langer, *Admitting the Holocaust* (Oxford and New York: Oxford University Press, 1995) 3. He explicates this concept further:

> Few, apparently, were prepared to concede (few still are) that in the other world of the Holocaust, what we consider evil was for the Nazis an *expression* of good, supported by a political and moral value system totally alien to our orthodox minds.

11. See Adorno, "Erziehung nach Auschwitz," 88.
12. The Austrian-American literary scholar Andreas Lixl-Purcell points out:

> As much as objective interpretations may succeed in providing us with analytical insights into the barbarism of Nazi politics, they cannot convey the subjective and emotional dimension. But it is exactly this private sense of solidarity and identification with the victims of the Holocaust that establishes a contextual bridge to understanding the past.

Cf. Andreas Lixl-Purcell, "Women's Holocaust Memoirs," *Leo Baeck Institute Yearbook* (1994) 237.

13. Ruth Klüger is currently working on an English translation of *weiter leben*, which will hopefully be out soon.

14. Grete Salus, *Niemand, nichts--ein Jude: Theresienstadt, Auschwitz, Oederan* (1958; Darmstadt: Verlag Darmstädter Blätter, 1981) 38.

15. Salus, 33.

16. Salus, 34.

17. Lucie Begov, *Mit meinen Augen: Die Botschaft einer Auschwitz-Überlebenden,* (Gerlingen: Bleicher, 1983) 182-83.

18. Kaplan, *Conscience and Memory*, 34.

19. Anja Lundholm, *Das Höllentor: Bericht einer Überlebenden* (Hamburg: Rowohlt, 1988)98.

20. Lundholm, *Das Höllentor*, 98.

21. Ruth Klüger, *weiter leben: Eine Jugend* (Göttingen: Wallstein, 1992) 97.

22. Klüger, 108.

23. Klüger, 107.

24. Lundholm, 136.

25. Klüger, 101.

26. Begov, 196.

27. Klüger, 106.

28. Klüger, 122.

29. Andrea Reiter, *Auf daß sie entsteigen der Dunkelheit: Die literarische Bewältigung von KZ-Erfahrung* (Vienna: Löcker, 1995) 122-23

30. Begov, 20.

31. Reiter, 71.

32. Reiter, 157.

33. Reiter, 161.

34. Kaplan, 49.

35. Adorno, 93.

36. See Adorno, 104.

37. See Adorno, 93.

11.

FROM NUYORICAN BARRIO LITERATURE
TO ISSUES ON PUERTO RICAN LITERATURE
OUTSIDE NEW YORK CITY:
NICHOLASA MOHR AND JUDITH ORTIZ COFER

Tenemos que sentir como puertorriqueños, funcionar
como americanos.
(We must feel like Puerto Ricans, behave like Americans.)
(Luis A. Ferré, former governor of Puerto Rico, October 12, 1969; qtd. in Varo 75.
   Translation is mine.)

What we must eliminate are systems of representation that carry with them the kind
of authority which, to my mind, has been repressive because it doesn't permit or
make room for interventions on the part of those represented. (Said qtd. in Mariani
& Crary 95)

Without Spanish one can say 'my parents are Puerto Rican, my grandparents are
Puerto Rican' but I doubt whether one can say 'I am Puerto Rican.' Without
Spanish one can respect Puerto Rican culture and eat whatever it is that mama put
on the table, but that's about all. (qtd. in Fishman 71)

Puerto Rican literature in the United States maintains a strong attachment to
New York City, the initial urban center of Puerto Rican immigration to the United
States. Although historically the largest Puerto Rican labor population resided in
that city, since 1980 the majority of Puerto Ricans in the United States have settled
outside the state of New York (Rodríguez 4). Even so, New York City continues to
be viewed as the intellectual nucleus of Puerto Rican culture in the United States,
partly because of several academic programs of Puerto Rican Studies in New York
and partly because of the lively Puerto Rican social and artistic centers there. The
Puerto Rican community in New York--with its social center firmly attached in the
barrio--is commonly referred to as "Nuyorican." The term Nuyorican is
representative of biculturality, or, rather, it stands for a Puerto Rican immigrant

culture. Initially the term was used with derogatory intention by Puerto Ricans on the island to refer to Puerto Rican immigrants in New York City. Eventually it included first and subsequent generations of Puerto Ricans born and raised in the City. Other Puerto Rican groups favor the term "Neorican," because it stresses the fact that the Puerto Rican culture that has developed in New York City is distinctively different from that on the island.

Since the late 1960's Nuyorican writers have taken upon themselves the task of documenting in printed form the history of Puerto Rican immigration to the United States (Acosta-Belén, Flores, Eugene Mohr). A pioneer in this movement, Nicholasa Mohr, born in New York City in 1935 of Puerto Rican parents, with her first work, *Nilda* (1973), went a step further with her choice of English rather than Spanish or "Spanglish" as the sole language of her novel. Spanglish, an ethnic-linguistic code-switching, compound form between Spanish and English, had become associated with life in the Nuyorican barrio. Mohr's choice of language proved to be pivotal in creating a division between the literature produced by Nuyorican writers and that of authors writing in conventional American English (usually for mainstream publishing houses). Certainly, in Mohr's case, the use of standard English may have been responsible for her editorial success with mainstream publishers. In fact, Mohr is praised as the only early Puerto Rican writer to have had a literary career in mainstream publishing houses (Kanellos 124), unlike other Nuyorican authors who, because of their choice of language, saw their works limited to regional or independent ethnic publishers.

Sixteen years after the publication of *Nilda*, Judith Ortiz Cofer published in 1989 her first novel, *The Line of the Sun*. The first novel published by the University of Georgia Press, *The Line of the Sun* was nominated for the Pulitzer Prize, awarded that year to Latino-Cuban novelist Oscar Hijuelos for *The Mambo Kings Sing Songs of Love*. Ortiz Cofer started her literary career as a poet in the 1970s and, like Mohr, she writes in conventional American English. Despite outstanding awards received by both authors and despite numerous references to their works in articles on Puerto Rican or Latino/a literatures, there are relatively few critical articles on Ortiz Cofer (Acosta-Belén, Grobman, Bruce-Novoa, Ocasio, Piedra) and Mohr (Flores, Natov & DeLuca, Heredia, Miller, Zarnowski). Critics still show a strong preference for bilingual-Spanglish Nuyorican authors although the concept of a "Nuyorican school" has begun to lose authority as other Puerto Rican and Nuyorican writers have moved outside New York City (Turner 4). This is the case of Ortiz Cofer, who was born in Puerto Rico in 1952 and lived in New

Jersey from the age of two. Today she resides in Athens, Georgia, where she is an associate professor of English and creative writing at the University of Georgia.

Ortiz Cofer's and Mohr's novels *The Line of the Sun* and *Nilda* stand out because of their treatment of ethnic memories, which include a close examination of gender and racial discriminations. The strong eye-witness character of their works shows a tendency toward a testimonial account of special ethnic memory shaped by the socio-cultural and linguistic signifiers of Puerto Rican and Neorican life in the United States. In addition, both Ortiz Cofer and Mohr present, through powerful female characters, a strong genealogical emphasis that appropriates biographical accounts in order to create new images of the Puerto Rican reality in the United States. The two writers place their female characters within a specific locale, mostly Puerto Rican or latino barrios, where the characters deal with sociological issues related to their roles within the conflictive zones of Puerto Rican and American cultures, such as issues of the rights of women.

There are differences between these two authors, however, in their approach to the Neorican culture. Mohr's work is clearly defined by her early decision to write in conventional English, although she draws heavily from characters and anecdotes in a barrio background.   That decision marked her as a marginal writer within the Nuyorican literary group, who established bilingualism or Spanglish as the sole communicative code for the Neorican culture. Mohr's stand also provoked a similar reaction among Puerto Rican intellectuals on the island, who have denied that her work is truly Puerto Rican, because it is not written in Spanish. Mohr has addressed both groups's criticisms in two articles in particular: "Puerto Rican Writers in the U.S., Puerto Rican Writers in Puerto Rico: A Separation beyond Language: Testimonio" and "The Journey toward a Common Ground: Struggle and Identity of Hispanics in the U.S.A.," which can be described as a personal manifesto of her independence from both Nuyorican and Puerto Rican literary styles.

Judith Ortiz Cofer continues Mohr's trend by writing in conventional English, but Ortiz Cofer does not intend to produce alternative definitions of Puerto Rican-ness, stemming from personal observations of Neorican cultural behavioral patterns. Her *The Line of the Sun* fits solidly within the post-colonial ethnic literary genre. From the epistemological perspective of the ethnic text, Ortiz Cofer's novel addresses contemporary issues common to women of all cultures, not specific to the understanding of Puerto Rican-ness, by stressing the post-modern reality reflected in the lives of her Puerto Rican female characters.   Cofer's and Mohr's respective degrees of commitment to Nuyorican aesthetics and socio-political discourse invite numerous critical considerations. One of particular relevance is their exploration of the process by which their own Puerto Rican, Nuyorican or Neorican cultural significations take place.

* * *

> As a writer of Puerto Rican parentage who was born, raised, educated, and is presently living in New York City, I often get asked, 'Why don't you write in Spanish?' And this question is asked not only by those persons of non-Hispanic background but also by the Puerto Ricans residing on the island of Puerto Rico. (Nicholasa Mohr 1989:111)

> To be Puerto Rican is to work on uncertain ground, the object always of some grander politics, the student of an intractable history. (Shorris 28)

The choice of language is a central issue in the construction of Puerto Rican-ness or Nuyorican-ness. The controversy is intense on both sides. In spite of strong political ties with the United States (Puerto Rico has been an American commonwealth since 1952), Puerto Ricans on the island have kept Spanish as the indispensable vehicle for both daily and official communication (only the federal court uses English as its official language). The challenge to keep Spanish is high, despite struggles against invasive American consumerism, and many fear that failure to maintain Spanish as a dominant language will allow English to become the "native" language of the island. Unlike the Nuyoricans, however, Puerto Rican on the island seldom acknowledge the fact that their defiant advocacy of Spanish is an expression of a dual national identity. Nuyoricans must respond simultaneously to the cultural stimuli of both Puerto Rican and American mainstream cultures that produce a chronic tension in the barrio. The existence of an "other-ness" within the hybridity of the Nuyorican culture reflects the post-colonial issues that the Puerto Rican community in New York City has experienced since its development around the 1920s. The existence of a similar dual national identity in Puerto Rico has been ignored, the attitude of most residents of the island indicates a preference to accept without undue comment the existence of their colonial heritage despite the imposition of American citizenship upon Puerto Ricans in 1917.

Nuyoricans, however, have recognized and continue to struggle against the colonial-ethnic label of their classification as "Nuyoricans." In fact, Nuyoricans experience racial marginality, or the so-called "ethnic other." That fact is reflected in the use of multiple ethnic labels applied to the Puerto Rican immigrant in the City of New York (e.g., "Spanish," "Hispanic," "Hispano," "Latin," and "Latino," and most recently, "Puerto Rican," without the usual American hyphenation used in reference to other underrepresented groups, as in African-Americans. (Nuyoricans have suffered other labels too, even racial epithets such as "Spics" and "Pork-chops.") Nuyoricans share with Puerto Ricans on the island, however, a strong sense of separateness from mainstream American socio-cultural institutions. In spite of pressures for incorporation of Nuyoricans into American culture, or at least incorporation into an English-speaking ghetto, historians and sociologists stress that Puerto Ricans in the United States "have shown a proclivity not to abandon their culture, language, and identity" (Rodríguez 16-17). Instead, Nuyoricans have created their own "migrational culture," centralized in bilingualism, and concretely in Spanglish. That code-switching language form represents life in an American ethnic ghetto. It also has taken on linguistic referents associated with life in the big U.S. city and is, therefore, representative of American traits. Most significantly, it also represents a compromise between the two cultures. The process shows a commonality in the Puerto Rican post-colonialist experience after World War I, which led to official incorporation of Puerto Rico as an American territory. Spanglish may also be viewed as a forerunner in the development of the modern concept of Puerto Rican-ness (both insular and continental).

The choice of English over Spanish or Spanglish increasingly has become a focus of interest among Latina and Puerto Rican women writers. This subject is very serious for Judith Ortiz Cofer, as it had been for Nicholasa Mohr since her open debates with Nuyorican and Puerto Rican intellectual circles. For instance, Ortiz Cofer confided to me during an interview conducted in 1993 her fear that her Puerto Rican-ness could be restricted by her choice of language or career: "I resent very strongly when someone decides that, because you live in Georgia, because you don't speak perfect Spanish, because your degrees are in English, you are not one of us." For Ortiz Cofer the construction of Puerto Rican ethnicity is excepted from any pre-established linguistic values assigned to the use of Spanish over English. Her choice of language, Ortiz Cofer insists, must not be taken as a political or ethnic position but as a reflection of the maturity of the Puerto Rican diaspora:

> I would like to be recognized as a Puerto Rican writer because I feel that it is a two-way street. I am indebted to my heritage for the material that it has provided me with; it is enriching to my imagination to have the cuentos [tales], the Spanish language, and the history of this rich place. I feel that I am paying the

debt back by translating that experience into a language that I hope will be read by
many more people outside the Puerto Rican community. (qtd. Ocasio 1994:738)

To approach the linguistic component inherent in the definition of Puerto
Rican-ness, *The Line of the Sun* uses a case study of sorts: Ramona and her
husband, Rafael, a sailor stationed in the United States, move their family to New
Jersey.   Because of Ramona's strong insistence, they take residence in a
predominantly Puerto Rican barrio.   Marisol, their daughter and narrator of the
novel, recalls her own story and the stories of other relatives; she also functions as
the bilingual Neorican who serves as interpreter between two cultures.   College-
educated, Marisol pays special attention to the difficulties encountered by her mother
and by other Puerto Rican women whose language barriers limit their access to
mainstream society.   From her perspective as an adult narrator, Marisol examines
her family's life as an example of immigrant Puerto Rican society, or the Neorican
family, self-restricted to the geographical and cultural limits of the barrio.   The high-
rise building, or "El Building," makes even more vivid the restraining confines of
Neorican culture.

Ramona clearly favors life in "El Building," although her former life in a rustic
island setting, makes these new living conditions seem extremely limiting.   She is
still dependent, however, on the concrete signs that determine her Puerto Rican-ness
and in the United States she finds that only in El Building:

> It was easy for Ramona to become part of the ethnic bee-hive of El
> Building.   It was a microcosm of Island life with its intrigues, its gossip groups,
> and even its own spiritist, Elba, who catered to the complex spiritual needs of the
> tenants.   Coming in from shopping, my mother would close her eyes and breathe
> deeply; it was both a sigh of relief, for the city streets made her anxious, and a
> taking in of familiar smells.   In El Building, women cooked with their doors open
> as a sign of hospitality. Hard-to-obtain items like green bananas from the Island,
> plantains, and breadfruit were shared. (170-71)

Ortiz Cofer draws a direct contrast between "El Building," with its signs of
Puerto Rican-ness, and the suburb, a unique American city dwelling concept.   After
two years in New York City, Ramona's husband, Rafael, had come to the realization
that "a street-tough Puerto Rican immigrant is not the same species as the usually
gentle and hospitable Islander" (170).   There is dichotomy in Rafael's statement: He
is defensively pro-American, but he recognizes that the Nuyorican has been tainted
by life in the United States.   Ramona rejects as irrelevant, however, Rafael's strong
claims that life in the barrio is dangerous and not conducive to the raising of their

two young children. Ramona rejects the suburb, presented by Rafael as the ideal family setting (which they can afford, since he has a good, stable income); she describes life in suburbia in clearly post-colonial fashion:

> He would take us for rides to Fairlawn, an affluent community where doctors, lawyers, and other Paterson professional lived. here was so much space, and you could even hear the birds. Mother glanced at the cold façades of the houses and shook her head, unable to image the lives within. To her the square homes of strangers were like a television set: you could see the people moving and talking, apparently alive and real, but when you looked inside it was nothing but wires and tubes. (172-73)

The iconoclastic stand against the idealistic fabrication of Puerto Rican life in el barrio is also present in Nicholasa Mohr's *Nilda.* As in Ortiz Cofer's novel, women are set apart from important structures of power outside the realm of their households. *Nilda,* however, places a more historical emphasis on the strong female-oriented culture developed by Puerto Rican immigrant women living and sharing similar experiences related to life in an ethnic barrio. As in Ortiz Cofer, Mohr's images of Neorican culture stem from the difficulties encountered by newly arrived women immigrants who find themselves immersed in a foreign environment dominated by the English language, and, therefore, restrained from achieving participation in broader mainstream social organizations.

The historical process of the development of Neorican women's culture appears amply documented in *Nilda.* As in *The Line of the Sun,* the representative of first generation Nuyorican is a young girl, Nilda. Like Marisol, Nilda's training in helping with the administration of the household begins early in her childhood. Nilda, because of her mother's limitations with English, becomes her mother's "business partner" in those rare instances when the mother has to leave the monolingual barrio. On those occasions, Nilda becomes aware of the racist attitudes of the English-speaking society, which begins to show a strong resentment against the Puerto Rican, a monolingual American-born citizen. A most revealing episode in *Nilda* is the scene in which Nilda suffers humiliation by a City of New York bureaucrat. While Nilda's mother is applying for welfare, the female bureaucrat makes a conceited effort to scold Nilda for the unkempt appearance of her nails and goes on to cut them:

> "Turn your hands over. Over, turn them over. Let me see your nails." Nilda slowly turned over her hands. "You have got filthy nails. Look at

> that, Mrs. Ramírez. She's how old? Ten years old? Filthy." Impulsively, Nilda
> quickly pushed her hands behind her back and looked down at the floor.
>
>   "Why don't you clean your nails, young lady?" Nilda kept silent.
> "How often do you bathe?" Still silent, Nilda looked at her mother. She wanted
> to tell her to make the woman stop, but she saw that her mother was not looking
> her way; instead she was staring straight ahead. (68)

Because of her inability to respond efficiently in English to this racist attack and
because of her fear that any negative reaction will affect her case, Nilda's mother
must endure Nilda's humiliation. She too is humiliated, since as Nilda's mother she
is responsible for Nilda's well-being, her authority and her capacity to function as a
mother challenged in front of her child.

In tracing the development of the women-oriented Nuyorican community,
Nilda displays a strong feminist discourse which can be viewed as an early form of a
Latina socio-economic feminism, highly dependent on the historical circumstances
that caused Puerto Rican immigration to the United States. The nature of the Puerto
Rican immigration (of Spanish-speaking, American-born citizens arriving as
economic immigrants from an American territory) is central to the developing of the
genealogical discourse in *Nilda*. Female characters face specific historical incidents
that determine their own adaptation to American mainstream society, which is also
experiencing radical changes at the time of World War II. One must recall that
adaptation to American mainstream society is continually challenged, however,
since as in the case of Nilda, she also has fresh in her memory the abuses that she
and her mother have suffered at the hands of official representatives of American
society. On the other hand, Nilda, as she begins to function better within the
English-speaking society, also recognizes the political-activist importance of her
bilingual skills.

Among critics, Latina feminist scholars have commented on the strong
presence of socio-linguistic and political issues in the works of Latina writers.
Gloria Anzaldúa, a Chicana writer and literary critic, for instance, has observed in
particular the significance of the use of English for the Latina writer, a choice
defined along racial lines as an important issue to "mujeres-de-color" (women of
color)

> To speak English is to think in that language, to adopt the ideology of the
> people whose language it is and to be 'inhabited' by their discourses. Mujeres-de-

color speak and write not just against traditional white ways but against a
prevailing mode of being, against a white frame of reference. (1990:xxii)

Ethnic exploration, including the handling of issues relating to racial and gender
discrimination, for the Latina author is sharply penetrating. She must deal with this
issue on a multi-faceted level: How are gender boundaries established within
American mainstream culture and within their own ethnic group; how is the social
construction of these gender roles achieved; and by what process can women of
color achieve an ideological stand?

Both Nicholasa Mohr's *Nilda* and Judith Ortiz Cofer's *The Line of the Sun*
address Anzaldúa's "prevailing mode of being," represented in the novels'
protagonists who encounter from the Nuyorican community opposition based solely
on societal limitations placed on them because of their gender and early age. This
opposition is significant, since in both cases these young characters are bilingual and
can fully function in mainstream society, whereas very few Puerto Rican-born
characters can do so.

In the case of Mohr, there is a strong tendency toward historical documentation
of the gender boundaries within American mainstream and Neorican cultures. More
than Marisol, Nilda develops under the strong influence of her experiences as a
teenager during World War II, reflecting the radical changes that are taking place
nationally as a result of the war and of the socio-economic conflicts faced by the
thousands of Puerto Rican immigrants in New York City. Nilda's responsibility to
serve as her mother's "partner" (a strong trait of Puerto Rican culture is the
expectation that children be involved in family matters), is increased by a weak
father figure; so Nilda assumes a dominant role that has been traditionally reserved
for men. Nilda's problem, however, is that her control is limited to the few instances
when her mother has to leave the barrio for official business. Within the limits of
the barrio, Nilda returns to the restrictions due to her status as a young girl, and her
bilingualism, which marginalizes her from the monolingual, Spanish-speaking
community.

Judith Ortiz Cofer takes a different social approach: the examination of the
process that constructs the gender roles. In line with Mohr's bildungsroman-type
character, Marisol is a typical youngster who, in addition to her normal growing
pains, must also face more serious issues arising from her very traditional Puerto
Rican upbringing in a latino barrio. The marginality of Marisol's growing-up
experiences (aggravated by the fact that she attends a private school where she and

her brother are the only latinos), produces in her (as in Nilda) a character who is constantly questioning her place among the two conflicting cultures: "On the streets of Paterson my mother seemed an alien and a refugee, and as I grew to identify with the elements she feared, I dreaded walking with her, a human billboard advertising her paranoia in a foreign language" (174). At the end, Marisol comes to grip with her biculturality, a sign of Neorican culture which, as in Marisol's case, is more a way of life: "I learned something during those days: though I would always carry my Island heritage on my back like a snail, I belonged in the world of phones, offices, concrete buildings, and the English language" (273).

Marisol appears to be a more developed character than Nilda, in the sense that her plight takes on a more allegorical dimension. At first Marisol is preoccupied solely with economic issues. Her father's income can provide the family with better living conditions; however, because of her mother's fear of suburban life style, they live in the barrio, but well beyond their neighbors' economic level. At the father's insistence, Marisol attends a private Catholic school where she and her brothers are the only children of recent immigrants. This compromise creates a dichotomy, reflecting the split between mainstream and Neorican cultures: "By dressing better and having more than any of the children in El Building, we were kept out of their ranks; by having less than our classmates at Saint Jerome's, we never quite fitted in that society, either" (178). Not only does Marisol feel that she is marginal to her dual societies, but she also becomes more active in her quest to devise signs (cultural or personal) that will facilitate the expression of her own experience. In fact, Marisol--as her name symbolically suggests: Mar(i)sol (sea and sun)--finds the ultimate way to create a balance in her life. At the end of the novel, an adult Marisol, like a traditional buildungsroman character, reflects on her childhood and realizes that her problems as a Puerto Rican raised in the United States were part of a normal growing process. However, unlike other teenagers, Marisol also understands that her biculturality gave her an early and highly developed maturity, reflected in her profound interest in relating closely to the experiences encountered by other members of her family: "In the years that followed I concluded that the only way to understand a life is to write it as a story, to fill in the blanks left by circumstance, lapse of memory, and failed communication" (290).

This process of self-representation by the Latina writer opposes mainstream imposition of the other-ness encoded in a process described by Edward Said as "decontextualization or miniaturization of the ethnic experience" (qtd. in Mariani & Crary 94). Ortiz Cofer and Mohr oppose on two levels such "decontextualization and miniaturization" of their own Puerto Rican-ness. First, like other Latina writers, they seek to produce what Anzaldúa describes as "the breaking down [of] paradigms...by creating a new mythos..." (1990:379). Indeed, both Ortiz Cofer and Mohr seek to reconstruct mainstream Puerto Rican-otherness by opposing the stereotypical "West Side Story Syndrome." By their experiential discourse of displacement they reject that mainstream representation of Puerto Rican or Nuyorican women and, by "ethnic" association, of all Latina women. Second, the process of a Puerto Rican representation independent of the abstract and inclusive Latino-ness brings within itself "a change in the way we [mujeres-de-color] perceive reality, the way we see ourselves and the way we behave," resulting in what Anzaldúa describes as "a new consciousness" (1990:379).

In keeping with that "new Latina consciousness," Ortiz Cofer's and Mohr's main characters are invariably Puerto Rican or Nuyorican women. In fact, both writers have produced a considerable number of fictional women protagonists or, as in the case of Ortiz Cofer, a collective mass of female poetic voices, who point to various stages of feminist ethnic activism against sexism and racial discrimination. Significantly, Mohr's short story collection, *Rituals of Survival: A Woman's Portfolio* (1985), locates Puerto Rican/Nuyorican women's lives within a socio-political context that provides a meaning to otherwise uneventful existences. Emphasis on the woman's perspective is reflected in the fact that each short-story in that collection has as a subtitle the name of its woman protagonist. These characters are a wide array of Puerto Rican and Nuyorican women, women representative of the Puerto Rican diaspora in New York City. Their stories, sometimes tragic and bitter-sweet, illustrate the formative phase of the Neorican culture, of which they had a central role in spite of the social limitations placed upon them by the chauvinist Puerto Rican patriarchy or by the racist tendencies of mainstream society.

On the other hand, Ortiz Cofer explores fully her own feminist Puerto Rican identity. As mentioned earlier, Judith Ortiz Cofer started her literary career as a poet. Published by mainstream media, her poetry equates the expression of her Puerto Rican self with social comments. The presence of a woman's voice addresses one key facet: the correlation between the Puerto Rican experience and her commitment to gender-related issues. Ortiz Cofer's own Puerto Rican-ness is independent of the mythical locus of the Nuyorican barrio. Her desire to engage in more direct discussions of the metaphorical representation of the Puerto Rican identity may have been responsible for her transition to prose and essay writings.

Nicholasa Mohr's social concerns are also evident. Like Ortiz Cofer, Mohr stands out as a marginal voice within the Puerto Rican and Nuyorican communities. First, she has been a frequent critic against the islanders who have rejected her work as not being truly Puerto Rican:

> We are no longer an island people. This reality has become increasingly incomprehensible to the Puerto Rican from the island. This new world, which we are still creating, is the source of our strength and the cradle of our future. (1987:160)

Second, Nicholasa Mohr's women characters, whether they are Puerto Rican or Nuyorican, do not exhibit the linguistic duality expressed by Spanglish, as it is in the work of other Nuyorican writers; the latter writers use Spanglish as a symbolical representation of the binary Nuyorican identity, dependent upon the constant opposition of Spanish and English. Another evidence of independence from traditional Nuyorican literature is the fact that Mohr does not reproduce "barrio life," nor does she present the Nuyorican barrio as a symbolical locus of special significance to her Nuyorican characters.

It is significant, however, that Ortiz Cofer's and Mohr's literary constructions follow semiological patterns shaped by socio-cultural signifiers of Puerto Rican life in the United States. Outstanding in that process are the strong genealogical discoursive structures produced by their women protagonists. From that perspective, for instance, Ortiz Cofer's whole poetic production could be characterized as her attempt to offer a re-construction of the Puerto Rican identity through techniques that draw heavily upon her autobiographical memory. For example, *Silent Dancing* (1990), a collection of poetry, short stories and personal essays, dwells on key moments of her childhood spent between Puerto Rico and New Jersey. The personal or autobiographical essays, or rather, the "creative non-fiction,"[1] as she insists that these pieces should be labeled, reproduce eye-witness accounts that promote further exploration of the duality of an "I" narrator, remembered as both the "other" and "self." Ortiz Cofer's experiences of growing up as a Puerto Rican in the United States (and those of other significant family members) subjected her to the same extended Puerto Rican locus of her fictional female characters. One example is found in the essay, "The Myth of the Latin Woman: I Just Met a Girl Named María," from her work, *The Latin Deli* (1993).

Ortiz Cofer recalls in "The Myth of the Latin Woman..." a personal incident which stresses her "other-ness ethnic" condition. The incident that gives name to the essay refers to her encounter with a drunk Irishman on a bus trip from London to Oxford University (where she was earning graduate credits). The Irish man "serenaded" her with his rendition of "María," a song from the musical "West Side Story."[2] This incident stresses the fact that there is no single specific place in which the Puerto Rican-otherness becomes evident. In other words, although Puerto Ricans have created mythical places for the experiencing of Puerto Rican-ness (e.g., the "Latin deli," associated with the social core of the barrio), Ortiz Cofer's experience reveals that any locale becomes a background to Puerto Rican-ness, since, as she points out in "The Myth of the Latin Woman...," "the island travels with you" (148).

In Mohr's short-story collection *In Nueva York*, originally published in 1977 and reprinted in 1993, the writer also appropriates intertextual testimonial narrations to support her well-defined political stand:

> My birth makes me a native New Yorker. I write here in the United States about my personal experiences and those of a particular group of migrants that number in the millions. Yet, all of these actualities seem to have little or no bearing on those who insist on seeing me as an 'intruder,' or 'outsider' who has taken on a foreign language: perhaps even taken it on much too forcefully, using it to document and validate our existence and survival inside the very nation that chose to colonize us. (1989:111-112)

Like Ortiz Cofer, Mohr creates Nuyorican women characters that do not depend on their connection to the barrio community for the development of their feminine psyche. In fact, their confrontations with mainstream prejudices (specifically racism) and with the male Nuyorican bias against women's rights link Mohr with other Nuyorican women writers as voices that "share a common expression, a declaration of the universal causes of women" (Estévez 173).

Another link with a feminist agenda is Mohr's use of her own autobiographical memory in the creation of her characters. For instance, her story "The Artist (Inez)" in *Rituals of Survival: A Woman's Portfolio* (1985), presents a feminist hero, Inez, a young Nuyorican woman who struggles against her family and her husband as they attempt to undercut her desires to became a graphic artist. Mohr herself is a trained graphic artist but the character is not identifiable with Nicholasa Mohr to the same extent that "María" is identifiable with Judith Ortiz Cofer.

***

> Writing is dangerous because we are afraid of what the writing reveals:
> the fears, the angers, the strengths of a woman under a triple or quadruple
> oppression. Yet in that very act lies our survival because a woman who writes has
> power. And a woman with power is feared. (Anzaldúa 1983:171)

In conclusion, Judith Ortiz Cofer's and Nicholasa Mohr's works depend on a feminist epistemological center that examines the relationship of the public and the private feminine self(s) with the representation of Puerto Rican-ness or Nuyorican-ness. The effect of a dual marginality is present in their opposition to the sexist "West Side Story Syndrome" of mainstream society and their "other-ness" as women writers in Puerto Rican and Nuyorican cultures and literatures (dominated, until recently, by male writers). That decentering of power structures may be exclusive to the feminine other-ness discourse. In fact, critic Gayatri Chakravorty Spivak claims that the feminist "deconstructivist can use herself (assuming one is at one's own disposal) as a shuttle between the center (inside) and the margin (outside) and thus narrate a displacement" (107).

Such a feminist discourse that can be labeled as depicting "ethnic feminine displacement" is evident in both Ortiz Cofer and Mohr. Ortiz Cofer, in particular, stands out for her experimentation with the interconnection of literary genres as a response to her recognition of a fragmented "Puerto Rican in the United States" identity. As in *Silent Dancing* and in *The Latin Deli*, for instance, ethnic depiction of that Puerto Rican semiological-based identity is for Judith Ortiz Cofer a point of departure in her examination of a post-modern urban feminine American psyche. For both Mohr and Ortiz Cofer the Puerto Rican community and its popular and economic cultures, produce symbols illustrative of a community formed of its own ethnic, social elements. Their most significant contribution to American literature is precisely that feminist deconstruction of the Puerto Rican reality that attains character as literary material, abandoning old sociological schemes promoted by Nuyorican writers or by the stereotypical and openly racist other-view of mainstream media.

Rafael Ocasio

Notes

[1] In an interview published by *Callaloo*, Ortiz Cofer comments on her concept of "creative non-fiction": "By calling them [her personal or autobiographical essays] creative non-fiction, by introducing the word "creative," I am admitting, so that there is no confusion, that what I am trying to

do is non-fiction in intent, that these incidents actually happened, but that the way I am transmitting them to the reader may be a recreation" (qtd. in Ocasio 1994:735).

[2] Puerto Rican writer Ana Lydia Vega has commented on a similar personal anecdote. She remembers that when she studied in France in the late seventies, her "French friends--who did not distinguish Puerto Rico from Costa Rica or Tahiti from Haiti--baptized me with the dubious nickname of Mademoiselle West Side Story" (113). (The emphasis is in the original Spanish.)

Works cited:

Anzaldúa, Gloria. "La conciencia de la mestiza: Toward a New Consciousness." *Making Face, Making Soul: Haciendo Caras: Creative and Critical Perspectives of Women of Color.* San Francisco: Aunt Lute Foundation, 1990. 377-389.

---. "Speaking in Tongues: A Letter to 3rd World Women Writers." *This Bridge Called My Back: Writings by Radical Women of Color.* Eds. Cherríe Moraga & Gloria Anzaldúa. New York: Kitchen Table, 1983. 165-174.

Estévez, Sandra María. "The Feminist Viewpoint in the Poetry of Puerto Rican Women in the United States." *Images and Identities: The Puerto Rican in Two World Contexts.* Ed. Asela Rodríguez de Laguna. New Brunswick: Transaction Books, 1987. 171-177.

Fishman, Joshua A. "Intellectuals from the Island." *Bilingualism in the Barrio.* Eds. Joshua A. Fishman and Robert L. Cooper. Indiana University, 1971. 7-73.

Kanellos, Nicolás, ed. *Short Fiction by Hispanic Writers.* Houston: Arte Público Press, 1993.

Mariani, Phil & Jonathan Crary. "In the Shadow of the West: An Interview with Edward Said." *Discourses: Conversations in Postmodern Art and Culture.* Eds. Russell Ferguson, William Olander, Marcia Tucker and Karen Fiss. New York: The Museum of Contemporary Art and Cambridge: The MIT Press, 1990. 93-103.

Mohr, Nicholasa. "Puerto Rican Writers in the U.S., Puerto Rican Writers in Puerto Rico: A Separation beyond Language (Testimonio)." *Breaking Boundaries: Latina Writings and Critical Readings.* Eds. Asunción Horno- Delgado, Eliana Ortega, Nina M. Scott, and Nancy Saporta Sternbach. University of Massachusetts Press, 1989. 111-116.

---. "Puerto Ricans in New York: Cultural Evolution and Identity." *Images and Identities:The Puerto Rican in Two World Contexts.* Ed. Asela Rodríguez de Laguna. New Brunswick: Transaction Books, 1987. 157-160.

---. *Nilda.* Houston: Arte Público Press, 1986.

Ocasio, Rafael. "The Infinite Variety of the Puerto Rican Reality: An Interview with Judith Ortiz Cofer." *Callaloo* 17:3 (1994): 730-742.

Ortiz Cofer, Judith. *The Latin Deli.* University of Georgia Press, 1993.

---. The Line of the Sun. Athens: University of Georgia Press, 1989.

Rodríguez, Clara E. *Puerto Ricans Born in the U.S.A.* Boston: Hyman, 1989.

Shorris, Earl. *Latinos: A Biography of the People.* New York: Norton, 1992.
    Spivak, Gayatri Chakravorty. *In Other Worlds: Essays in Cultural Politics.* New York:
    Methuen, 1987.

Turner, Faythe. "Introduction." *Puerto Rican Writers at Home in the USA: An Anthology.* Ed.
    Faythe Turner. Seattle: Open Hand, 1991. 1-6.

Varo, Carlos. *Puerto Rico: Radiografía de un pueblo asediado.* Ediciones Puerto Rico, 1973.

Vega, Ana Lydia. "Saludo a los niuyoricans: La cantaleta policacofónica de la puertorriqueñidad."
    Cupey X:1-2 (January-December 1992): 110-116.

II Works Consulted:

Acosta-Belén, Edna. "A MELUS Interview: Judith Ortiz Cofer." *MELUS: The   Journal of the*
    Society for the Study of the Multi-Ethnic Literature of the United States 3:18 (Fall 1993):
    83-97.

---. "Puerto Rican Literature in the United States." *Redefining American Literary History.* Eds. A.
    LaVonne Brown Ruoff and Jerry W. Ward, Jr. New York: Modern Language Association,
    1990. 373-378.

Bruce-Novoa, Juan. "Ritual in Judith Ortiz Cofer's *The Line of the Sun. Confluencia* 1:8 (Fall 1992):
    61-69.

---. "Judith Ortiz Cofer's Rituals of Movement." *The Americas Review* 3-4:19 (Winter   1991): 88-99.

Flores, Juan. "Puerto Rican Literature in the United States: Stages and Perspectives." *Redefining*
    American Literary History. Eds. A. LaVonne Brown Ruoff and Jerry W. Ward, Jr. New York:
    Modern Language Association, 1990. 210- 218.

---. "Back Down These Mean Streets: Introducing Nicholasa Mohr and Louis Reyes Rivera." *Revista*
    Chicano-Riqueña 2:8 (1980): 51-56.

Grobman, Laurie. "The Cultural Past and Artistic Creation in Sandra Cisneros' The *House on the*
    Mango Street and Judith Ortiz Cofer's *Silent Dancing. Confluencia* 1:11 (Fall 1995): 42-49.

Heredia, Juanita. "Down These Streets: Exploring Urban Space in *El Bronx Remembered and The House on the Mango Street. Mester* 2-1: 22-23 (Fall 1994/Spring 1995): 93-105.

Miller, John. "Nicholasa Mohr: Neorican Writings in Process: 'A View of the Other Culture.'" *Revista/Review Interamericana* 9 (1979): 543-54.

Mohr, Eugene. The Nuyorican Experience: Literature of the Puerto Rican Minority. Westport: Greenwood, 1982.

Mohr, Nicholasa. *In Nueva York*. Houston: Arte Público Press, 1993.

---. "The Journey toward a Common Ground: Struggle and Identity of Hispanics in the U.S.A." *The Americas Review* 1:18 (Spring 1990): 81-85.

---. *Rituals of Survival: A Woman's Portfolio*. Houston: Arte Público Press, 1986. Natov, Roni & Geraldine DeLuca. "An Interview with Nicholasa Mohr." *The Lion and the Unicorn: A Journal of Children's Literature* 11:1 (1987): 116-121.

Ocasio, Rafael. "Judith Ortiz Cofer: La deconstrucción de la invisibilidad latina o la dialéctica de la representación puertorriqueña." *El poder hispano: Actas del V Congreso de Culturas Hispánicas de los Estados Unidos*. Eds. Alberto Moncada Lorenzo, Carmen Flys Junquera, and José Antonio Gurpegui Palacios. Universidad de Alcalá, 1994. 499-506.

---. "Puerto Rican Literature in Georgia? An Interview with Judith Ortiz Cofer." *The Kenyon Review* XIV:4 (Fall 1992): 43- 50.

---. "Speaking in Puerto Rican: An Interview with Judith Ortiz Cofer." *Bilingual Review/Revista Bilingüe* XVII:2 (May-August 1992): 143-146.

Ortiz Cofer, Judith. *Silent Dancing*. Houston: Arte Público Press, 1990.

Piedra, José. "His and Her Panics." *Dispositio* XVI:41 (1991):71-93.

Zarnowski, Myra. "An Interview with Author Nicholasa Mohr." *The Reading Teacher* 45:2 (October 1991): 100-106.

---. "Growing Up Puerto Rican: The Fiction of Nicholasa Mohr." *Dragon Lode* 9 (1991): 5-8.

12.

FETISHIZED BLACKNESS: RACIAL DESIRE
IN CONTEMPORARY JAPANESE NARRATIVE AND CULTURE[1]

Flipping television channels late one insomniac night in Tokyo in the winter of 1990, I happened upon a Japanese dancing duo performing in black face, singing, outfitted in the trendiest of costumes: baseball caps with brims turned to the back, expensive sneakers, and baggy trousers. That same year, a friend who was visiting Japan entered a dance hall which to his surprise appeared to be peopled almost exclusively by black youths. Even more to his surprise, upon closer scrutiny he realized that the "black" young men were Asian: Japanese with darkened faces, some with dread locks and some with fades, performing hip hop dance steps and breaking to rap music.

From the mid 1980s through the 1990s, the best-selling novelist Yamada Eimi, who is herself married to an African-American man, published book after book replete with detailed erotic depictions of Japanese women with African-American lovers; books that were primarily consumed by young Japanese women. At basically the same time, Ieda Shôko, a journalist of sorts, published two (supposed) exposés of Japanese women's erotic dalliances with African-American men[2]. Contemporaneous with the popularity of hip hop style among mostly young Japanese men, has been the consumption of blackness by young Japanese women, both in narrative form through texts like Yamada's, and in material form, when some women seek actual erotic encounters with African-Americans.

The encounter of teenage and young adult Japanese men and women with rap music, hip hop style, and signs of blackness, as well as the portrayals of African Americans in popular narratives, are multifaceted reconfigurations of these variant signs, bound to global commodity exchange, Japanese racialism and Japanese national identity. The contemporary pop-culture Japanese rendering of hip hop and rap consists of a fascination with the aural and visual styles (the sounds, movements, body language and outfits), and an African-American symbolic presence signaled by fetishizing black skin and hairstyles. This disposition of hip hop style requires *as its foundation* a separation of hip hop and rap from the specifics of American racialism, and reconstruction bounded by Japanese racialism. Similarly, the iconography that informs the appearance of African Americans in narrative text has a meaning specific to its Japanese context. Abetting a wide range of racialist stereotypes, the borrowing of elements of style sundered from content is facilitated because blacks are foreigners in Japan, rather than others within[4]. Attitudes towards American blacks are not the direct outgrowth of tensions within mainstream society (although earlier discourses on racial purity are). Japanese refabrications of elements of black youth culture are thus primarily limited to ones that operate on the level of signs; signs originated elsewhere and split from their referents; signs that then resignify within the Japanese context, as informed by Japanese internal racialist and gendered tensions. Accordingly, there is an increased potential for reductive mythic images of African Americans. For both the young women seeking African-American lovers, (in text or in body), and the young (primarily) men who dress themselves in hip hop style, blackness is frequently affixed to an antecedent erotic subtext which fetishizes blackness as symbolic of phallic empowerment.

The phenomenon of non-black youth dressing themselves in "black style" is not unique to Japan. In the United States white teenagers have also adopted the clothing, mannerisms, hairdos, vernacular, and other markers of hip hop style. In Japan special salons advertise their expertise in "dread-hair" (*doreddo hea*) - a process which may cost dearly in time and money; in America white girls may plait their hair in small braids[5]. What is strikingly different in Japan, is that black skin is incorporated as an essential signifier of "hip hop style." Japanese youth enamored of hip hop regularly darken their complexions with make-up, especially when they go out dancing. Not only does the writer Yamada depict black men as the erotic objects for her narrative heroines, but she herself was videotaped on a television show, *New Yorker*, preparing for a tour of the South Bronx, applying dark foundation make-up, and combing her hair with an Afro-pik[6].

Recent works by John Russell have mapped out a domain of Japanese representations of blacks which he holds to be directly imported from the West[7]. But present day Japanese "black face" is usually not determined by the American historical counterpart. In the United States, the history of white entertainers in blackface has marked the darkening of the skin in imitation of African Americans as "racist": the recent debacle of Ted Danson at the New York City Friar Club roast of comic Whoopi Goldberg in October 1993 affirms that blackface remains a taboo in contemporary America[8]. The American version was a caricature, and made use of certain coded images and props, such as white gloves and exaggerated lips. American blackface did not seek realistic representations of African Americans[9]. While such exaggerated versions can also still be seen in Japan, some Japanese black face, on the other hand, emulates hair and clothing styles, (akin to the "white Negro" phenomenon in the States) but also fetishizes skin color in an attempt to mask the Japanese self with a *realistic* black visage. Russell has argued convincingly that the new popularity of black style in Japan, (that takes its place alongside the contemporary narrative portrayals), reproduce old stereotypes, yet I think that for some Japanese youth, - and in the ambivalences as written in some narrative text - reconfigurations of themselves in black images mark a processing of blackness that is qualitatively different from earlier representations, and reveal a subtext of racial and erotic desire.

That the blackening of the bodily self has become a desired index in Japan upsets conventional twentieth century inferential symbolic homilies on black skin. While, as Tricia Rose has argued, hip hop originates from within a commodity-driven urban African-American youth subculture, (availing itself of already circulating recorded music, audio and video technology, and fashion), it also originates as a venue for black youths' subversive voice[10]. In America the massification of rap and hip hop style to access a broader, white market inevitably entails a process of a partial elision of hip hop's subversive origins in the service of "sanitized" white narratives, and further exploits the existing collusion with commodity culture.[11] In the Japanese reproduction, while many of the origins of hip hop and rap are erased, they are erased differently; most notably, they have not been "whitened."

Although rap and hip hop have been successfully utilized by corporate advertisers throughout the world, each reproduction represents a hybrid of the dominant local culture and the imported African-American subculture. Hip hop becomes universalized (a global phenomenon), yet is ceaselessly remade regionally through its interaction with variant social, political, ideological and other contexts. This decentering and unification of desire for, and the capacity to acquire goods are situated within the globalization of capital production in the contemporary period. Goods sold to a targeted region must *resonate* with an extant aesthetic and/or appeal on an imagistic level to a perceived need/desire. Marketing campaigns must redirect existing desire towards novelty commodities.

The dispensation of goods in late capitalism frequently employs an erotic subtext: sex apparently bolsters sales. Wolfgang Haug has argued that when commodities are divorced from any utilitarian value, they compete on the level of illusion and appearance: an image is created and sold through the suggestion of erotic sensualism (or libidinal urge). Apparel, for example, is frequently sold through recourse to "a language of clothes conveying sexual feelings.[12]" Haug's erotic subtext has particular relevance for Japanese black style - of which hip hop is a sub-style. In Japan the sexual message encoded in "black" style is directly identified with phallic empowerment for both men and women, a consequence of Japanese racial attitudes towards American blacks. Other co-present subtexts, such as rebellion against adult mainstream society, provide youth with, in Umberto Eco's words, a text for "semiotic guerrilla warfare" against the world of their parents[13].

Hip hop style, which is marked in Japan with black skin, is interwoven with the phallus as a signifier of a subtext of masculine, heterosexual *body* power. Young men seek to incorporate this power through remodeling themselves in imitation of hip hop artists. For young women, evident in narratives by female authors such as Shôko and Yamada, black style includes the acquisition of male African-American lovers, bound to the same subtext of phallic empowerment, but transgressive of assumed (racially exclusive) Japanese male access to their sexual bodies, and belittling of Japanese masculine identity. The doubled perception of threat/desire produced through the fetishization of blackness is a product of contemporary Japanese representations of self and mechanisms of othering, nuanced by reforming gender/power distribution.

For the older generation "whiteness" was a signifier for American economic, ideological, and political, putative superiority, against which murky, Japanese "yellowness" was a sign of being below the standard. As the nation-state Japan is increasingly perceived to have surpassed American capitalist initiative, a somnambulant anti-Japanese sentiment has reawakened in America; in Japan, the younger generation has begun to challenge the monolithic myth of white supremacy. In the shadow of a reviving Japanese nationalism are other perceptions straining against the delineations of a racialism bounded by the antipodal notions of black and white. Youth reproduction of themselves in black style, and depictions of female sexual coupling with African Americans, signify a potential transnational identity, supplementary to a previously introjected, Western imperialist black/white binary paradigm, revelatory of a desire and a propensity for racial identificatory slippage. The transidentified Japanese- "colored" self however *also* appropriates American racialist stereotyping, for an ambivalent self-identification. To rephrase, the Japanese self is integrated with its "coloredness," and thereby with blackness, while it simultaneously introjects the Western (white) imperialist gaze. Naming, sampling, hip hop dress, turning hair into dread locks, darkening of the skin, and the acquisition of black lovers in cultural and narrative texts, all function to produce an ambivalence in Japanese youths' embrace of African-American style: individual and national identity, (self-as-Japanese), and transidentity, (self as allied with color) are proclaimed and erased[14].

Japanese Racialism, Narrative Collusions.

Racial othering in Japan, as elsewhere, is promoted, as David Goldberg has asserted regarding the general structure of racialist essentialism, as a mode of exclusion based on a perceived natural (physical, bodily) difference, which conceptually unifies both self and other in homogeneous groupings[15]. Japanese racialism[3] has historically marked differences between Asians by positing a variety of discourses on physical (bodily) distinctions, which include the notion of "pure blood lineage" and an association of purity and acculturation with light skin; discourses which also mark inhabitants of the nation-state Japan as "other." John Dower writes in his *War Without Mercy* that "the Japanese themselves looked down on all the other 'colored' races. ...they had esteemed 'whiteness' since ancient times.[16]" The "classical" valorization of "whiteness" in Japan, however, must also be differentiated from black/white racialism: whiteness marked a non-laboring class from a laboring one, and not one race from another.
John Russell has shown that the dominant pre-second world war images of Africans and African Americans circulated in Japan were fettered by the binarism of black equals savage/white equals civilization[17]. Such delineations buttressed the extant Japanese racial ideology that had represented darker Asians as inferior. Modern Japanese racial ideology is thus classical in what Etienne Balibar identifies as the anthropological universal of marking difference along the axis of humanity (culture) and animality (nature).[18]

Russell has argued convincingly that images of American blacks in Japan have frequently reproduced American racialist stereotypes, evidenced by the popularity of the *Story of Little Black Sambo*, and the modern yet still reductive portrayals of African Americans as "sexual objects, studs, fashion accessories and quintessential performers," imagistic changes which Russell dismisses as "more old wine in new bottles.[19]" In Yamada's narrative depictions, for example, in keeping with modern trends her representations of black men comprise a sampling from a variety of *contemporary* stereotypes. "Black Silk" from the anthology *I am Beat* (*Boku wa biito,* date), introduces jazz-musician Percy as:

> Lately, Percy is Maria's exclusive property. He escorts her everywhere. Decked out in a linen suit, Panama hat on his head, he's dressed like a good old-time sax-player. But he doesn't look old-fashioned, because Percy is a very young black man with a superfine, beautiful body.[20]

(Note that Percy is called Maria's property.) "My Heart in Rhyme" depicts a black American who is both rap-artist and jazz musician (a composite figure of generally separated African-American musical forms):

> Moving to the music, Barney began to rap. A year ago he fell in love with a fine woman but then his life got totally crazy and that was that. Even though he loved her sooo much, jealousy got in the way and it didn't go well at all. The words went something like that. Barney performed it in front of Phyllis, gesturing and posturing, making her laugh.[21]

No survey of black characters would be complete, it seems, without the requisite association of African-American men with certain forms of music, dance, and of course, drugs:

> ...not just gambling. You probably remember Dealer Victor. It so happened that there was some fine coke at his house and we had a party and got high. If I try to remember how many white lines I sniffed, there's this fantasy in my head. The fantasy is, I bring along these two cute girls who take me to bed, sandwiched in between them, too much.[22]

The tales cited above reproduce partialized representations of black men culled from the repertoire of popular media images - men who then function as the erotic object for the female protagonist. Two other short tales from the collection, "X-Rated Blanket" and "Taste Of...." are soliloquies on the pleasures of love-making from, respectively, a woman's and a man's point of view.[23] While neither narrative explicitly identifies the object of passion ("X-Rated Blanket") nor the narrator ("Taste Of...") as black, it can be easily inferred. The narrator of "Taste Of...." plays the harmonica and smells like barbecue sauce, while the yearned-for George in "X-Rated Blanket" has a voice described as "like a southern melody."[24] In Yamada's work, however, that which clearly identifies a male character as black, is when he is portrayed as an excellent lover. For it is black men who, in Yamada's words, possess the "genius" of love-making; repeatedly she compares the sexual skill of lovers in text through reference to their race.

Such portrayals certainly substantiate Russell's conclusion that the vast majority of "expanded roles" remain within set domains (musician, athlete and stud), yet I think that for some Japanese youth, and for Yamada as well - as I will show- African Americans as signs are encoded with additional, and new, significations: the images of African Americans are not inevitably the same old thing, but something *different* (even if they are still also informed by antecedent discourses). For many young Japanese, admiration replaces former fear and distaste, as evidenced by the quote "I am mesmerized [*akogareta*] by black people."[25] *Akogareta*, to yearn for, or be in awe of, has been used in the past affixed to things foreign to mean "desirous of," but until very recently African Americans were definitely not considered part of desired (*akogareta*) America.

Twelve years ago, when working as a production coordinator for Japanese television and commercials, I would be asked to find American extras to appear in various minor roles. "American" unequivocally meant white; black extras were reserved for the illustration of criminal activities. Asian faces would not do, because Asian faces don't signify "America" within Japanese codes. Twelve years ago, producers, "talent" and crew would whisper to me their fears of black people, known to them only through American media and filmic portrayals of African Americans holding guns to the heads of putatively normative, law-abiding whites, asking, "Why are black people so violent?" Twelve years ago, the *akogareta* United States constructed by Japanese television advertisements was exclusively white. Today, a different, yet still "desired America" is *also* signified by [hip hop styled] African Americans, or African-American men as (heterosexual) lovers, often consumed only in the pages of erotic narrative and popular texts. The reimaging of America to include ethnicity begins within America itself, but is reconfigured to suit Japan's positioning, supplemental to a black/white binarism, revealing moments of slippage and indeterminacy, mirroring the concurrent subtle repositionings of dominance between the two nations.

Twentieth century Japanese national racial identity was constructed in the shadow of the Western white/black binarism, into which Japan could not neatly configure itself. Japanese (and other Asians) inhabited an in-between space of being neither white nor black, facilitating a certain degree of identificatory irresolution.[26] Japanese racial identity frequently took on a relationalism: "colored" in comparison to whites, "pale" against blacks. For the writer Natsume Sôseki, (within Japan, perhaps the most acclaimed modern Japanese writer), catching a reflection of his own countenance while visiting London in 1900 was a lingering moment of racial shame and self-hatred. Sôseki described in a letter how he saw a midget with a strangely-colored face approaching him while he was taking a walk nearby his boarding house, only to awaken to the shocked realization that the midget was his own reflection in a mirror. In her 1994 essay, "Fearful Terrain: The Underground and the Continent in the Works of Natsume Sôseki," Katsuyo Motoyoshi wrote,

> Frantz Fanon would have had no trouble understanding .... [B]efore the ironic, and perhaps uncomfortable laugh, before the shocking flash of recognition, who was that "midget" that Sôseki has seen? ...[T]he identity of the midget caught in Sôseki's glimpse cannot be understood, if the reflective surface of the mirror is falsely equated with transparency. Here, the mirror stands for a specific intervention, that of the Western imperialist gaze which has been interiorized by Sôseki.[27]

In 1933 the writer Tanizaki Jun'ichirô, another giant of the modern Japanese canon, noted that although the Japanese had long esteemed whiteness, "this whiteness of ours differs from that of the white races": Japanese whiteness, he asserted, is clouded by a taint of irrepressible shadows, and therefore,

> [W]hen one of us goes among a group of Westerners it is like a grimy stain on a sheet of white paper. ...A sensitive white person could not but be upset by the shadow that even one or two colored persons cast over a social gathering.

> [During the American Civil War] when persecution of Negroes was at its most intense, the hatred and scorn were directed not only at full-blooded Negroes.... [Even] those with the slightest taint of Negro blood...had to be ferreted out and made to suffer....[H]ow profound is the relationship between shadows and the yellow race.[28]

Frequently Japanese situated themselves medially along the familiar evaluative axis of white supremacy/black inferiority, yet Sôseki's misrecognition of himself, and Tanizaki's empathy for Western racialism, illustrate how the Western imperialist gaze has also been introjected when beholding the self, and collapsed within extant discourses on colored others.

American forces occupied Japan in the immediate postwar period, soon centralized in Okinawa, creating a "colonized" site where black and white Americans became "others within."[29] It was a limited, specialized site, however, which did not infiltrate mainstream society. Interracial marriages and liaisons between soldiers and native women of Okinawa were common, but Okinawans themselves were (and are) excluded from the category of the (conceptualized) pure Japanese.[30] The Americans' sources of income were independent of the Japanese economy, and offered no threat of monetary competition to dominant classes. The Japanese Home Ministry organized local associations of prostitutes (poor women) in the exclusive service of the occupation troops, in an attempt to maintain the "racial purity" of the dominant classes.[34] In the aftermath of the war Japan as nation was positionally "feminized" and metaphorically "raped" by the occupation forces: deprived of self-governance, forced into surrender and capitulation to the Western other, upsetting the terms of power/masculinity.

In the mid 1940s the writer Sakaguchi Ango (1906-55) envisioned a future Japan bereft of Japanese men, peopled by American men, Japanese women, and their (mixed-blood) children.[32] In Shinoda Masahiro's film *MacArthur's Children*, set during the occupation, a central female character is raped upstairs in the very house where, and at the moment when, the village administration is downstairs entertaining the occupation troops. The young boys from whose viewpoint the film is narrated, speak in awe of the massive size of American (black and white) penises.[33] 'e Kenzaburô's "Prize Stock," ("Shiiku," 1958), similarly employs a child narrator to describe the awesome spectacle of a naked black man, "the black soldier possessed a magnificent, heroic, unbelievably beautiful penis."[34]

In the postwar, against the assumedly superior American (material) penis and phallus (symbolic empowerment), Japanese men were collectively demasculinized. Prewar Japanese/American collusive productions of each other had already situated Japan within a binary system as a shadowed, unknowable and mysterious other, persistently occupying the same polarity, and alterity, as the feminine.[35] The valorization of "whiteness" notwithstanding, African-American soldiers paradoxically *also* occupied the dominant position vis-a-vis a surrendered Japan.

As modern Japanese racialism renders blackness alongside the natural and the bestial, it has been accommodating to a production of blackness commingled with "body-ness" and uncontrolled and excessive sexual drive, differentiating the slightly tainted whiteness of the yellow race from the deeply polluted black race. Yamada's first work (which won the *Bungei* literary prize), *Bedtime Eyes, (Beddotaimu Aizu,* 1987) depicts the love affair between Kim, a Japanese cabaret singer, and Spoon, an African-American soldier who is selling military secrets. The basis for Kim's attraction is Spoon's "bestiality" which affirms her "purity," as translated by Russell:

> From his arm pits came a strange smell. A corrupt odor, but definitely not unpleasant. As if by being assaulted by a dirty thing, I am made aware I am a pure thing. That kind of smell. His smell gives me a sense of superiority. It makes me yearn like a bitch in heat driven by the smell of musk.[36]

Michael Dyson's commentary on white imaginaries of black masculinity and sexuality is also true of Japanese racialism:

> Few images have caused more anxiety in the American sexual psyche than the black male embodiment of phallic prowess. A sordid range of stereotypes, jealousies and fears have been developed around black men wielding their sexuality in ways that are perceived as untoward, unruly, or uncontrolled.[38]

The widely-disseminated stereotype of black men possessing mythic phallic power has its foundation in an association of black skin with a masculinized primal.[38] The protagonist of the contemporary author Shimada Masahiko's "Momotaro in a Capsule" collusively visualizes the black phallus as a symbol of supreme masculine prowess while denigrating his own, Japanese, inadequate genital endowments:

> From the time he was twelve, Kurushima idolized the brave beautiful phalluses of primitive sculpture. Phalluses like oversized nightsticks: heavy, gleaming, black, hard, glaring provocatively heavenward, brimming with a fearless laughter, as if they had a special connection with some omnipotent god. "Wish I had a cock like that." ...Whenever Kurushima eyed his [own], he grew depressed. "My genitals were made for masturbation."[39]

The bodily myth of black American masculinity that permeates Japanese representations is the extant iconical ideation which paves the way for contemporary narrative and popular depictions. In Yamada's *Harem World* (*Hâremu wârudo*, 1990) protagonist Sayuri introduces her black lover Stan to her Japanese lover Shinichi, who agonizes,

> A black man - the so-called very incarnation of sexuality. He had heard that once a woman tasted that, she would never return to Japanese men. [Sayuri] had said that the size of his [Shinichi's] penis was not a problem, but if she knew how good that one [the black man's penis] was, then she surely would switch [to a black lover].[40]

Today, anxiety expressed over the black penis in Japanese magazines, television shows and narrative texts is, as above, still often accompanied by a negative assessment of Japanese penises as inferior. In 1992, a young black man, identified as Luke, is an advice columnist for a popular magazine, *Video On Stage*. One Japanese youth writes, "Luke, please listen to my problem. I am mesmerized by brothers like you, I go to tanning salons and I'm determined to do my very best at dance and fashion. But [my penis is] small."[41] His inadequate penis is, he complains, the reason why he has just been dumped. While Luke asserts that technique is more important than size, he concludes by assuring the readers that his own penis, however, is of enormous proportions. The prewar image of a bestial black man is reconstituted as a sex symbol, and the once threatening black phallus (and suppressed erotic curiosity) is reimaged as *overtly* desirable, and commodified.

The supreme mark of difference which inverts the conventional superior/ inferior binarism (which would situate Japanese men in the empowered position) is thus repeatedly the "perfect black penis." Yamada's heroines, or young Japanese women in general, may be empowered by manipulating this transcendental (black) penis (as both signifier and material object). Boasting of a prior tryst with one of her many black lovers, Sayuri proclaims "his dick is the best... Do you think white people have dicks?"[42] The homage paid the black penis by Yamada's heroines is attended by an equally vigorous devaluation of the Japanese penis. In *Bedtime Eyes,* Kim describes Spoon's penis:

> His dick bore no resemblance to those reddish, nasty cocks that white men have; and it was also different from Japanese men's child-like, pathetic ones which were completely incapable of self-assertion unless they were stuck inside some helpless Japanese pussy.[43]

Although Sayuri of *Harem* claims it is more than the size of the sexual organ that defines sexual prowess, talented love-making remains the province of African Americans, related to their mental and emotional simplicity and irrationality. From *Bedtime Eyes*:

> The only solution he knew was fucking. How are we going to do it? How can I satisfy you? What do you mean there are other methods besides fucking? She was sure this was what Spoon was saying to himself. An immature child framed in a big body. My adorable Spoon.[44]

The appetite of *Bedtime*'s Spoon (frequently also portrayed as childlike, as in the quote above) for sex is matched only by his heavy drinking and cocaine-sniffing. It is his animality, opposition to mainstream culture and lack of restraint that attracts Japanese lover Kim.

For both young Japanese men and young Japanese women, the meaning of blackness is inseparable from a fetishization of blackness, symbolized by the phallus. The psychoanalytic term "fetish" has been substantially broadened in academic discourses, increasingly detached from a corporeal materiality, and utilized, for example, to describe the psychic mechanisms which dominate perpectivist imaginings of (and appended anxieties over) sexual difference and colonial desire.[45] My use of fetish is meant to be inclusive of the establishment of a replacement object to stand in for the missing penis in protection of the index of male subjective identity because not just the phallus as symbol, but the penis itself, are woven directly into the signification of blackness in the contemporary Japanese context. My usage is also inclusive of its broadened application; appropriate to the polysemic symbol of black skin in Japan today. When Japanese male inferiority is centralized in the penis, and black men are equated with phallic power, the outfits imagistically bound to African-American black youth promise to transform the wearer into stud. The establishment of a fetishized object averts (or displaces) the threat (of emasculation, or feminization, or disempowerment); in Japan black skin is both metonymy and metaphor, mimicry and menace, not as an appendix to the lacking other, but as a reconfiguration of the lacking self in the empowered, masculinized image of the other. For young men, to possess the black phallus (in its symbolic presence within hip hop outfits and darkened skin) is to wield the weapon that threatens white masculinity; a black phallus affixed to the Japanese body would invert the "original feminization" by the occupation troops, and the ongoing valorization of European/American whiteness over Japanese yellowness.

It bears repeating that the (black) phallus is symbolically present in black skin with which Japanese male youths have conflated their selfhood.

Copresent with male desire for the phallic power of blackness, is the threat that Japanese phallic inferiority will displace the Japanese male from his (naturalized) position of power over Japanese women. By choosing an African-American lover, encoded with an extant text of phallic empowerment, and rejecting the economic and social stability of a Japanese husband, the Japanese woman has availed herself of a passive-aggressive act of resistance. For her the power of the black phallus is marshaled to further threaten (already destabilized) Japanese masculinity. Her agentive choice of a black lover is an act of resistance against Japanese (and white) male sociocultural domination.

A second letter to columnist Luke is from a Japanese teenage girl who confesses to a desire to have sex with black men, and asks advice on how to solicit them.[46] It is not that the young woman is enamored of a particular man who is black, but rather that she wants to try sex with any black man. Blackness for this young woman is desired for its symbolic meaning. In *Banana Chips Love* , a popular miniseries videotaped on location in New York City in 1991, a Japanese woman who has apparently mastered the art of living abroad in Manhattan, peripherally establishes the program's internationalism by regularly appearing flanked by an entourage of African-American men.[47] She, the program intimates, is the epitome of sophistication and independence from Japanese tradition, and the black men on her arm(s) represent her subjective, erotic agency.[48]

A comic from a men's pornographic magazine is illustrative of male anxiety awakened by Japanese women's choice of "foreign" lovers. Two young men sit at a bar lamenting their miserable sex lives. One sobs that his girlfriend has been stolen by a "black alien"; the other commiserates that his girlfriend is having an affair with a married "entity X." Sighing over their intact virginity and the growing scarcity of available Japanese women, the two young men exchange glances, and the comic ends as they embrace, one saying, "Gee, the more I look at you the cuter you get," to which the other replies, "My, you too," and the final caption reads, "The anxiety over Japan's future continues."[49] Japanese female choice of African-American lovers here emasculates Japanese men: in the cartoon blackness functions as an icon of desired and omnipotent heterosexuality, against which the Japanese men have become homosexualized - not through choice, but simply by being displaced from heterosexual practices.

The treatment that Yamada's heroines bestows upon Japanese men in text is quite different from that given their black lovers, and can be brutal and sadistic. Undertones of sadism that color her treatment of black men in text become dominant overtones in her heroines' abuse of their Japanese partners. A process of emasculation begins at the site of empowerment, apparent in the comparisons of penises quoted above. *Harem World's* Shinichi feels disempowered when confronted by Sayuri's black lover:

> [Shinichi] seethed with violent jealousy towards the black man confronting him. Lurking deep inside his breast was a powerful conviction of his inferiority - in comparison to their [black men's] legendary physical prowess and large sexual organs.[50]

In her 1988 *Kneel Down and Lick My Feet,* Yamada writes the story of dominatrix Shinobu. Far from the enshrined phallic icons associated with Yamada's black studs, Shinobu describes her (Japanese) clients' penises: "They just look like a bunch of wriggly vegetables out of some cartoon."[51] Referring to her clients repeatedly with words like "pathetic," "jerk," and "slave," Shinobu has a decidedly negative opinion of men in general, but her sharpest criticism is reserved for Japanese men:

> I think men are quite delicate. If I say the wrong thing at the wrong moment, it's all over for them. If there were a man who could talk to a woman in bed the way I talk, women would come just listening to him. But there aren't many men like that, men who can say enough of the right things in bed. Relatively speaking, foreigners are better at it. Men who can speak in a way that is both obscene and refined, crude and sincere. Most Japanese men don't have it in them.[52]

Boasting that her line of work affords her a peek into the most natural male state - one which the wives and girlfriends of her clients are sadly ignorant of - she gleefully admits to finding pleasure in the (temporary) power reversal. Quite to the point, she asks rhetorically, "Show me another job where you can abuse men and have them thank you."[53] Contemptuously, she compares her job to that of bar hostesses, concluding that not only do hostesses have to serve their clients, they also make less money. Shinobu's pleasure in the power reversal is abundantly clear in the following description of her session with a Mr. Yamamoto:

> I sit on the red velvet throne with my legs crossed. Stark naked, the man approaches. He sits at my feet. He sure does look like a slave. In real life, the guy is president of a big company and spends his time bullying his employees.

'Queen Shinobu, it is an honor to be your humble plaything today.'

'You are a despicable little slave.'[54]

Hammering away at Japanese men, both in her asides and the depicted tortures, the scornful tone with which Shinobu attacks the symbol of masculine identity reaches its zenith in a scene which consists of an extremely graphic description of needles being inserted into the penis of a pathetic, paying (Japanese) client.

Shinobu's economic survival is predicated on a male need to be tortured - a sexual "perversion" that requires female compliance with male directives. The senior Queen, called Mama, is the only one not too shocked and revolted to satisfy the client who requests that needles be inserted in his penis. Shinobu narrates,

> Mama began to speak in a loving voice, in that dim room oozing with insanity. It was enough to make me shiver, in spite of myself. Times like this, I really admire Mama. She's a real pro.[55]

Mama's capacity to repress revulsion or distaste, to subsume her own needs and sexuality in fulfilling those of her paying client, is what marks her as professional. The power wielded by the "queens" of *Kneel Down and Lick My Feet* is inseparable from male economic supremacy, a facade which reinforces (in a disguised format) subordination of women. In "the real world," client Yamamoto is a powerful man. The private world of the club, which (temporarily) reverses power roles at the request of the male, does not affect their social status outside of the club.

The Japanese woman, who is socially, economically, politically and otherwise subordinate to her male counterpart, liberates herself from subordination (by removing herself from sexual relation to Japanese men), and threatens Japanese male heterosexual subjective agency by taking on an African-American sexual partner (as do Yamada's heroines). Her act of resistance, however, sidesteps the direct issue of Japanese male dominance. Removing Japanese men as lovers/husbands from her immediate, personal circumstances places the woman outside the Japanese norm, and does not, in the short term at least, directly affect the systems of power distribution between the sexes in mainstream society.

Shared Subordinations: Gender and Race

For the young Japanese woman, notions of her own racial "in-betweeness" as
Asian, and the extant encoding of the (black) phallus with power inform her desire
for black men, (be it in text or in material body). This desire is further complicated
by additional discourses that discover confluence in women's and black's shared
subordinate positionality, alongside mutual, and mutually naturalized, notions of
bodily excess. The metaphor of the primal is only one of many metaphors
employed in racialist portrayals of blacks which have reappeared in various
discourses on women. As Nancy Leys Stepan has argued, in the nineteenth century,
scientists turned to a reading of the biological differences between the sexes which
placed women in an analogous position with so-called lower races, locating both
women and non-whites in the category of inferior other:

> Women and lower races were called innately impulsive, emotional, imitative
> rather than original and incapable of the abstract reasoning found in white men.
> Evolutionary biology provided yet further analogies. Woman was in
> evolutionary terms the "conservative element" to the man's "progressive,"
> preserving the more "primitive" traits found in lower races. ...
>
> In short, lower races represented the "female" type of the human species, and
> females the "lower race" of gender.[56]

Yamada writes women much as she does black men, as lusty, volatile,
physical beings held captive by overpowering appetites, and marginalized by
dominant (Japanese and white male) economic power. Her texts blaze with erotic
descriptions of women pursuing sexual fulfillment with a blatant disregard for
anything, or anyone, or any morality, which might interfere with that pursuit.
Repeatedly, the narrators of Yamada's modern tales of love write their pleasure
through the medium of the body, experiencing the world from an entirely sensual
vantage point. Upon entering Yamada's narrative topography, spatial and temporal
guideposts grow vague, rendered inconsequential in a world described in purely
sexual/sensual terms.   Desire propels the narratives directly, with little or no
attention to plot. While her longer fictions offer sketchy storylines and general
information about their protagonists, her short works abandon even such
minimalist pretensions towards structure. In *Bedtime Eyes* the circumstances of
Kim's and Spoon's lives are only mentioned in passing, while attention is lavished
on the steamy details of their affair. Yamada's much shorter "X-Rated Blanket," is
a single-consciousness detailed narrative soliloquy upon the unnamed heroine's
rapturous sexual intercourse with her lover George:

> My body collapses into a shape mirroring the space between his arms. Like
> mine, his body caves and coils. When my skin makes a depression, his skin
> touching that spot rises to fill it in. When my nipples are erect they are buried
> by his body. We love each other exactly like liquids.
>
> This is loving. My artless mind thinks so: the grinding of naked bodies against
> each other, leaking, sparking, blending, all of this. Is there any finer way to
> love? Crying, yelling, laughing. These things all happen at once; is there
> anything else so preposterous.[57]

Yamada's narratives of pleasure have no room for more mundane concerns.
Readers spiral through repeating patterns of desire (absence) and fulfillment
(presence), as lovers meet, gaze, touch, kiss, make love, eat, drink, smoke, and
part. In Yamada's work, underlying instinctual (libidinal) drive clearly motivates
the female characters, and the work itself, through an interplay of desire and
satiation. Varied instinctual appetites dominate the lives of Yamada's women with
a tactile urgency, producing what can be described as a conventionally "female"
body in their presentation of women as creatures of nature and sexual appetite
turned insatiable once unleashed. In her discussion of gender difference, Wendy
Hollway has noted that in some cultural systems (and possibly underlying other
systems' insistence on female asexuality) women's sexuality is believed to be
"rabid and dangerous and must be controlled."[58] Appetites of all sorts tether
Yamada's women securely to their bodies, and sever them from acculturation.
Beasts to male humanity, Yamada's heroines make a theater of their bodies,
publicly and defiantly caressing their sexuality. Her texts, songs to the purely
physical, are also ripe with ambivalent dissolutions of difference between
Japanese women and their African-American lovers. The shared subordinated
status, that for both women and black men has been naturalized in the body, sets
the stage for acute ambivalences throughout Yamada's narratives.

> Stan expressed affection towards Sayuri very ingenuously. When affection
> became sexual desire, he exhibited a colossal genius, marshaling fingers,
> tongue, sighs and words to suit his purposes.[59]

The word which I have translated above as "ingenuously" is the Japanese *sunao*,
used repeatedly by Yamada to describe the naive, unstudied sexuality of both
Japanese women and their black lovers. While undoubtedly some passages suggest
that Yamada's heroines taste for black men is inseparable from a desire to affirm
their own difference, their non-blackness, there are also repeated suggestions that
her female narrators share with their black lovers a body bound to the sexual, the

physical, and the abject. Yamada celebrates the physical in passages that challenge
those who would denigrate this as bestial:

> All we do is make love...maybe people will say we are like animals. But do
> animals desire their partners like this? Can they know the art of feeling the flesh
> tingle even as one is satisfied? Every bit of him is enveloped in smooth skin.
> There, in that core, he is. Can an animal hunger to taste that, as though lapping
> broth?[60]

In *Harem World*, the black body is incorporated into the Japanese one, genetically
endowing (the female) Sayuri with a naturalized sexual prowess. Sayuri pays
homage to the phallic superiority of black men in the same breath as she claims
kinship with African ancestors. Boasting of a prior tryst, Sayuri proclaims:

> "His dick is the best!"

> "He's black?"

> "Well of course. Do you think white people have dicks? My African blood
> (*kokujin no chi*) was all stirred up. My ancestors were certainly not slaves. They
> were African nobility, royalty.'[61]

When one of Sayuri's longtime Japanese lovers is shocked to learn that she is half
black, her black lover Stan responds, "You make love with Sayuri, don't you. You
should have known [that she was part black] - no one should have had to tell you
such a thing."[62]

Yamada's tentative gesture towards rewriting "womanhood" (and possibly
enacting a personal liberation) celebrates her own positioning as female at the
margins of mass society. The partialized view of the African-American male
mirrors the representation of "gendered female" that permeates Yamada's
narratives. In her works, likeness works magnetically, alternating between fierce,
irresistible attraction and powerful repulsion. Yamada's textual engagement of
black male characters is inseparable from their symbolic functions, (as is the
teenage girl's erotic interest), as threatening to Japanese phallocentrism, and as
indicative of female erotic agency. Her works also take their place within and
reinforce the commodity aesthetic of African-American men.

Semiotics and Plundered Body Images

Following Eric Lott's general analysis of blackface, while representations of African Americans in Japan reduce the black other to spectacle, they also may represent the attempted incorporation of an image of the other[63], and/or an expression of an unconscious erotic desire for the other. Reconceptualized in consideration of Japanese female agentive solicitation of black male lovers, erotic desire is not repressed, but flaunted. Hebdige has noted that in Britain, blacks can be seen as the ultimate symbol of the other within the dominant culture, and therefore aspects of black style can be sampled by the white subculture in an act of defiance against dominant social mores, resulting in a semiotic dialogue[64]. To recast Hebdige's analysis within a formulation acknowledging a fundamental power imbalance as the cornerstone for the fetishization of blackness, hip hop style in Japan is not a dialogue between Japanese and African-American youth, but a plundering of an empowered body image. As noted in the introduction to this essay, most of the interaction between Japanese and African-American youth is indirect (because there are still so few African Americans bodily in Japan). Accordingly, the object of desire is generally encoded within, and limited to interaction with the variant signs.

The writer Shimada Masahiko cites Yamada's narratives as examples of easily accessible, easily circulated and easily consumed prose, narrative in the service of market economy [65]. One can also frame Shimada's argument in the concrete arena of the Japanese economy. As the yen exchange rate rose, and Japanese women became more prosperous, they were free to globetrot, and sample sex as consumers throughout Southeast Asian, in poor American black communities, as well as the Caribbean islands.

A student of mine reported that during a recent visit to Japan he noticed, and queried his Japanese companion about the increasing numbers of young Japanese women seen arm-in-arm with black men. His companion responded that it was the latest fad: Japanese women sought black men because they looked good on one's arm, akin to the latest pocketbook, or other fashion accessory. As accessory African-American lovers are reduced to reflections of Japanese symbolic desire. Alone in her bathroom, the female narrator of Yamada's "X-Rated Blanket" looks at herself in the mirror[66] and sees the reflection of her own desire when she fantasizes about lover George, "Twisted, I am wet; water floods high enough to wet my eyes. That's how I clearly recognize my own desire when I look in the mirror." The self-referential aspect of her desire for George resonates with how, according to Haug, commodities function to reflect back the inner desire of the consumer[67]. Just as the desire inflamed by advertisements' manipulations of the libido cannot be sated through acquisition of goods, so too Yamada's narrator confesses that sex with George is always accompanied by more desire, "As the sensation of satiation fills me - the satisfaction of having at last become one - I savor an intense pleasure tinged already with the mingling of a new, ongoing hunger."[68] The consumption of her lover yields only temporary satisfaction because, like goods sold by image and not concrete use-value, the symbolic desire targets an imagination, not a reality.

The varied incorporations of the imaginary black other by Yamada's heroines is, moreover, facilitated by her use of *katakana* (the syllabary used to write foreign words of non-Chinese origin). Frequently, the voices of characters in texts are expressed in New York African-American vernacular slang written in *katakana*. The flexibility of the Japanese language, and its ability to absorb other languages in *katakana* - a process which often renders the words unrecognizable to the country of origin - complements Yamada's writing of African-American culture. In the following example of Yamada's Japanized English, loan words are translated back into English:

> *Diira* (dealer) *bikutâ* (Victor) *o oboete iru darô. Aitsu no ie de wa tamatama suteki na, kôku* (coke/cocaine) *ga haitte pâtii* (party) *hiraite gettohai* (get high). *Howaito* (white) *rain* (line) *o nanbon hiita ka omoidasôto sureba, atama no naka wa fantajii* (fantasy). [69]

This is no longer American urban slang, but Japanese. While *katakana* is used more and more by many of today's young writers, and is used to transliterate most words of non-Chinese foreign origin, (which account for increasingly larger proportions of the written text), Yamada's renditions can also be read as an attempt to appropriate the linguistic idioms of (New York urban) African Americans. In her works reference to the genitals - male or female - are almost exclusively in *katakana* renditions of American slang, as are most of the names of her male characters and the titles of her works (Spoon or Stan as character names, and *Double Joint* or *Harem World* as titles, for example). Japanese proper, relational, hierarchical, and gender-based, does not provide her with a voice for her special brand of sexual bravado.

Yet *katakana* is part of the Japanese language while it is also suggestive of the foreign. Vocabulary lifted from its context is slipped into Japanese syntax, which gives it the appearance and atmosphere of American slang, while in fact, it remains Japanese. The manner in which Yamada incorporates the black other in text parallels the structures that inform *katakana* usage in the modern period. While signaling the presence of the other in text, (or indicating emphasis, much like italics), *katakana* simultaneously orders what is written within the parameters of Japanese linguistic structure and pronunciation. African Americans likewise function to mark a difference cataloged by a reproduction of marginality.

While Yamada's literary intention appears to mirror the "writing-the-body" project of some European and American feminists[70], and to seek a personal and political sexual liberation, by not challenging the underlying binaries of phallocentrism, she instead reproduces sex/gender and racial discourses dependent on existing structures of empowerment and resistance. Aligned with the African-American man through racialist and gendered marks of difference, Yamada labors at incorporation, laying claim to a kinship, yet is reduced to writing battles for power between two colonized (subordinate) categories of people. These characters then objectify and dominate each other, reproducing a discourse of colonization. Desire in Yamada's texts is thus never more than the desire of the other. Dominant culture and phallocentric society imprison and restrain Yamada's heroines and their black lovers, while her characterizations reproduce respectively, the "engendered body" and the "racialized body" of the very axioms they stand in opposition to. It is the production of her "engendered" self as woman-body that leads to Yamada's depiction of an association with self-as-black (colonized); in both cases the end result is (perhaps unwanted) collusion with dominant Japanese racialism and phallocentrism.

Undoubtedly, for many Japanese, the unshaken sense of their own Japanese identity (validating economic and political power over others within and without) is so solid that the appearance, or look, or atmosphere of other can be donned like a hat or coat, which can be just as easily shed, leaving no mark or impact on the idea of self as Japanese. The experience of "playing black" does not necessarily alter, or affect, this racialism. A Japanese *Video On Stage* columnist rambles through a discourse unified only by media images of blacks around the world: a brief reference to starvation in Somalia is followed by an explication of the English word "wicked," after which Spike Lee's *Malcolm X* is (positively) reviewed. [71]

Yet in its insistence on a (constructed) difference, signaled by the intentional sign of ethnic otherness, black skin, many youth situate themselves oppositionally against the myth of Japanese racial homogeneity. The putative kinship between African-American men and Japanese women, or the reimaging of the young Japanese male that employs indices of blackness, mark a desire for racial slippage, and a valorization of "coloredness" that is supplementary to the Western black/white binarism; a binarism which does not represent Asian "yellowness." At the same time, difference may be affirmed through the surety that the outfits, and skin darkening do not erase their own Japaneseness. As a young magazine columnist put it, "mesmerized by black people... I cannot turn black. Of course not." [72]

The selling of black style has the potential to unsettle discourses on Japanese racial purity. The "de-sanitization" of desired (*akogareta*) America to incorporate blackness, and the positioning of blackness as a signifier connoting desire, destabilize the familiar constructs of racially-biased evaluative systems. Remodeling the Japanese self in an African-American image reproduces an indeterminacy and interlocation in Japanese racial self-identification. Reconfiguring blackness as desirable also provides greater possibility for African-American (bodily) presence in Japan, which generates interactive dialogue rather than unilateral plundering of image.

The very new popularity of black lovers among young Japanese women (not Okinawans, but Tokyoites), (and as depicted in narratives by writers such as Yamada), constitutes a further site of resistance to Japanese myths of homogeneity: interracial coupling challenges Japanese male ownership of Japanese women, and threatens to defile "pure" blood lineage (the essence of Japanese superiority). Although at the time of writing of this essay, as Karen Kelsky claims, most of these young women neither marry their African-American lovers, nor birth babies of mixed-heritage, some do (as has Yamada), and others will [73]. If, and when, the liaisons sought by Japanese women with African-American men progress beyond accessory to husband, their children will produce, of necessity, a site of resistance that will further challenge Japanese "homogeneity" by broadening the categories of heterogeneous voices within.

Nina Cornyetz

Notes:

[1] In order to better suit the focus of the present collection of essays toward a reading of literary, and not strictly cultural texts, this essay has combined edited versions of two previously published essays: "Fetishized Blackness: Hip Hop and Racial Desire in Contemporary Japan," *Social Text* 41 (Winter 1994): 113-39; and "Power and Gender in The Narratives of Yamada Eimi," in *The Woman's Hand: Gender and Theory in Japanese Women's Writing*, Paul G. Schalow and Janet A. Walker, eds. 425-457 (Stanford: Stanford University Press, 1996).

[2] Ieda Shôko, *Ore no hada ni muregatta onnatachi* (Tokyo: Shôdensha, 1985) and *Ierô kyabu* (Tokyo: Kôyû Shuppan, 1991).

[3] See my "Fetishized Blackness: Hip hop and Racial Desire in Contemporary Japan" for a more thorough discussion of this issue. See Andrew Jones, "Black Like Me"*Spin* 9:7 (Oct. 1, 1993): 74-8, for a good description of the hip hop trend in Japan. For studies of African-American hip hop and rap see Tricia Rose, *Black Noise: Rap Music and Black Culture in Contemporary America,* (Hanover, N.H.: Wesleyan University Press, 1994) and her "Orality and Technology: Rap Music and Afro-American Cultural Resistance," *Popular Music and Society* 13:4 (Winter 1989); Elizabeth Blair, "Commercialization of the Rap Music Youth Subculture," *Journal of Popular Culture* 27:3 (Winter 1993): 21-33; and Ted Swedenburg, "Homies in the 'Hood: Rap's Commodification of Insubordination," *New Formations* 18 (Winter 1992): 53-66. Swedenburg argues that American rap reorders back into a "black" context "white" music (rock and roll, for example) from which black origins have been elided, and samples old rhythm and blues in positive acknowledgment of the origins of African-American contemporary music. In Japan rap and hip hop are severed from the specifics of American racialism, and (inevitably) from the reordering into a "black" context, and frequently montaged with Japanese lyrics and rhythms. Japanese rap and hip hop are thereby usually divested of specific references to the economic, political and other material and ideological contexts germane to being African American in the United States. There are occasional instances when Japanese rappers use rap as conscious political oppositional statements, reframed within the context of specific Japanese insubordination. See Jones, "Black Like Me,"for an interview with one such Japanese rapper.

[4] See my "Fetishized Blackness: Hip Hop and Racial Desire in Contemporary Japan," for more on how Japanese popular culture commodifies "blackness." In Japan, a contemporary focus on "surface" becomes entwined with the mature capitalist disengagement of style from content, facilitating extreme forms of disjunctive montage which reverberate with the formal aspects of hip hop's reconfigurations in Japan.

[5] Japanese salons advertise expertise in African-American hairstyles, such as dread-locks, high-tops, fades, and so forth. An advertisement on page 87 of a popular magazine,*Video On Stage* 6 (Nov. 1, 1992) claims, "We do 'club hair' including 'dread-hair' *[doreddo hea]*." See "Reviled For Their Love of Hip-Hop Style," *People Weekly* 41:4 (January 31, 1994): 60-1 for reportage on white youth dressing themselves in "black" hip hop style. All translations from Japanese source materials are mine unless indicated otherwise.

[6] Telecom Japan, *New Yorker*, personal copy of edited footage.

[7] John Russell, "Narratives of Denial: Racial Chauvinism and the Black Other in Japan,"*Japan Quarterly* 38:4 (October 1991): 416-28, and "Race and Reflexivity: The Black Other in Contemporary Japanese Mass Culture," *Cultural Anthropology* 6:1 (February 1991): 3-25. These two essays by Russell are important, pioneering discussions of modern Japanese discourses on blackness.

[8]There was a public outcry and scandal when the actor Ted Danson appeared in blackface, and made racial jokes. Typical samples of the media response include: "Whoopi, Ted, We Are Not Amused," *Los Angeles Times,* 13 Oct. 1993; "Racial Jokes Spur Apology From Friars," *New York Times,* 10 Oct. 1993; "What Are You Laughing At?" *San Francisco Chronicle,* 17 Oct. 1993.

[9] I am indebted to Eric Lott's "Love and Theft: The Racial Unconscious of Blackface Minstrelsy," *Representations* 39 (Summer 1992): 23-49, and John G. Blair's "Blackface Minstrels Cross-Cultural Perspective," *American Studies International* 28:2 (October 1990): 52-65, for my understanding of the fetishization of blacks by American and English blackface minstrels. I have intentionally reconfigured the word, "blackface" into two separated words, "black face" when referring to contemporary Japanese practices to distinguish the two practices. See Russell "Narratives of Denial" and "Race and Reflexivity" for discussions of representations culled from American ones. Although such images still exist, most of the youth darkening their complexions in today's hip hop style do not imitate these exaggerated models.

[10] Telephone conversation with Tricia Rose, 27 July 1994. See Rose's *Black Noise,* especially the second chapter, "'All Aboard the Night Train': Flow, Layering, and Rupture in Postindustrial New York," 21-61. On page 41 Rose states, "Hip hop has always been articulated via commodities and engaged in the revision of meanings attached to them."

[11] Elizabeth Blair argues that rap has entered a stage characterized by the "sanitization" of hip hop subculture as it makes its appearance in mass culture. The process of sanitization includes a negation of its association with the (specific) conditions of being black in America, partly by situating whites along side blacks as producers and consumers of rap. See her "Commercialization of the Rap Music Youth Subculture," especially 31-2. This also follows Hebdige's analysis of subculture in Britain. Hip hop, which originated as a challenge to the dominant (white) culture by a disenfranchised (black) class in America, was first incorporated by white youth subculture, and then appropriated by capitalist production at large, mass produced and in the process defused of much of its subversive attributes. See Dick Hebdige, *Subculture: The Meaning of Style* (New York: Methuen and Co., 1979). Rose also cites Hebdige in her discussion of rap's commercialization in *Black Noise,* 40-1.

[12] Wolfgang Haug, *Critique of Commodity Aesthetics: Appearance, Sexuality and Advertising in Capitalist Society,* trans. Robert Bock (Minneapolis: University of Minnesota Press, 1986), 56.

[13] Quoted by Hebdige, 105.

[14] See my "Fetishized Blackness: Hip hop and Racial Desire in Contemporary Japan," for a more thorough discussion of "trans-identification" in Japanese adaptations of hip hop and rap.

[15] David Theo Goldberg, "The Social Formation of Racist Discourse," in *Anatomy of Racism,* David Theo Goldber, ed. (Minneapolis: University of Minnesota Press, 1990), 306.

[16] John Dower, *War Without Mercy: Race and Power in the Pacific War* (New York: Pantheon Books, 1986), 12. The valuation of white complexions existed in the tenth century when it was employed to distinguish the economically-dominant, non-laboring Heian aristocracy from the working classes. In the modern period, members of the outcaste group know as *burakumin,* Korean-Japanese, Okinawans, the Ainu and other aborigines, children of mixed racial parentage, and more recently, Southeast Asian and Chinese immigrants fall into the category of "other within." For essays on discrimination in modern Japan see Hirota Masaki, *Sabetsu no shosô (Various Aspects of Discrimination), Nihon kindai shisô 22* (Tokyo: Iwanami, 1990). On the *burakumin* see George De Vos and H. Wagatsuma, eds., *Japan's Invisible Race* (Berkeley: University of California Press, 1967). On minorities in Japan see Edward Fowler, "Minorities in a 'Homogeneous' State: The Case

of Japan," in *What Is In a Rim: Critical Perspectives on the Pacific Region Idea*, Arif Dirlik, ed. 211- 233 (Boulder: Westview Press, 1993).

[17] See Russell's "Narratives of Denial," and "Race and Reflexivity."

[18] Balibar, Etienne, "Paradoxes of Universality," in *Anatomy of Racism*, 290.

[19] See Russell, "Narratives of Denial," 5-7, and "Race and Reflexivity," 19, 21. Most of the Africans and African Americans with whom prewar Japan had contact were the slaves and servants of European/American traders.

[20] Yamada Eimi, "Kuroi kinu (Black silk)," in *Boku wa biito (I am beat)* (Tokyo: Kadokawa shoten, 1988), 43.

[21] Yamada Eimi, "Boku no ai wa in o fumu (My heart in rhyme)," in *Boku wa biito (I am beat)*, 73-4.

[22] Yamada Eimi, "Daburu jointo (Double joint)," in *Boku wa biito (I am beat)*, 96.

[23] Yamada Eimi, "Seijin muki no môfu *(X-Rated Blanket)*," 5-15; and "Taste of (Boku no aji)," 189-210, both in *Boku wa biito (I am Beat)*. *X-Rated Blanket* is available in translation by Nina Cornyetz in *New Japanese Voices* (New York: Atlantic Monthly Press, 1991), 50-4. Pagination and quotations here reference the Japanese language text.

[24] "X-rated Blanket," 14.

[25] *Video On Stage*, 77.

[26] While some Japanese clearly recirculated stereotypes, as argued by Russell in "Race and Reflexivity" and "Narratives of Denial," (and thus appear identified with whites) others deplored American racism and allied themselves as people of color with African Americans, both prior to and immediately following the Second World War. See Dower. For studies of Japanese and Okinawan racialism see Michael Molasky, "Burned-Out Ruins and Barbed Wire Fences: The American Occupation in Japan and Okinawan Literature" (Ph.D. diss., University of Chicago, 1994); and "Poetry of Protest from Occupied Okinawa: Arakawa Akira's 'The Colored Race'" (unpublished essay, 1994).

[27] Motoyoshi Katsuyo. "Fearful Terrain: The Underground and the Continent in the Works of Natsume Sôseki" Paper presented at "The Politics of Exclusion in Modern Japanese Literature and Culture," Workshop, Boston, 25 March 1994, 2.

[28] Tanizaki Jun'ichirô, *In Praise of Shadows*, Thomas J. Harper and Edward Seidensticker, trans. (New Haven: Leete's Island Books, 1977), 31; 31-2.

[29] While Japan as a modern nation has not undergone colonization (and conversely colonized Korea, Manchuria, and occupied much of Southeast Asia and China in the modern period) the experience of the United States occupation in the immediate postwar has been partly analogous to colonization.

[30] Okinawa was invaded by the Shimizu Clan from the Japanese islands in the seventeenth century, and remained a Japanese colony until the Pacific War. After the war, Okinawa was under United States Sovereignty until it was "returned" to Japan in 1972. See Molasky for Okinawan/Japanese literary processing of the occupation.

[31] Dower, 308.

[32] Sakaguchi Ango, *Sensô to hitori no onna (The War and a Woman)* Vol. 4, 171-188; *Darakuron (Essay On Depravity)* Vol. 14, 511-22; and *Tennô shôron (Short Essay on the Emperor)* Vol. 14, 523-4, in *Sakaguchi Ango zenshû* (Tokyo: Chikuma bunko, 1990).

[33] Shinoda Masahiro, *Setouchi shônen yakyû dan (MacArthur's Children*, 1984). English subtitled version, 1985 distributed by Pacific Arts Video, Beverly Hills, California. The actual rape of Komako, the woman, becomes a metaphor for the "rape" of Japan as a nation by the American occupation. Komako is raped by her brother-in-law, Tetsuo, who assumes the "right" to access her

physical body after her husband is (erroneously) proclaimed a war casualty, paralleling the assumption of rights and privilege by Americans to the nation-state Japan.

[34] O'e Kenzaburô, "Prize Stock," in *Teach Us to Outgrow Our Madness,* John Nathan, trans. (New York: Grove Press), 152.

[35] Because the Western subject is putatively male, and Japan has been conceived of as the "other" to this subject, Japan is in effect feminized. This postulation is reinforced by the erotic absence of the Japanese male in heterosexual Western constructions, making the works of Marguerite Duras a glaringly obvious exception to this rule.

[36] Quoted by Russell, "Narratives of Denial," 423. The original is on page 13 of Yamada Eimi, *Beddotaimu aizu* (Tokyo: Kawade shobô shinsha, 1987) Many of Yamada's female protagonists *also* labor to dissolve this difference and form a community aligned with black men through shared marks of bodily "otherness." For a more detailed discussion of the relation between femaleness and blackness in Yamada's texts see my "Power and Gender in the Narratives of Yamada Eimi."

[37] Michael Eric Dyson, *Reflecting Black: African-American Cultural Criticism* (Minneapolis: University of Minnesota Press, 1993), 169.

[38] Frantz Fanon, "The Fact of Blackness," 108-26, and Nancy Leys Stepan, "Race and Gender: The Role of Analogy in Science," 38-57, both in *Anatomy of Racism* .

[39] Shimada Masahiko, "Momotaro in a Capsule," in *Monkey Brain Sushi* , Terry Gallagher, trans. (Tokyo: Kôdansha, 1991), 113.

[40] Yamada Eimi, *Hâremu wârudo* (Tokyo: Kôdansha bunko, 1990), 100. The title is a "Japanized" pronunciation of (originally) English words, written in the phonetic syllabary for transliteration of non-Chinese, foreign words. Transliteration of the title back into English renders two possibilities, *Harem World* or *Harlem World.* In Japanese the dual meaning is most likely intentional. In the afterword Yamada claims she was inspired by Spike Lee's film "She's Gotta Have It." Referred to hereafter as *Harem World.*

[41] *Video On Stage,* 76. The column is called "*Mr. Luke no mi no shita sôdan,*" which rewrites the common idiomatic "discussions pertaining to one's circumstances (*mi no ue*)" with "discussions pertaining to the lower half of the body (*mi no shita*)."

[42] *Harem World,* 8.

[43] *Beddotaimu Aizu,* 14.

[44] Bedtime Eyes, 61.

[45] The basis for fetish can be read as anxiety related to sexual performance, identity, masculinity, and by extension, power. The fetishized object transforms the threatening sexual lack into eroticizec presence and allows for the circulation of desire. In Japan, as elsewhere, the "black phallus" becomes an index of a eroticized power, alternately perceived as a threat, or as an object of desire. As Griselda Pollack has argued, in her "Fathers of Modern Art, Mothers of Invention,"*Differences* 4:3 (Fall 1992): 107-8, following John Ellis, Freud's "penis" (anatomy-bound material object), as explicated in his "Fetishism (1927)," *Collected Papers 5,* James Strachey ed. (New York: Basic Books, 1959), 198-204, can be recontextualized within an expanded symbolic context. "[F]etishism is not just a disavowal of a lack of penis; it is potentially also to be understood as a contorted from of masculine resistance to a whole system, the phallic structuring of sexual difference. ...Fetishism can then be understood as a structure of substitution of signifiers determined in relation to the phallus/ language/difference/ power, which is not exclusively tied...to a sexual difference which is ...a matter of masculine versus feminine." Homi Bhabha has further "detached" the penis from its corporeal context by reading the commingled perception of threat and the desire felt by the colonist when confronted with the native as imbued with the same psychic mechanisms as inform the

construction of the fetish. For Bhabha, black skin becomes the sign of difference which engenders anxiety, and the fabrication of discourses of likeness/presence and dissimilarity/lack (metaphor and metonymy). See "The Other Question," 66-84 and "Of Mimicry and Man," 85-92, in *The Location of Culture* (New York: Routledge, 1994). Fetish has also been used to explicate the psychic mechanisms of commodity exchange. Karl Marx's "The Fetishism of the Commodity and Its Secret," *Capital* Vol. 1 (New York: Vintage Books, 1977), 163-77 paves the way for Haug's Marxist/psychoanalytic analysis of commodity exchange.

[46] *Video on Stage,* 76.

[47] *Banana Chips Love,* Tokyo: Fuji Television, 1992. Videotape. A popular miniseries about Japanese protagonists shot in New York City.

[48] Recent newspaper and magazine articles have reported on the new phenomenon of young Japanese women's reluctance to marry, and the dilemma experienced by their male counterparts who, on the other hand, are eager to settle down. In general, it is the years before they marry that young Japanese women enjoy their greatest economic and experiential freedom. Most live with their parents and work at office jobs, affording them plenty of money for travel and shopping. Because women's education is less directed towards career goals, women are freer to study liberal (and/or traditional) arts such as literature, music, and language. Once married, the majority quit their jobs, become the heads of their households, and dedicate themselves to rearing children, housework, and domestic needs. Babysitters and daycare centers are an exception: when help is needed women usually turn to their own mothers, in-laws, or other (female) family members. Because Japanese men are required to spend long overtime hours at work, and often commute well over an hour each way to and from their offices, it is logistically impossible for most men to more than nominally participate as fathers. Relationships (sexual and other) with non-Japanese offer these young women (and those Japanese men who have foreign partners) release from (certain) expectations: both partners are somewhat alleviated of the burdens of cultural norm (although other racial and national expectations exist). American men, for example, are expected to be more *"yasashii"* (indulgent, gentle). The brief explication here on sex/gender roles and the status of women in contemporary Japan cannot do justice to the topic. Nor should the reader assume correlation between premodern or modern Western and Japanese gender politics, and the class issues which inform these politics. In premodern Japan, neither upper nor lower class women were exclusively responsible for childcare or cooking, but were primarily responsible for the management of "stem households" *(e)*. The relegation of cooking and childcare to women is a twentieth century reformation. A few good sources in English for a general introduction to political, economic, social, literary and other contemporary and historical positionings of women in Japan, modern and premodern gender roles, women's status, and sexual politics are: Gail Lee Bernstein, *Recreating Japanese Women, 1600-1945* (Berkeley: University of California Press, 1991); Ueno Chizuko, "The Position of Japanese Women Reconsidered," *Current Anthropology* 28 (1987): 575-84; Sharon Sievers, *Flowers in Salt: The Beginnings of Feminist Consciousness in Modern Japan* (Stanford: Stanford University Press, 1983). More recent studies can be found in the English supplements to the *U.S.-Japan Women's Journal,* numbers 1-6, 1991-1994. See especially Karen Kelsky, "Postcards from the Edge: The 'Office Ladies' of Tokyo," *U.S.-Japan Women's Journal, English Supplement* 6 (March 1994): 3-26, and "Intimate Ideologies: Transnational Theory and Japan's Yellow Cabs," *Public Culture* 6 (1994): 465-78, for discussions of Japanese women's relationships with non-Japanese men, particularly relevant to this essay.

[49] *Goro,* February 1992, 173.

[50] *Harem World,* 117.

[51]Yamada Eimi, *Kneel Down and Lick My Feet,* excerpt in *Monkey Brain Sushi,* Terry Gallagher, trans., 191. All quotes are from this excerpted translation. The original text is *Hizamazuite ashi o oname* (Tokyo: Shinchôsha, 1988).

[52] *Kneel Down and Lick My Feet,* 195.

[53]*Kneel Down and Lick My Feet,* 189,

[54] *Kneel Down and Lick My Feet,* 190.

[55] *Kneel Down and Lick My Feet,* 201.

[56] Nancy Leys Stepan, "Race and Gender: The Role of Analogy in Science," in *Anatomy of Racism,* 40.

[57] "X-Rated Blanket," 8-9; 13.

[58] Wendy Hollway "Gender Difference and the Production of Subjectivity," in Julian Henriques et al, eds. *Changing the Subject: Psychology, Social Regulation, and Subjectivity* (New York: Methuen, 1984), 232.

[59]Yamada, *Harem World,* 149.

[60]Yamada, "X-Rated Blanket," 11.

[61]Yamada, *Harem World,* 8-9.

[62]Yamada, *Harem World,* 150.

[63]Lott, 23-49.

[64]Hebdige, 44-5.

[65] Inoue Hisashi, Takahashi Gen'ichirô and Shimada Masahiko, *"Soshite, ashita wa dô naru ka," Kono issatsu de wakaru Shôwa no bungaku, Shinchô* special edition (February 1989): 447-50.

[66]Yamada Eimi, "X-Rated Blanket," 59

[67] Haug, 52.

[68] "X-Rated Blanket," 14.

[69]Yamada Eimi, "Double Joint," 96.

[70]As, for example, in Hélène Cixous and Catherine Clément, *The Newly Born Woman.* Betsy Wing, trans (Minneapolis: University of Minnesota Press, 1986). The focus of some feminists has been not simply to describe how woman is absent in phallocentric systems (absent because representations of woman are never more than distorted mirrors of man), but to celebrate women's body (and sexuality) as a potential site of resistance. For Cixous, and other feminists, women's desire constitutes an uncolonized space (one of many gaps inherent in the system) wherein woman can write herself. Writing-the-body (primarily the sexual body) through a language that deconstructs such binaries, and replaces unitary meaning with multiplicity and diffusion, becomes for Cixous, an act of personal and political liberation (63-132).

[71]*Video On Stage,* 77.

[72]*Video On Stage,* 77.

[73]Kelsky, ""Intimate Ideologies: Transnational Theory and Japan's Yellow Cabs," 473.

Abstracts of Arguments

Ch. 1: Religious Skirmishes and the Ethnic Outsider

Although multi-cultural composition readers claim to "expand horizons," this essay argues that some ethnic literature not only fails to play the good host(ess) to the ethnic outsider, but also risks perpetuating stereotypes or incurring the hostility of these readers. Concentrating on the differing responses to Grace Paley's short story, "The Loudest Voice," the essay demonstrates a wide variety of interpretations based on reader's religious (Christian and Jewish) background and suggests the realization of universality sought by anthology editors may not be attained unless works which sensitize readers to the differences of various cultures and ethnic groups are carefully selected rather than assuming that all texts offer equally valid doorways into the worlds of the "other."

Ch. 2: Sam, Walter Lee and The Powerless Black Male

This essay examines Lorraine Hansberry's Walter Lee Younger (*Raisin in the Sun*) and Athol Fugard's Sam Semela (*Master Harold.......and the boys*) as black men whom their societies would emasculate. Despite the forces that would strip of their power and manhood, both characters deal with their powerlessness by dreaming, and the essay contends that by asserting their dreams of social progress, they both ultimately defeat the majority that has planned their downfall or tried to keep them enslaved.

Ch. 3: Cather's America, A Nation of Nations

This essay argues that while most of Willa Cather's contemporaries, writers and intellectuals alike, throw ethnic groups reaching the American shores into the famous melting pot, Cather maintains her uniqueness by allowing these groups to maintain their national and cultural identities as they busy themselves building a nation together. A composite of nations, Cather's America is strongly characterized by ethnic harmony. Her appreciation of ethnicity in fact grows from novel to novel, finding its finest and most delicate expression in *Death Comes to the Archbishop* where she projects a picture of an America harmonious with the description of the country as "a nation of nations."

Ch. 4: Speaking Through Silences: Italian /American Women

By placing the work of Agnes Rossi within the context of Italian /American women's literature, this essay examines the writing strategies employed by Rossi and how they serve to compel her readers to question the kind of recognition sought by Italian Americans and members of other overlooked or undervalued ethnicities.

Ch. 5: Loss and Growth of Identity in Resort 76

This essay explores the methods utilized by Shimon Wincelberg in his Holocaust play to examine the Nazi prejudice against Jews. By creating a situation in which a Nazi is forced to live among Jews in a Polish ghetto, Wincelberg develops an ironic state of affairs which forces the anti-Semite, who discovers to his horror that he too possesses Jewish blood, to re-evaluate his feelings about Jews and about his own identity.

Ch. 6: Zora Neale Hurston's Aesthetics

This essay draws attention to Hurston's problematization of race and to her oblique -- and frequently paradoxical -- approach to politics, both in her fiction and non-fiction writings, contesting the generalized view of Hurston's work as politically uninvolved. Special emphasis is laid on contrasting the evolution of Hurston's ideas about ethnic discrimination in her novels, with the evolution of her aesthetics.

Ch. 7: Rediscovering Nation, Resisting Oppression: U. S. Third World Literature

Against assertions of the United States as a melting pot society or the liberal pluralist ideologies of contemporary multi-culturalism and postcolonial theory who forward visions of racial harmony and national unity, this essay contends that a prominent element of U. S. minority or third world literary discourse continues to be the construction of a national consciousness geared toward the resistance of racial oppression as internally colonized national political subjects.

Ch. 8: What God Has Put Asunder: The Politics of Ethnic Barriers

This essay looks at the river Niger as a geographical separation which some Africans argue was genuinely designed by God to keep opposing ethnic groups apart. Nigerian writers Chukwuemeka Ike and Isidore Okpewho are analyzed as the author tries to understand the lack of acceptance between tribes who live in the same country but yet see each other as enemies, from vastly different cultures and possessing vastly different worth.

Ch. 9: East West Paradigms: *Obasan* and *Disappearing Moon Cafe*

This essay offers a discussion of the ways in which Joy Kogawa's *Obasan* and Sky Lee's *Disappearing Moon Cafe* inscribe the silenced history of Japanese Canadians and the Chinese Canadians, respectively, in archeological / genealogical modes that disrupt the continuist narrative of Canadian multi-cultural history. In doing so, the texts also destabilize the opposition between East / West traditional paradigms of identity / location by denouncing the exclusionary bias of historical and cultural definitions of space, and positioning the writing subjects on the margin of Canadian *and* Japanese / Chinese historical narratives.

Ch. 10: Women Before Hell's Gate: Survivors of the Holocaust and Their Memoirs

Following Theodor Adorno's dictum that the most important task of education is the prevention of future Auschwitzes, this essay examines the holocaust memoirs of women and what they have to teach us fifty years after the events they describe. The dehumanizing impact of the camps and the ways in which survivors tried to rehumanize themselves in order to survive is the centerpoint of the authors argument as he explains how the chroniclers of Holocaust events win our admiration and respect through their willingness to share with readers the most traumatic events of their lives.

Ch. 11: Nuyorican Barrio Literature

This essay presents the works of Judith Ortiz Cofer and Nicolasa Mohr as paradigms of the literary process shaped by the socio-cultural concept of Puerto Rican life in the United States. Both authors place emphasis on the Puerto Rican exile by means of testimonial discourse, an ideal method for American ethnic depiction.

Ch. 12: Fetishized Blackness: Racial Desire in Contemporary Japanese Narrative and Culture

This essay explores the symbolic significance of "blackness" as depicted in contemporary Japanese popular narrative and cultural texts. The fetishization of blackness is analyzed within the context of Japanese racial identity - surplus to the dominant paradigm of a black/white binarism - and Japan's post-occupation, ambivalent relations with America.

Notes on the authors

Michael J. Meyer, editor, holds a Ph. D. from Loyola University, Chicago and teaches English elective courses at Hong Kong International School in Hong Kong where he has lived since 1993. A former assistant editor of *The Steinbeck Quarterly*, Meyer has published chapters on Steinbeck in several volumes and was the editor of Rodopi's *Literature and the Grotesque* in 1995. His full length study of Steinbeck's use of the Cain and Abel myth in his canon is presently under consideration by the University of Alabama Press, and Scarecrow Press will publish his update of the official Steinbeck bibliography in 1997 or 1998.

S. Krishnamoorthy Aithal is professor of English at the Indian Institute of Technology, Kanput. He has published articles in scholarly international journals including the *ACALS Bulletin, American Notes and Queries, American Studies International, The British Journal of Aesthetics, Critical Quarterly, Essays in Poetics, Eire - Ireland, English Studies, Explicator, Indian Journal of American Studies, Indian Literature, International Fiction Review, James Joyce Quarterly, Language & Style, The Literary Criterion, Neophilologus, North Dakota Quarterly, Southwestern American Literature*, and *Studies in Bibliography*. He also has edited a collection of essays, *The Importance of Northrop Frye* and served as a visiting scholar at the New Mexico Institute of Mining and Technology, Socorro, NM (1985-1986) and at the Northrop Frye Centre, Toronto (1991). His PhD was awarded by Indiana University in 1968 and postdoctoral research was conducted at the Newberry Library in Chicago in 1992, both under the auspices of a Fulbright grant sponsored by the United States Information Agency.

Nina Cornyetz is assistant professor of Japanese at Rutgers University. Her work focuses on the issues of gender, ethnicity, and sexuality in modern Japanese narrative and culture, and she has just completed a book, *Dangerous Women: Phallic Fantasy and Modernity in Izumi Kyôka, Enchi Fumiko, and Nakagami Kenji*.

Eva Darias-Beautell is a Lecturer at the Universidad de La Lagunas in Tenerife, Spain where she has also held a four-year research scholarship in Canadian Studies. Dr. Darias-Beautell has published several published several articles on Canadian literatures and cultures in national and international journals, and a book on the writings of Japanese Canadian Joy Kogawa is forthcoming. She is presently working on contemporary Canadian fiction.

Peter Erspamer received his Ph.D. from The University of Wisconsin - Madison and has taught at Winona State University, the University of Missouri - Columbia and Fort Hays State University. He is the author of *The Elusiveness of Tolerance: The "Jewish Question" from Lessing to the Napoleanic Wars* published in 1997 by the University of North Carolina Press.

Ana Maria Fraile-Marcos is associate professor at the Universidad de Salamanca (Spain) where she is presently teaching a graduate course on African-American literature. Her doctoral dissertation, "Zora Neale Hurston y su apotacion a la literatura afroamericana," was submitted at the Universidad de Salmanca, where it has recently been published on CD Rom. Other works in the field of African-American Literature are her books, *Zora Neale Hurston: 'Mi Gente! i Gente!'* and *Langston Hughes: Oscuridad en Espana.*

Edvige Giunta received her PhD from the University of Mianii, Florida, and is assistant professor of English at Jersey City State College, New Jersey. She has publsihed many articles and reviews on Itlaian / American literature and cinema and has written an afterword for the reprint of Tina de Rosa's novel, *Paper Fish,* by the Feminist Press (1996). She is also serving as guest editor of a special issue of *VIA: Voices in Italian Americana* devoted to women (1996).

Tim Libretti is Asst. Prof. of English at Northeastern Illinois University in Chicago. He received his PhD from The University of Michigan at Arbor and previously taught at Colgate University and at his alma mater. He is currently working on a manuscript entitled *U.S. Literary History and Class Consciousness: Rethinking U.S. Proletarian and Third World Minority Literatures.*

Obododimma Oha teaches in the Department of English and Literary Studies at the University of Calabar, Nigeria. He received his Ph.D. in Stylistics from The University of Ibadan, Nigeria. He is a poet and a playwright, and also does research in literary semantics, war rhetoric, gender, and media discourses. His essays have appeared in international journals and books published in the United States, the United Kingdom, Nigeria and Canada.

Rafael Ocasio (Ph.D., U Kentucky, 1987) is an Associate Professor of Spanish, director of the Latin American Studies Program and Chair of the Department of Modern Foreign Languages and Literatures at Agnes Scott College, Decatur, Georgia. His principal areas of research are Afro-Cuban and revolutionary Cuban children's literatures and contemporary issues on Puerto Rican literatures. He has published critical articles and interviews in the following journals: *Cuadernos Americanos, Confluencia, The Lion and the Unicorn, Archiv Orientalni, Romance Quarterly, Callaloo* and *The Kenyon Review*, as well as articles in reference *Guide to American Literature, Masterpieces of Latino Literature*, and *Latin American Writers on Gay and Lesbian Themes*. He is currently at work on a critical study of the late Cuban novelist, Reinaldo Arenas, whose contributions in Latin sexual discourse and political activism are in neeed of review.

Karen Surman Paley is a lecturer in the English department of Boston College and a doctoral candidate at Northeastern University where she is working on an enthographic dissertation on teaching the eprsonal narrative. He work in Composition has been publsihed in the *Journal of Advanced Composition* and *Assessing Writing* and two essays on Chaucer apepared in *Diversity* and *Dreaming*.

Eric Sterling earned his PhD in English, with a minor in drama and theatre from Indiana University, Bloomington. He presently teaches at Auburn University / Montgomery in Alabama, and his publications include articles on William Shakespeare, Edmund Spenser, Arthur Miller, Edwrad Albee, Rolf Hochhuth, and Henry Mackenzie.

Charles Trainor received his PhD from Yale University and is the author of *The Drama and Fielding's Novels* (Garland, 1988). He is currently Professor of English at Siena College in Loudonville, N.Y.

Ch. 11: Nuyorican Barrio Literature

This essay presents the works of Judith Ortiz Cofer and Nicolasa Mohr as paradigms of the literary process shaped by the socio-cultural concept of Puerto Rican life in the United States. Both authors place emphasis on the Puerto Rican exile by means of testimonial discourse, an ideal method for American ethnic depiction.

Ch. 12: Fetishized Blackness: Racial Desire in Contemporary Japanese Narrative and Culture

This essay explores the symbolic significance of "blackness" as depicted in contemporary Japanese popular narrative and cultural texts. The fetishization of blackness is analyzed within the context of Japanese racial identity - surplus to the dominant paradigm of a black/white binarism - and Japan's post-occupation, ambivalent relations with America.

MLN

Modern Language Notes

*M*LN pioneered the introduction of contemporary continental criticism into American scholarship. Each of the first four issues of every volume centers on the critical works of a particular language. The fifth issue is devoted to comparative literature. Published five times a year: January (Italian), March (Hispanic), April (German), September (French), & December (Comparative Literature).

FORTHCOMING CONTENTS (VOL. 111, NO. 4. September 1996)
Critical Departures: *Salammbô's* Orientalism • *Ut mus in pice*: Brody, Montaigne et la "lecture philologique" • Dialogues of the Deaf: The Failure of Consolation in *Les Liaisons dangereuses* • Descartes et les automates • "Fils de rien" • Scénographie du dialogue balzacien • The "Counter-Public Sphere": Colette's Gendered Collective • Louis-René des Forêts: "Face à l'immémoriable" • Dialogue or Domination? Language Use in Proust's *A la recherche du temps perdu* • Puzzles and Lists: George Perec's *Un Homme qui dort*

Prepayment is required. **Annual subscription (5 issues):** $33.00, individuals; $85.00, institutions. **Three year subscription to single-language:** $31.00, individuals only. **Foreign postage:** $5.20, Canada & Mexico; $13.50, outside North America. **Single-issue price:** $9.00, individuals; $18.00, institutions. Payment must be drawn on a U.S. bank in U.S. dollars or made by international money order. MD residents add 5% sales tax. For orders shipped to Canada add 7% GST (#124004946). **Send orders to:** The Johns Hopkins University Press, P.O. Box 19966, Baltimore, MD 21211. **To place an order using Visa or MasterCard, call toll-free 1-800-548-1784, FAX us at (410) 516-6968, or send Visa/MasterCard order to this E-MAIL address:** jlorder@jhunix.hcf.jhu.edu

 Published by The Johns Hopkins University Press

EA6